An Introduction to Epistemology

Introducing Philosophy

Introducing Philosophy is a series of textbooks designed to introduce the basic topics of philosophy for any student approaching the subject for the first time. Each volume presents a central subject of philosophy by considering the key issues and outlooks associated with the area. With the emphasis firmly on the arguments for and against a philosophical position, the reader is encouraged to think philosophically about the subject.

An Introduction to Epistemology

Charles Landesman

Hunter College and The Graduate School
of the City University of New York

BLACKWELL
Publishers

First published 1997

2 4 6 8 10 9 7 5 3 1

Blackwell Publishers Inc.
238 Main Street
Cambridge, Massachusetts 02142
USA

Blackwell Publishers Ltd
108 Cowley Road
Oxford OX4 1JF
UK

Library of Congress Cataloging-in-Publication Data has been applied for.

ISBN 0–631–20212–9; ISBN 0–631–20213–7 (pbk.)

British Library Cataloguing in Publication Data

A CIP catalogue record for this book is available from the British Library.

Commissioning Editor: Nathalie Manners
Desk Editor: Cameron Laux
Production Controller: Lisa Eaton

Typeset in 11 on 13 pt Bembo
by Graphicraft Typesetters Ltd, Hong Kong
Printed in Great Britain by Hartnolls Ltd, Bodmin, Cornwall

This book is printed on acid-free paper

To Arlyne, with love

Contents

Introduction

For some years I have taught an introductory course in epistemology, the theory of knowledge, to both undergraduate and graduate students. It has not been easy to identify philosophical texts that are accessible to students who have no background in epistemology, that appeal to students with a wide range of interests, that are interesting, and that encourage further explorations of the field. In recent years, I have used Bertrand Russell's marvelous book *The Problems of Philosophy* as the core text in my course. This book is a model of how to combine interesting, historically rich discussions of elementary and fundamental epistemological problems with philosophical insight. It was first published in 1912, however, so I found myself adding to my lectures on Russell's text discussions of recent ideas that Russell had no opportunity to consider. I tried to cover similar territory, while taking into account philosophical trends that have recently appeared on the scene. I then decided to try my hand at writing a text that would be as accessible as Russell's to those interested in exploring the fascinating, though complex, problems that philosophical reflection on human knowledge brings to our attention. This book is the result.

It consists of seven chapters, each of which tackles a major topic in epistemology. In each one, I present some of the leading ideas that have influenced how philosophers approach the topic and include my own point of view. An issue that keeps cropping up is the question of skepticism. Do we really have the knowledge we think we have? The philosophical questions that are stimulated by skeptical reflections are not merely technical issues within the analytical tradition in philosophy; they are deep concerns about the human condition. One of the first philosophical works that I read during my first year in college was Berkeley's *Three Dialogues between Hylas and Philonous*. His views about the nature of human knowledge and of the reality we are trying to know about struck me then, and still strike me now, as strange and mysterious; yet they were presented as conclusions of powerful arguments that I did not then know how to challenge. My ruminations on Berkeley's philosophy over the years have kept alive in my mind and heart the thought that the world may be quite different from the picture of it that I am inclined to accept.

In his *Meditations*, Descartes began his consideration of the problem of knowledge by putting forth arguments tending to justify a radical form of skeptical doubt. Descartes was not himself a skeptic; indeed, his book is an effort to reply to the doubts it began by raising. But it was Descartes who put the problem of skepticism on the agenda of modern philosophy. As I survey recent trends in philosophy, I am struck by how strong the skeptical tradition still is, even though it does not often present itself as such. Over a century after Descartes published his great work, Kant, in his *Critique of Pure Reason*, introduced into philosophy the idea of the thing in itself. Things in themselves consist of the way the world really is, independently of how we may happen to think of or experience it. The idea of the thing in itself raises the possibility that our thoughts about the world may be radically mistaken. Thought is one thing, reality another; and there is no guarantee that thought truthfully represents reality.

Kant denied that we actually have knowledge of things as they are in themselves. We can know things only as they appear to us, and the picture of the world that we form on the basis of the appearances is constructed according to categories of thought that pay no regard to things in themselves. Kant did not think that he was a skeptic; in fact, he believed that he had developed an adequate reply to the radical skepticism that his great predecessor David Hume had formulated in his *Treatise of Human Nature*. Nevertheless, Kant's view that the mind, and not things as they are in themselves, determines the structure of human knowledge is a kind of skepticism: the mind-independent objective reality we aim at apprehending in everyday life, in science, and in religion forever eludes our grasp.

Many recent philosophers have accepted much of the skeptical point of view, often without realizing it, when they reject the idea of the thing in itself. Recent trends in philosophy, such as pragmatism, logical positivism, naturalized epistemology, constructivism, and postmodernism, attempt to get by without the idea of an objective, mind-independent reality that can be known by means of our cognitive faculties. We are now in the midst of a revival of pragmatism, according to which the purpose of thought is not to represent the world as it is in itself, but to enable us to cope with problems. *Purpose of text*

This book makes an attempt to come to grips with a variety of skeptical arguments by defending realism, both the commonsense and the scientific versions. By 'realism' I mean the view that there exists a mind-independent reality that we can have knowledge of, even though the way it appears to us by means of our senses may often fail to match the way it really is. This is the view that Descartes finds reason to support at the end of his *Meditations* and that Locke defends in his *An Essay Concerning Human Understanding*. The ideas of Descartes and Locke will play a major role in the chapters that follow. *Break down of Chp.*

Let me now say a few words about the topics that will be covered. Chapter 1 is concerned with the question of how sense perception manages to give us access to the objects that affect our senses. It discusses both direct realism, which says that in sense awareness we are able to inspect the objects that appear, and representative realism, according to which our access to objects is indirect and is mediated by inner sensory experiences.

Chapter 2 is concerned with the question of the accuracy with which sensory experience represents objects. To what extent do the ways that things appear match the ways that they are in themselves? Locke's famous distinction between primary and secondary qualities is discussed. As an example of a way in which experience fails to match reality, the topic of the nature and status of color is considered.

In chapter 3 the topic of skepticism with regard to the senses is discussed, together with certain responses to skepticism, such as idealism and constructivism. I appeal to G. E. Moore's proof of an external world as a successful way of replying to skeptical arguments. Chapter 4 takes up the question of our knowledge of our own mental life, and in the course of this discussion, Descartes's famous "I think, therefore I am" is criticized.

In chapter 5 I discuss Hume's problem of the rationale of induction, as well as the arguments pro and con scientific realism. Chapter 6 takes up the problem of whether there is any knowledge that is independent of sense experience and defends Kant's view of the synthetic a priori against recent criticism. Chapter 7, finally, considers the nature of epistemology and, in particular, criticizes efforts to replace traditional epistemological inquiries by psychology. It ends on the topic of the ethics of belief; this is the question of whether we are obliged to pay attention to evidence, and only to evidence, when deciding what we shall believe, especially as regards religious matters.

In the Further Readings at the end of each chapter, I have omitted publication details for those philosophical classics that appear in numerous editions.

1

Sense Awareness

1. The Original Understanding

Let us begin thinking about human knowledge by reflecting upon
our original understanding of the human knower and his or her
situation in the world. We think, first of all, that we are human
beings who have bodies some of whose parts we classify as sense
organs. We think that the world we live in consists of objects of
various sorts, all of which occupy particular positions in space and
time. We think of these objects as composed of various stuffs –
water, wood, iron, plastic, and so forth – and as having various
properties that we can observe, such as colors and shapes. In
addition to these properties, the objects bear a large variety of
relations to one another. Furthermore, they undergo changes;
things happen to them; they move from one place to another;
they interact with one another. The term 'ontology' is the name
of that branch of philosophy that investigates the sorts of things
that actually exist. Thus far, the ontology of our original understanding consists of material objects (bodies, things), the stuffs of
which they are composed, their properties and relationships, and
the events they undergo. I almost forgot. There is one group of
things I did not list within this ontological framework: namely,
we ourselves who drew up the list. Perhaps you think that we are
already incorporated in the list under the category of material
bodies. It is true that we *have* bodies. But is it plausible to identify
the human person with their body? Let us put this question aside
for a while. We shall merely add the category of person to our list

and leave undecided whether this is a fundamental category in its own right or a subcategory under material objects, or whether it is to be understood in some other way.

How do human beings get to know about the existence of the items that fall within these categories? The answer that the original understanding offers is that we learn about them by means of our senseorgans. Each sense organ is the physical basis for a sense: the eyes the basis for vision, the ears for hearing, and so on. By means of our senses we become aware of material bodies and events and their properties and relationships in the spatiotemporal world. Sense awareness, it seems, is the foundation of our knowledge of whatever there is in the world.

Let us take an example. You are looking for your brown gloves. You open the drawer, and there are the gloves in your field of vision; you see them. Do you now know where they are? Perhaps the light was dim, and you were unable to get a good look at their color. So you do not think that these are your brown gloves. Thus, even though something may fall within your field of vision and become an object of visual sense awareness, you still may not know what it is.

Suppose you turn on a nearby lamp in order to obtain a better view of the gloves. Now their brown color appears to you. Do you now know that here are the gloves you were looking for? Well, consider this thought-experiment. Suppose an animal – your dog, for example – was also looking at the brown gloves. It too had the gloves and their color within its field of vision. It had the same sort of sense awareness of the gloves that you have. Does it know that these are brown gloves? Of course not. In order to know that these are brown gloves, one must not only have the gloves in one's field of vision, but one must judge that these are brown gloves. The possession of knowledge of this sort involves not just sense awareness, but also the power of judgment. This sort of knowledge is of the kind called 'knowing that', by contrast with 'knowing how'. Knowing that involves a judgment, an assent to a proposition, to something capable of being either true or false. In sense awareness, something is, we think, present to us; it is, we may say, given to us. In sense awareness, we are receptive to the objects and events in our surroundings. But knowledge in the form of knowing that is more than mere receptivity;

it involves acts of mind in which the material provided by sense awareness is interpreted. In the case at hand, the things I see are classified as gloves, and their color is classified as an instance of brown. In the judgment that these are brown gloves, they are also identified as being in a certain place ("Here they are") and as positioned at a certain time (through the tense of the verb, "are").

Thus the judgment involves the use of certain concepts such as 'glove' and 'brown'. Since the term 'gloves' is in the plural, the concept 'more than one' also comes into play, and implicit in this concept is the concept of number. In addition, our understanding of the spatial and temporal frameworks in which material objects and events are located is utilized. Thus the capacity to acquire knowledge by means of the senses depends upon possessing the relevant concepts and frameworks. Many questions arise, not the least of which is how these various items come into our possession in the first place. Another question concerns the propositions that we assent to in judgments and that are capable of being true or false. Do we need to add these to the categories of our ontology? Do judgments, concepts, propositions, and frameworks belong to new categories, or are they among the categories already specified? The ontology of the things known seemed simple and unproblematic. But once we begin to reflect upon knowledge itself, new candidates for our ontology come into view.

How shall knowledge itself be understood? Does our original understanding have anything to contribute here? Is knowledge simply judgment? A judgment could turn out to be false. Perhaps I thought that these gloves are blue when they are really brown. I certainly don't know that they are blue, since one cannot know to be true what isn't true. When we come to know that a certain proposition is true, we have, as it were, captured a truth. Since judgments are capable of being false as well as true, we cannot simply identify knowing something with an act of judgment.

Perhaps knowledge should be identified with judgments that are true. It is true that these gloves are brown; so, when I judge that they are brown, do I not know that they are brown? But there are cases of true judgments that do not provide knowledge. I can hit upon the truth accidentally. For example, you ask: "How many pennies are there in my pocket?" I guess "Six," and I happen to be right. It was just a guess, not something I knew.

Knowing is not judgement, or vice versa

one can be correct accidentally

Know, is at least true judgement + ?

Knowledge is at least true judgment, but it is also something more. What is missing? Here is another question to which we shall return later.

Among the propositions that are candidates for knowledge are propositions to the effect that certain things exist or do not exist. For example, there exists a pair of brown gloves in the drawer. Or, there are no such things as unicorns. Judgments of both existence and nonexistence contribute to one's ontology by specifying which types of things we think exist and which do not. On the basis of these examples, gloves belong to our ontology, whereas unicorns do not.

Is it really true that sense awareness is the sole basis for our knowledge of what exists? Well, we all believe in the existence of things that do not fall within the purview of the senses. For example, I believe that there will be a presidential election in the year 2000. That is an event that belongs to the future and will not be observed until it happens. But if I *now* know that it will occur, then I know of the existence of something that does not now or has not in the past been an object of sense awareness. I also believe that Columbus sailed to what was later called America in 1492. That is a past event that was once observed but has not been observed by anyone for more than 500 years. These examples show that we believe in the existence of certain events even though they have not been objects of *our* sense awareness.

We also think that there are conditions of the universe that could never entirely fall under anyone's sense awareness, past, present, or future. For example, according to the law of gravity, every body in the universe exercises a force of attraction upon every other body. A law of nature such as this is a uniformity that transcends the possibility of direct verification through the senses, in that it refers to objects and their relations which no one will ever have the opportunity to observe. In addition, the law makes reference to a *force* of attraction, something which may not be observable at all. In our thinking about the world, it is not uncommon for us to assume the existence of various items that cannot be objects of sense awareness, such as atoms and electrons, the unconscious, God and the soul, numbers, absolute space and time, the highest good, and so forth. So in whatever way sense awareness constitutes the basis of human knowledge and belief, it does not do so simply by being directed at all such objects. The verification of the existence of various types of objects, if it involves sense awareness, seems to involve much more besides.

Thus far we have discussed sense awareness rather uncritically, as if there were no problem in understanding its true nature and the way in which it works. We certainly think we acquire much of what we know about the world through the senses; yet skeptical philosophers, from the ancient world to the present time, have pointed out that our senses frequently deceive us. They have argued that the way things are made to appear by means of our senses does not always match the way things really are. Something can look to be of one color, yet really be of another. Something can look smaller than it really is. A straight stick placed in water looks bent. Parallel lines such as railroad tracks seem to converge. These and countless other cases represent a frequent lack of correspondence between appearance and reality. But if sense awareness is unreliable, how can it provide the certainty which we associate with knowledge? Let us turn now to consider the ways our senses actually operate in generating our judgments about the surrounding world.

"How our senses operate"

2. Sense Awareness and Direct Realism

At the very moment that I am writing these words, I am able to see the telephone that is sitting on my desk out of the corner of my eye. It has a certain familiar shape; its color is white; it has a red hold button, and the remaining buttons are gray. When I think about this and similar states of affairs from the standpoint of our original commonsense pre-philosophical, pre-scientific understanding, these are some of the things I am inclined to believe. When I use my eyes to see something, a certain scene is presented visually; this scene includes various objects (such as the telephone, its receiver, and the connecting line) and their relationships and properties. The objects are viewed in a larger setting (for example, the telephone is on the desk, which is situated in front of a bookcase), and this larger setting is itself situated in a fragment of the world that is not itself fully presented at the moment of sense awareness.

Moreover, the knowledge about the scene that I acquire through sense awareness is not a product of hard thinking or complex calculations. I do not need to use much effort to obtain it. I simply report the facts that are presented to me. That the telephone is white and the hold button red are things I know not because I have inferred them from other facts, but because sense awareness has allowed me to inspect the very facts themselves. When I think of the things I know by inference or by calculation or by means of the testimony of others, I am convinced that sense awareness is a basis for knowledge that is direct and immediate; it makes it possible for me to inspect the very facts themselves. I think I know that Columbus sailed to America for the first time in 1492. But that is not a fact that I have observed. My access to it is very indirect. The author of the history book in which I first read about it himself learned about it by reading other books and documents. Ultimately the basis for this knowledge is the firsthand observations of others a long time ago; my current belief is the product of a sequence of events which began over 500 years ago. I am in no position to inspect the facts themselves. Instead, I inspect sentences in a book that assert these facts, and I assume that these assertions are reliable. Our original understanding affirms that the knowledge of objects given in sense awareness is direct, because sense awareness is an inspection of the very facts which that knowledge represents.

There is something else of great importance that our original understanding also affirms. It says that the facts that are inspected in sense awareness are objective and independent. What this means is that these facts do not depend upon anything about the person doing the inspecting. These facts would still exist even if no one was inspecting them. That there is a telephone on the desk, that it is white, that it has this particular shape, and so forth are facts that exist whether or not anyone is apprehending them via sense awareness. Suppose, for example, that I experience a momentary blurring of vision. The telephone then looks blurred to me. But I do not ascribe that blurry look to the telephone, but to me, the observer. The blurry effect is due to me; it is not a feature of the telephone. It is subjective and dependent. But the white color of the phone and its shape are not effects due to the observer, but objective, independent features of the object. That is what I think prior to adopting a critical philosophical perspective, anyhow.

The ontological assumption that lies behind the thesis of objectivity and independence is that we exist in a world that for the most part we have not made. The world is already there, and sense awareness is a means of apprehending fragments of what is already there. We do not think of sense awareness as having a creative function. It does not bring into existence the facts apprehended and inspected by its means. It is not an activity like painting or sculpture whereby objects are produced which never existed before. Instead, it seems as if we are purely passive in sense awareness; we merely record information that is directly accessible.

The term 'direct realism' will be used to represent these theses implicit in our original understanding. According to direct realism, sense awareness is a way of apprehending objects and their features and relationships that are objective and independent and that belong to a wider world, parts of which are also capable of becoming objects of sense awareness, and this mode of apprehension is direct and immediate, the independent facts apprehended being inspected rather than inferred.

There is an interesting implication of direct realism that has yet to be mentioned. What I know about the past before I was born and what I know about the future must be learned by inference and interpretation, because such facts are not available for inspection. But something that I can inspect must exist now, at the time at which I am inspecting it. I cannot inspect something that does not exist simultaneously with the inspection of it. If we think of the world as spread out not only in space but also in time, then this thesis of simultaneity says that what are apprehended in sense awareness are those fragments of the world which exist at the same time as those fragments that include the awareness that is apprehending them.

Our original understanding consists of our commonsense view of the objects of knowledge in relation to the knowledge of them. We have found that reflection upon examples of visual sense awareness confirms that a certain set of theses which have been labeled 'direct realism' formulates some of the thoughts implicit in our original understanding. However, in the previous section, I mentioned one fact that has been used by skeptical philosophers to challenge direct realism: namely, the fact that sense awareness frequently leads us into error. Something can appear, for example, to have a size or shape or color other than the size or shape or

color it really has. How does our original understanding cope
with error?

We must first take note of a distinction which has not been
made explicit as yet between sense awareness and the beliefs and
judgments that are founded upon it. In sense awareness, certain
items are presented or given – for example, the telephone, its color
and shape, and its various parts. In sense awareness, such items
are made available for inspection. However, we may or may not
decide to record what is presented to us. It may not be of interest
to us, or we may not pay any attention to it. In fact, most of the
items within the scenes that visual perception presents are not
attended to and not recorded. The records we make of what we
see are highly selective; we do not have "world enough and time,"
to quote Marvell, to notice everything amidst the passing show.
These records are the judgments we make about the scenes that
are presented. When the judgments are retained in our memory,
we call them beliefs. Thus, the visual presentation of the telephone and its color is one thing, and the belief that this is a
telephone and that it is white is another thing. The belief is,
indeed, founded upon the presentation, so there is an important
connection between them. But they are not the same.

With this distinction before us, we are in a position to recognize that there is a corresponding distinction to be made with
respect to error. There can be errors in sense awareness where the
appearance deviates from the thing that appears. This type of
error is illustrated by the straight stick that appears bent when
placed in water. But there can also be errors in the judgments and
beliefs based upon sense awareness, as when one judges that that
stick *is* bent. A deviation between appearance and reality does not
necessarily produce an error in judgment. Thus, although the
stick looks bent to me, I am not misled, because I am familiar
with the phenomenon of refraction.

Suppose that I am misled, however, and think that the stick is
really bent. How is this possible? One explanation that many
philosophers have found to be plausible is this. When I look at the
stick in water, what is presented to me is not a straight stick, but
rather an image of a bent stick. I then inspect this image, realize
that it is bent, and, being unfamiliar with the phenomenon of
refraction, judge that the stick is actually bent. This explanation

introduces into our ontology a new item that we have not previously mentioned: namely, a visual image. If the explanation is to do its job, the image must be an item that is distinct from the object of which it is the image. In the case before us, the image presents us with something bent, whereas the object we are trying to apprehend is straight. The image is one thing, the object another. We inspect the image in order to figure out the nature of the object.

But this explanation is not consistent with direct realism. Direct realism says that we inspect the object itself to determine its properties, that our knowledge of the object is direct and is not founded upon any inference; it is simply a report of the facts directly presented. But the explanation denies that, in this case at least, there is any inspection of the stick in the water. The object of inspection is the image that intervenes between the stick and our judgment. Our awareness of the stick is indirect; it is founded upon our direct awareness of the image.

Moreover, we do not think that the image which we inspect is something that is objective and independent, as is the stick. If no one were observing the stick, there would be no image of a bent stick. The image arises because of the peculiar way in which the rays of light are bent by the water and by the ways in which these rays affect our eyes. But these effects upon our eyes and the images that are produced would never have occurred if we had not been looking at the stick. So the object of direct inspection lacks the objectivity that direct realism ascribes to it.

The direct realist may reply by rejecting this explanation. Or instead, he or she may say that this explanation applies only in the exceptional case when there is a deviation between appearance and reality, but it does not apply in the more usual case when there is no deviation. In the usual case, we inspect the object itself; only when there is a deviation do images come into the picture.

Whatever we are inclined to think about this debate, one thing has become clear: our original understanding is not immune to criticism. In fact, its critics believe that our original understanding and the theses implicit in it are logically incoherent. The direct realism it affirms is not consistent with the possibility of error that it also affirms. So let us take a closer look at sense awareness to determine whether our original understanding can be successfully defended.

[handwritten: indirect access to objects mediated by inner sense experiences]

3. Representative Realism *[handwritten: (A closer look at sense awareness)]*

Our discussion of sense awareness has thus far used examples drawn from vision to illustrate the theses of direct realism and the problem of error. However, when we consider the other senses, direct realism loses much of its plausibility. Consider, for example, the sense of touch. By means of touch, I am able to learn about certain properties of the bodies within reach, such as how hot or cold they are, how solid they are, how smooth their surfaces are, and so on.

Suppose, for example, I wish to discover how hot a recently baked potato is. I touch it and find that it is still quite hot. What has happened here to enable me to acquire this knowledge? Let us consider what we can find out about the origin of this knowledge just by reflecting upon the situation without bringing in information gathered from scientific sources. Upon touching the potato, I felt something in my fingertips. There was a very particular sensation, a sensation of heat in my finger that was brought about when my finger came into contact with the potato. The sensation told me that the potato was still quite hot. We can say that the sensation in my finger carried the *information* that it was hot. When one thing carries information about another thing, then the first thing is said to *represent* the second thing. So the sensation represents to me that the potato is hot.

[handwritten in margin: is this any different from the mechanics of vision?]

How does it come about that the sensation is able to carry this information and to perform this representative function? Before I touched the potato, I already knew what sorts of sensation correspond with various degrees of heat and cold. I knew how the potato would feel if it was cold, or if it was warm, or if it was hot. I use this preexisting *background information* to extract the information that the potato is hot from the occurrence of the sensation.

It as if I reasoned as follows. The background information provides me with the general premise that sensations of such and such a sort are caused by objects that are hot. Then there is the singular premise that a sensation of just this sort has been produced by this potato. From these two premises I conclude that the potato is hot. Of course, I do not usually consciously assert these two premises and then consciously draw the conclusion. The

[handwritten margin note: Judging the pot. as hot comes from a backdrop of pre existing knowledge of temperature ranges.]

processes that generate this conclusion when I feel this sensation usually occur below the threshold of consciousness. I just touch the potato and find myself believing that it is hot. We do not know exactly how the background information enters the picture or how it is applied to the occurrence of the sensation to generate the belief.

In spelling out what we have learned about tactual sense awareness, we are in a position to realize how little we know about the whole process. Here are some examples of things we would have to know in order to possess a complete picture, things which simple reflection cannot determine. First, what happens when I bring my finger into contact with the potato to produce the sensation? What is there in the potato that corresponds to just that type of sensation? We say that there is heat in it, but what exactly is heat? What happens in my finger, and perhaps in other parts of my body (such as my brain), that causes this sensation? Once the sensation has occurred, we would like to know how the relevant background information comes into play. Our minds are well stocked with information of all kinds. How does it come about that only the information relevant to the question at hand comes to the fore? To use a computer metaphor, how does the unconscious mind manage to look in the right directory and pick out the relevant file? In addition, we would like to know something about the origins of the background information: is it something that we have previously learned, or is it innate? And finally, once the relevant background information is available for use, how is it applied to the sensation to generate the conclusion?

[handwritten margin note: Is background knowledge learned or innate?]

These various questions are scientific. We label as 'scientific' those inquiries which go beyond what is available to simple reflection and our original understanding. The answer to these questions about how knowledge based upon tactual sense awareness is attained brings in psychology, physiology, and physics. The scientific study of touch brings together those sciences whose theories contain information about the interaction between the human organism and the bodies that come in contact with it.

But even without the aid of science, we are able to recognize that direct realism is not entirely correct in the case of tactual sense awareness. When I touch the potato and feel the sensation, I am able to determine the heat of the potato only indirectly, via the

sensation which carries the relevant information. The direct, immediate object of inspection is not the heat in the potato, but the
sensation felt in the finger. It is my consciousness of this sensation
that grounds my belief about the potato. Of course, not all of
direct realism is shown to be in error by these considerations.
Although the sensation is subjective and dependent, the object we
know about, the potato and its degree of heat, is objective and
independent. I shall use the term 'representative realism' to describe
the theory of our knowledge based upon tactual sense awareness.

Representative realism is able to explain certain sorts of error
that we are capable of making. It distinguishes the appearance
from the reality by reference to the difference between the sensation and the object that causes it. Thus, there are the following
possibilities of error. The sensation may fail to match the object,
thus producing false belief: for example, the potato may feel cold,
even though it is really hot. Or even if the sensation matches the
object, I may misinterpret it and thus judge incorrectly. And I
may misinterpret it either because of faulty background information, or because of faulty inference of the conclusion from correct
background information, or because of faulty application of correct background information to the sensation, or because of various combinations of these possibilities.

The criticism of direct realism and the transition to representative
realism that has been made with respect to tactual sense awareness
clearly applies to taste and smell as well. Our knowledge of the
tastes and smells of various objects and of the objects themselves
is a product of the sensations these objects cause in the sense organs.
I can find out that something is a lemon, for example, by tasting
it and finding the characteristic sensation of lemons in my tongue
and mouth. I can discover that there is cabbage cooking in the
kitchen by the sensation in my nose caused by the chemicals that
the cabbage gives off as it is cooked. In these cases as well, our
knowledge of the object is a product of our consciousness of the
bodily sensation that the object causes.

The case is more difficult with respect to hearing and vision.
The reason is that these two senses do not operate by producing
sensations that have a location in a part of the body of the perceiver.
When I hear something, the sound I directly hear does not, like the
sensation of heat that I am directly conscious of, have a specific

bodily location. In fact, the sound seems to be as objective and independent as the object that produces it. In hearing a sound, I am not conscious of the occurrence of a sensation of which I am the bearer; at least, such consciousness is not a product of simple reflection. Let us probe more deeply into these two senses.

4. Sound

When a tree falls in the forest and there is no one around to hear it, does its falling actually produce a sound? This is a question that is frequently raised when people begin wondering about the status of the immediate objects of the senses. What exactly is the source of our puzzlement? We do not ask the same question about pains, for example. The question, If a sharp knife is moved with great force through space but no living animal body is there to be cut by it, does it actually produce a pain?, is never raised. We know that pains are subjective and dependent, and that they do not occur in the absence of a living, sentient organism.

The puzzle arises in the case of sound because of a tension between two ways of thinking about it. There is, first of all, our original understanding, according to which sound is something objective and independent. The tree when it falls makes a sound; the sound it makes is, it seems, a happening that is directly produced by the falling tree and needs no perceiver for its existence. Suppose I ask you: "Did you hear that thunder?" When you say that you hear it too, I assume that the thing you heard is the very same thing that I heard. I do not think that I am the bearer of the sounds that I hear in the way that I am the bearer or owner of the pains I feel.

The second way of thinking about sound invokes theories that we owe to scientific extensions of our original understanding. When the tree falls and we hear a sound, we want to know how it comes about that events such as a tree falling bring about events such as the hearing of a sound. The original understanding, which is limited to what we can learn by simple observation and reflection, without bringing science or philosophy into the picture, has nothing to say on this issue. What the science of sound says is that when the tree falls it vibrates, and that these vibrations cause waves in the air which strike our ears, causing various changes within the ears, the nerves, and the brain. These specific events, whose nature is still under investigation, cause us to hear a sound just as the corresponding events for vision cause us to see a colored object.

Where does the tension arise between these two ways of thinking about sound? There does not appear to be a formal contradiction between our original understanding and the scientific results. The problem arises when we ask this question: When the tree falls in the forest, does it cause just the waves in the air, or does it cause the sound as well as the waves? The explanation of how our hearing the sound comes about makes reference only to the air waves; sound enters the picture only as something heard, not as something that is among the items that cause the hearing. To suppose that the falling tree causes the sound as well as the waves is to assume the existence of something unnecessary to the explanation. So it seems reasonable to assume that the sound itself is the result of the physical and physiological processes initiated by the falling of the tree. The sound comes into existence with the hearing of it and is an integral constituent of the hearing of it. It would not exist if not heard and thus is something subjective and dependent. It is more like a pain in this respect than like the tree. It is a consequence of this line of reasoning that when I say "I hear the tree fall," the event that I report hearing is something objective and independent, whereas when I say "I hear the sound made by the falling tree," the thing I report hearing is subjective and dependent. Scientific thinking does not merely extend our original understanding, it corrects it.

This way of thinking about the matter has made use of a certain assumption, or rule. I pointed out that it would be unnecessary as far as the explanation is concerned to suppose that the falling tree directly caused the sound to occur as well as the air waves. Since the belief in the existence of sounds that are objective and independent is unnecessary, it is wrong to adopt it. The assumption that is made here is frequently referred to as 'Ockham's razor', in honor of William of Ockham (1285–1349), who is thought to have said that entities are not to be multiplied beyond necessity. As used in this argument about sound, the principle says that in our efforts to discover the causes of some phenomenon, we should not assume the existence of any entities that are not necessary to explain its existence. Since objective sounds are not among the causes of our hearing of sounds, we should not assume the existence of objective sounds. Ockham's razor, also known as the 'principle of simplicity', says that we should adopt the simplest causal explanation of some phenomenon among all the available explanations that are supported by and consistent with all the evidence.

Ockham's razor is a principle that is relevant to our _ontological commitments_. Ontology is the attempt to give an account of the types of items that exist. An ontological commitment occurs when some theory that we adopt either asserts or implies the existence of some type of item. We have then, in adopting the theory, made an ontological commitment to the existence of items of that sort. In the argument above, our use of Ockham's razor has told us that we should not make an ontological commitment to the existence of objective, independent sounds. There are sounds, of course, but they are subjective and dependent.

The argument that I have presented here in favor of the subjectivity of sound may be challenged as follows. You have assumed, it might be objected, that if there were objective sounds, they would be something different from the sound waves caused by the falling tree. Since only the air waves play a role in the hearing of the sound, there is no need to suppose that there are objective sounds in addition. However, this assumption is false. The falling tree produces air waves; that is not in question. But the sounds that we hear _are_ these air waves. Sounds are identical with – they are nothing more than – the physical waves which cause us to hear them. Thus, since objective sounds are nothing in addition to the waves, it is not a violation of Ockham's razor to believe that they exist.

A difficulty with this objection was pointed out by George Berkeley (1685–1753) in the first of his *Three Dialogues between Hylas and Philonous*. The sounds that we hear, that we can be conscious of and inspect, are items of which we can say that they are "*loud, sweet, acute or grave.*"[1] But an air wave is "merely a vibrative or undulatory motion in the air,"[2] and it is absurd to suppose that a motion can be loud or sweet or acute or grave. In short, many of the things that are true of sounds are not true of motions, so sounds cannot be plausibly identified with motions.

Perhaps the objection can be modified to avoid this difficulty. We can say that there are two kinds of sounds: an objective sort, which consist of motions, and a subjective sort, which we hear and which can be described as loud or sweet or acute or grave. According to Berkeley, this modification fails, because it implies the absurdity that there are sounds that can never be heard: namely, the objective sort.[3] In addition, the modified argument clearly violates Ockham's razor. Once we admit that there are subjective sounds which we hear, there is no role for objective sounds to play.

The conclusion is that hearing resembles the three other senses that we have examined in involving the occurrence of a sensation: I am able to hear the tree fall in the forest only because I am able to hear the sound it makes. The hearing of the sound is as much a sensation as is the feeling in my fingers when I touch a hot potato. Just as the sensations in my fingers carry the information that the potato is hot, so the sensation of sound carries the information that the tree fell. There is this difference, however. Unlike the sensations involved in touch, taste, and smell, almost all auditory sensations lack a felt bodily location; it does not seem as if the sounds I hear occur in any part of my body. I say "almost all," for if the sound is very loud or intense, it may be accompanied by a painful feeling in the ears. and sometimes vibration is felt

That there are bodily sensations involved in touch, taste, and smell is knowledge available in our original understanding. That the hearing of sound is a sensation, however, transcends the data available to our original understanding. To establish that, it was necessary to bring in premises drawn from science. Thus the fact that representative realism, not direct realism, applies to hearing is a scientific conclusion. And since its establishment also involves a philosophical principle of simplicity (whose validity we have merely assumed), the defense of representative realism in the case of hearing involves bringing together theories drawn from both science and philosophy. Let us now turn to the last of the five senses, vision.

5. Visual Sense Awareness

Thus far, we have found that representative realism fits the facts of the case better than direct realism for four of our five senses.

What about vision? Isn't it true that when we see something, the very thing we see is there, before our eyes, available for inspection? I do not see the telephone by first becoming aware of something else; I am directly conscious of it. Unlike the case of touch, there is no conscious doubleness in vision. In touch, I feel the sensation, then judge that the potato is hot. The sensation is one thing, the potato another. In hearing, I first hear the sound, then judge that a tree fell; I become aware of the objective fact indirectly by a direct awareness of the sound that the falling tree made. But in vision, I see the telephone and its color directly; there doesn't seem to be any conscious item involved that represents the object and its color. Vision, so it would seem, is direct. In seeing something, we are in direct contact with the material world. It appears, then, that vision is an exception to the account that we have found applicable to the other senses.

However, as we saw earlier, there are frequent deviations between how things look and how they really are. These are not confined to cases such as the stick in the water that looks bent. They occur frequently in veridical cases as well. Changes in the lighting of a room produce changes in the medley of colors that the furnishings display. Changes in position produce changes in the apparent shapes and sizes of objects in the visual field. We seldom take explicit note of these changes because we are usually interested in the real, relatively unchanging features of things, rather than the flux of appearances. Were we to suspend our practical, objectively oriented interests in objects, however, we would become conscious of frequent deviations between appearance and reality. The Impressionist painters, particularly, were interested in the play of light and colors, in how objects appear to the attentive observer. Recall too how frequently the true colors of objects are obscured by the dim lighting in a room. Recall how often one must place something in a better light to determine its exact shade of color. Remember how even the identity of things is obscured in the dark.

These reflections convince us that the ways in which things are presented in our visual experience are very variable and quite frequently fail to match with exactness what we know of their objective features. They also convince us that there is such a thing as visual experience, which consists in the ways that objects manifest themselves to us visually. Such experience is something that would not exist if living, sentient organisms graced with the sense of sight did not exist. This suggests that there is room even in vision for representative realism. The ways objects look are subjective and dependent and represent to us the ways they are in themselves. We are led to distinguish between things as they are in themselves and their appearances.

When we bring our scientific knowledge of vision into the picture, we find that seeing works much like hearing. In neither case are bodily sensations prominent, although sensations in the ears or eyes may occur when the stimulus is very intense. In both, the experiences that occur are produced by the effects of physical stimuli (sound waves in the case of hearing, light waves in the case of sight) upon our sense organs. Just as the sound that a thing makes is a sensory event that is subjective and dependent, so the apparent colors and shapes and other visually presented qualities of bodies are subjective and dependent. Just as sounds carry information about the sounding bodies and so represent them to us, so do visually apparent qualities. The items that we are directly conscious of in our field of vision, the colored, shaped objects of various sizes which bear various spatial relations to one another, are not the material objects themselves that, according to the original understanding, we see. They are, rather, constituents of our experience of material objects that would not exist if we did not exist. Even though the material world exists independently of us, the way it appears to us, the visual field through which we see fragments of it, is subjective and dependent. Visual awareness incorporates sensations, just as do the forms of awareness of the other external senses.

We can sum up this survey of the five external senses as follows. Our knowledge of the external world based upon the five types of sense awareness is not, as direct realism would have it, a mere passive recording of facts available to our inspection. It is a highly indirect affair that depends upon sensory events available to our inspection which carry information about material bodies, their properties, and relationships that we are somehow able to extract so as to formulate beliefs about the things we perceive. Representative realism is the outcome of our reflections so far.

But if we are not passive recorders of directly given, independent facts, then we face a new question. If the judgments and beliefs that are grounded in our sense experience are to count as knowledge, they must be true, as we saw in the first section. If they are true, then in some way they correspond to, or faithfully reflect, the facts. But how sure can we be that they do faithfully reflect the facts? Our judgments formulate the information contained in our sensory experiences. How accurate is this information? Its degree of accuracy depends upon the degree to which our sensations faithfully represent things as they are in themselves. Are we actually able to know things as they are in themselves?

Further Readings

George Berkeley, *Three Dialogues Between Hylas and Philonous*, First Dialogue.

Paul Grice, "The Causal Theory of Perception," in *Studies in the Way of Words* (Cambridge, Mass.: Harvard University Press, 1989), pp. 224–47.

John McDowell, *Mind and World* (Cambridge, Mass.: Harvard University Press, 1994).

Bertrand Russell, *Our Knowledge of the External World* (New York: W. W. Norton, 1929).

Gilbert Ryle, "Sensation and Observation," in *The Concept of Mind* (London: Hutchinson's University Library, 1949), ch. 7.

Wilfrid Sellars, "Empiricism and the Philosophy of Mind," in *Science, Perception and Reality* (London: Routledge and Kegan Paul, 1963), pp. 127–96.

2

Appearance and Reality

1. Primary and Secondary Qualities

In this chapter, we shall discuss one of the most prominent and influential efforts in the history of philosophy to answer the question of the accuracy of the representations that enter into our sense awareness of bodies. This is the distinction between primary and secondary qualities formulated by John Locke (1632–1704) in his *An Essay Concerning Human Understanding*. The period in which Locke lived witnessed a revival of the atomism that was first formulated in ancient Greek philosophy by Democritus and Leucippus. According to the atomists, the material world consists of perceptible objects which themselves consist of minute, imperceptible particles. These particles, or atoms (Locke called them "corpuscles," and he called the theory of matter which was based upon them the "corpuscularian hypothesis") were believed to have certain qualities in common: each is extended in space; each fills space, or in Locke's terms, each is solid and impenetrable; each has a definite shape and size; and each is capable of motion and rest. The larger objects formed of collections of atoms, such as the things we are capable of seeing and touching, also possess these qualities of solidity, extension, shape, size, and mobility. Locke called these qualities of bodies the "primary qualities."

In addition to atoms, nature consists of space and time, which are the media in which the atoms exist and move. Locke's ontological commitment as far as material nature is concerned is to the existence of material atoms, collections of atoms clumped together, their primary qualities, and the space and time which house them. This view of nature was not original with Locke. He did not think of himself as one of those "Master-Builders, whose mighty Designs, in advancing the Sciences, will leave lasting Monuments to the Admiration of Posterity." He would not compare himself with Newton or Boyle. He speaks of himself instead as being "employed as an Under-Labourer in clearing Ground a little, and removing some of the Rubbish, that lies in the way to Knowledge."[1] His main concern was with human knowledge; his use of the corpuscularian hypothesis was motivated by the clarity it brought to the question of the accuracy of our sensory representations.

For Locke, the distinguishing and defining feature of a primary quality is that it is "utterly inseparable from the Body."[2] The primary, or fundamental, qualities of bodies are those that, according to the corpuscularian hypothesis, must be present whenever you have a material object. One of the primary qualities, solidity, is specially important, because it distinguishes matter from empty space. Another, extension, distinguishes matter from mind. Of course, Locke's version of the atomic theory is quite primitive when compared to the versions developed in recent times. As our conception of nature evolves, there is every reason to expect that the list of primary qualities will change accordingly. But for the sake of simplicity, we will stay with Locke's list.

When we come in contact with bodies via sense awareness, other qualities achieve prominence. In fact, associated with each sense are certain qualities that only that sense conveys directly. Vision provides awareness of light and color, hearing of sounds, taste and smell of tastes and smells, and touch of heat and cold. Locke called these the "secondary qualities," which are "Such *Qualities*, which in truth are nothing in the Objects themselves, but Powers to produce various Sensations in us by their *primary Qualities*, i.e. by the Bulk, Figure, Texture, and Motion of their insensible parts."[3]

Let us take color as an example. When I look at a tomato, it appears red to me. A particular shade of red is given in my sense awareness of the tomato. I then judge that the tomato is red. However, according to Locke, we must distinguish between the red that I am directly aware of and the red that I attribute to the tomato. The red I am directly aware of, the actual red that I

The rod I see is subjective
The red ascribed is a power of the tom.

inspect, belongs solely to the sensation. It is something subjective and dependent. The red that I ascribe to the tomato is quite different; it is just a power, or capacity, of the tomato to cause that sensation in me when I look at it. That power is founded upon the particular primary qualities which the atoms of the tomato possess. It is founded upon them in the sense that an object with that atomic structure will reflect into my eyes the light which will cause the sensation of that shade of red. A full explanation of why I see that shade of red will have to refer to those aspects of the atomic structure of the object that determine the type of light that affects my eyes. Neither the tomato itself nor any of its constituent atoms possesses as a quality the shade of red that I am directly conscious of.

Locke would offer a similar account of the remaining secondary qualities. One way in which his view can be formulated is this. There are really two sets of secondary qualities. One set consists of colors, sounds, and so on insofar as I am conscious of them. These exist in the sensation only and are subjective and dependent. The other set is made up of qualities that are predicated of objects, and these consist merely of powers of bodies to produce in us certain sensations. They are not exactly objective and independent, because their nature is specified in terms of their subjective effects. They are relational qualities that belong to objects insofar as they bear certain relations to sentient creatures.

We have arrived at the point at which Locke's view of the accuracy of our representations can be explained. He says: "The *ideas of primary Qualities* of Bodies, *are Resemblances* of them, and their Patterns do really exist in the Bodies themselves; but the *Ideas, produced* in us *by* these *Secondary Qualities, have no resemblance* of them at all. There is nothing like our *Ideas*, existing in the Bodies themselves."[4]

His point is this. With regard to certain features of bodies, the primary ones, there is a general match between appearance and reality. Thus, when I look at the cover of my copy of Locke's *Essay*, it looks rectangular. Not only does it *look* rectangular, it really *is* rectangular. But although its color looks to be brown, the color that it presents to me is not and cannot be the color of the object in itself. For in itself, independently of its relationships to other things, it has no color at all. And when we bring into consideration its relations with creatures capable of perceptual awareness, the only sense in which it is brown is the attenuated sense that it is capable of producing in sentient creatures an experience with that shade of brown as an ingredient.

In other words, the information embodied in the representations of sense awareness is generally (though not invariably) accurate with respect to the primary qualities, but is always inaccurate with respect to the secondary ones. The world contains colors and sounds, tastes and smells, heat and cold, only because there exist sentient creatures to perceive them. But the world as it is in itself, existing independently of sentient creatures, contains none of these qualities.

[margin note: In the absence of sentient creatures, there's no color, sound, taste, heat, cold, etc.]

Locke's view implies that our senses are fundamentally and ineradicably misleading when it comes to secondary qualities. He thinks that these failures of appearance to match reality lead us to make errors of judgment and belief. In speaking of the secondary qualities, he says that they "are commonly thought to be the same in those Bodies, that those *Ideas* are in us, the one the perfect resemblance of the other, as they are in a Mirror; and it would by most Men be judged very extravagant, if one should say otherwise."[5] I believe that the color I am directly conscious of when I look at a tomato is an objective, independent property of the tomato. In that, I am mistaken. For the color is just a subjective effect of the light reflected from the tomato upon my visual system. Locke's view implies that sense awareness is fundamentally deceptive, not only in the failure of the appearances to match reality, but also in its causing us to form false beliefs throughout our waking lives.

[margin note: sense awareness is fundamentally deceptive]

Next, we will consider Locke's reason for thinking that the secondary qualities differ from the primary ones with respect to the question of the accuracy of representation.

2. Color

[handwritten annotation: Reason that Secondary qualities differ from primary ones]

Earlier I mentioned some examples of the ways that our senses deceive us, such as the straight stick that looks bent in water. According to our original understanding, this type of failure of appearance to match reality occurs infrequently. Moreover, since

Locke says we are always misled by sense

we seldom fall into error even in such cases, mistakes in judgment are even less frequent. According to Locke, by contrast, our senses deceive us on every occasion; the appearances of the secondary qualities never match the reality. But since we think that they do match the reality, we invariably make errors in judgment.

When I say, for example, that the book is brown, the judgment that I make says that the book possesses the very color that I am directly conscious of, the color that is presented in my sense awareness of the book. But the book does not possess that color. So, taken as we intend it, the judgment is false. There is another judgment that we might make in the same words that says that the book possesses the power of causing a sensation of brown in sentient creatures. But that is not the judgment that we intend to make when we think that the book is brown. So what we actually think is false, and the judgment that is true is not one that it occurs to us to assert. Therefore, as long as we remain within the original understanding, the information about the external world that is transmitted to us in sense awareness includes a great deal of misinformation. We are, so Locke's view implies, thoroughly misled in our beliefs about nature.

Locke's reason for claiming that the secondary qualities are not objective in the way the primary ones are is formulated succinctly in these words: "Why is Whiteness and Coldness in Snow, and Pain not, when it produces the one and the other *Idea* in us; and can do neither, but by the Bulk, Figure, Number, and Motion of its solid Parts?"[6] In this argument, he is pressing an analogy between pain, on the one hand, and color, on the other. Both the pain caused in us when we come into contact with the frigid snow and the white color we become aware of when we look at it are caused in the same way, by the action of the snow's primary qualities upon our sense organs. We admit without any hesitation that the pain is subjective and dependent. We have no inclination whatsoever to ascribe the pain to the snow, rather than to us. But since our awareness of color is brought about in the same way as our feeling of pain, we should agree that the color is subjective and dependent as well.

secondary qualities are subjective

The following objection to Locke's argument is likely to occur to us immediately. Even if we agree that our awareness of the color is brought about, like the awareness of the pain, by the action of

challenge:
color is obj. of color
awareness is subj.)

the snow upon our sense organs, even if the *awareness* is something subjective and dependent, it doesn't follow that the color we are aware of is subjective and dependent. The white color is the object of our awareness. Although the awareness is subjective, its object need not be. After all, Locke does not claim that the snow is subjective and dependent even though we are aware of it. So with what right does he claim that its color is subjective and dependent?[7]

In order to reply to this objection, we need to make use of the principle of simplicity in much the same way as we did in the discussion of sound (in chapter 1, section 4). Locke thinks that the only qualities we need to assume in the snow in order to explain how it causes us to see white are the primary qualities. The white color that we see plays no role at all in this explanation. So there is no reason, according to the principle of simplicity, to commit ourselves to the existence of objective color. Our awareness of color is a consequence of the action of the atomic structures of bodies upon our visual organs. Color itself is not a property of the atomic structures of bodies; neither Locke's corpuscularian hypothesis nor the atomic theory of modern physics supposes that the colors we see are properties of the atoms or of collections of atoms. To continue to believe that bodies have the colors we see is a useless supposition that plays no role in any explanation of our experience.

refute:
the object is not composed of color) so color b/c a bi-product subj).

I would, however, like to suggest a modification of Locke's approach that will succeed in showing how radical a viewpoint he is espousing when compared to that of the original understanding. I pointed out in the previous section that, according to Locke, there are two kinds of colors: the colors we are directly aware of, which exist only in sensation, and the colors that are defined as powers of bodies to cause sensations in us. But I find no such duality in our use of color terms. When I say "This is red" and then say "This looks red," the word 'red' has the same meaning in both cases. This absence of semantic duality is illustrated when I say "This has the red color that it looks to have." This assertion implies that the red in the appearance or sensation is the same as the red ascribed to the object.

Even though objects do possess the powers to cause sensations in us, as Locke believes, our concept of color is not the concept of a power any more than is our concept of shape. Our understanding of what color is, is acquired through our direct acquaintance with colors in sense experience. Colors are just those very items that sighted people experience whenever their eyes are open, and those very items are not powers. So instead of saying with Locke that material things have colors, although the colors they have are not the same as the colors that sense awareness acquaints us with, it would be better to say that bodies have no colors at all, and that the only colors there are, are those we are acquainted with in sense experience.

This modification of Locke's view will very likely be found objectionable by physical scientists who study color. If bodies do not have color at all, what, then, are they studying? Color and sound are topics within physics. There are successful physical theories explaining the nature of color and sound. So there is no plausibility in the claim that there is no color in the external world. For example, the great physicist Max Planck has written: "Physical definitions of tone, color and temperature are no longer derived from the immediate impressions of the corresponding senses. Tone and color are defined in terms of frequencies or wavelengths."[8] According to this view, color is to be identified with some of the physical features in nature responsible for our sense awareness of color. Planck suggests, in this passage, that color according to the modern physical definition consists of light waves. Others have suggested that color consists of those aspects of the atomic structures of bodies that explain the reflection, absorption, and emission of light.

When physical scientists discuss color, what they are actually speaking about are some of these physical features that contribute to our visual awareness of color, as well as other related physical factors. However, none of these physical factors can actually be identified with color, for one very simple reason: colors are items that we can see – we are directly acquainted with them – whereas these physical features such as light waves and atomic structures are imperceptible – they are items postulated in scientific theories for their explanatory utility. The visible light that we see is not the same thing as the imperceptible light waves postulated in physical theory.

When Max Planck speaks of the physical definition of color, he is, in effect, using the word 'color' for something different from what we represent by that term. The concept that such a definition introduces is not the same as the concept of color that we have arrived at through sense awareness. It would be better, and less confusing, to have different terms for the different concepts. Perhaps the items introduced in the physical definition could be called "color★," and particular instances of it labeled 'red★', 'green★', and so on. Then we can say that what the physicists are talking about are not colors but colors★. We can then formulate our modified Lockean position by saying that even though bodies possess colors★, they do not possess colors. But then the question comes to mind: Does nothing have color? If colors are not objective and independent, perhaps they are subjective and dependent. Let us consider this possibility.[9]

3. Color Skepticism

Locke's view of the secondary qualities suggests that the colors we see are subjective and dependent; they exist in the sensory representations, and only in the sensory representations, that are constituents of our visual sense awareness of the external world. Although no material thing is red, the color red that we see is ascribable to the sensation that occurs when we look at something that looks red.

However, there are weighty reasons not to go along with Locke here. In the first place, the forms of speech we use to refer to our sensory representations do not imply Locke's view. When I say, for example, that something looks red, my assertion does not imply that anything is red. The thing that looks red may not be red; nor is anything else said to be red. Even if, as I have argued, when something looks red, there exists a visual sensation of red, this way of speaking does not imply that the look or the sensation is itself red. To say that something is a sensation of red does not require us to say that it is a red sensation, anymore than saying that something looks like snow implies that the sensation consists of snow.

In the second place, the Lockean view is not consistent with any plausible theory of the mind and its relation to the body. When philosophers and psychologists speak of the mind, they mean to refer to that which connects and unifies the various thoughts, emotions, desires, beliefs, and sensations that occur in human experience. There are many views about what this connecting factor is, and there is not enough room here to survey all of the prominent theories. So the best I can do is to illustrate the argument against Locke by mentioning two of the dominant theories of mind.

The first is associated with the philosopher René Descartes (1596–1650), according to which the mind is a substance distinct from the body. It is sometimes called 'mind–body dualism', on the ground that it asserts that mind and body are two separate principles. Descartes did not deny that mind and body interact. When, for example, I look at something red, events in my body cause a sensation of red to occur; but the sensation itself is a mental event that is numerically distinct from any physical event. Also, when I decide to move my hand, my decision is a mental act of the will that causes changes in the brain and nervous system that cause my hand to move.

According to Descartes, a fundamental difference between mind and body is a consequence of their different relation to extension, one of Locke's primary qualities. To say that something is extended is just to say that it is spread out in space. A body or material thing is essentially a thing that is extended, whereas the mind is unextended; the essential feature of the mind is that it is a thing that thinks.[10]

The second view of the mind that I shall mention here is the materialist position that the mind just consists of the brain and nervous system, and that events going on in the mind are really just brain processes. The most prominent representative of materialism among Descartes's contemporaries was the English philosopher Thomas Hobbes (1588–1679). Materialism in one version or another has become the dominant view of the mind in recent philosophy.[11] Dualists reject materialism on the grounds that there is no intelligible way to understand how mental states could be brain processes. How can a thought which has a certain content and meaning be the very same thing as a burst of electricity or a chemical change among the neurons of the brain? Materialists have exercised a great deal of ingenuity in their efforts to show that there is nothing absurd in this identification. They argue that if mental events could be brain processes, then the principle of simplicity requires that they be identified with brain processes.

Locke's claim about the subjective reality of colors and the other secondary qualities fits with neither dualism nor materialism. Let us consider dualism first.

According to the dualist view, a sensation of red is an event occurring in the mind. Now it is not obvious what this phrase 'in the mind' can mean for a dualist, since the mind is unextended and cannot have anything 'in' it in the spatial sense. What the dualist should say is that even though the mind is not extended, it is a thing or substance capable of undergoing changes, and a sensation of red is just one of those changes. To say that something is in the mind is just to say that it is one of those changes that the mind is undergoing, or one of those states that it exemplifies.

Consider the color red. There is a strong association between red (or any other color for that matter) and extension. Many philosophers have thought it quite obvious that anything that is colored is necessarily extended, that any thing or object that exemplifies a color must be something that is spread out in space. If that is so, then, if the sensation of red is itself a red thing, it too must be extended. But then something extended would have to be attributed to a thing which is not extended. This would make the thing that is not extended into an extended thing. So a dualist cannot consistently claim that colors have a subjective reality. The fact that something looks red implies that there is some mental event which itself could *not* be red. *dualist view*

Since the materialist replaces the unextended mental substance with the extended brain, there is no similar logical incoherence in his claiming that mental states are colored. However, there is nothing in our current understanding of sensory processes that suggests that when something looks red to someone, there is actually a red patch occurring in his brain, or nervous system, or in his retina or optic nerve. What are occurring are various chemical and electrical events, but there is no reason the suppose that any of them exemplify the color red. So neither the materialist nor the dualist can find any room within the mind for color.

A theory of the mind that rejects both dualism and materialism, that allows mental states to be extended but denies that mental states are to be identified with brain states, could, in theory, find a place for color. There actually is such a theory, sometimes called '*neutral monism*', which was suggested by some remarks of David Hume (1711–76) and developed by William James (1842–1910) and others.[12] According to neutral monism, reality consists of items of a sensory sort: items that in themselves are neither mental nor physical but are like the extended patches of color or the sounds that we encounter in sense experience. The difference between mind and matter is not intrinsic to this neutral stuff but is determined by the ways that these items are arranged. Mind consists of bundles of items arranged in one way, and matter of such bundles arranged in another way.

Neutral monism is the outcome of a radical version of empiricism. It is not among the theories of mind that are now considered candidates for a true theory. The reason is that efforts to construct minds and bodies as represented in the original understanding from these neutral sensory data have not been successful. The cost of giving up our concepts of matter and mind has been thought greater than the benefits produced. The main benefit of radical empiricism is its alleged ability to avoid skepticism. We shall see later, however, in chapters 3 and 5, that skepticism may be rebutted in other ways.

The outcome of this discussion is that if the claim that color has a subjective, dependent existence means that colored things exist 'in' the mind, then that claim is mistaken. Of course, if it is just taken to mean that things look to be colored, then it is true but compatible with the view argued for here that nothing mental is colored.

Earlier I argued that nothing physical is colored; colors have no objective reality in the external world. If the mental and the physical exhaust what there is, then the conclusion is that nothing has color, nothing at all. There are no colored objects in the external world, and no colored objects in the mental world. Color is neither objective and independent nor subjective and dependent. Every judgment in which we assert of something that it has a color, such as "This tomato is red" or "Snow is white" is, literally, false. Let me call this view '*color skepticism*'.[13] It is the outcome of various modifications and corrections imposed on Locke's theory of the secondary qualities.

Although I think that color skepticism is true, it usually meets with intense expressions of disbelief from those hearing of it for the first time. How can one possibly think that nothing has color? Don't we see colored items? How can we disregard the evidence of our senses in such an extreme and radical way? Certainly, if anything is a reason for thinking that something exists, the evidence of our senses is. In vision, we see colored things. There is no stronger reason at all for believing in the existence of something. Let us consider this argument at greater length.

4. Observation and Acquaintance

The notion of the evidence of the senses is somewhat ambiguous. In everyday life, such evidence consists in the reports we make about what we have observed. We observe this and that and the other thing, and our judgments about what we have observed and our recollection of them and the records we have made of them serve as evidence for many of our beliefs. Thus, for example, I observe a certain expression on someone's face and judge that the person is angry.

Our judgments formulating what we observe – 'observation reports' – are by no means infallible. The expression which I report as an angry look may instead be an expression of some other emotion. Macbeth thought he saw a bloody dagger, but he soon realized that it was just "a dagger of the mind, a false creation, proceeding from the heat-oppressed brain" (Act II, sc. 1). So the mere fact that there are many observation reports that say that this, that, or the other thing has a certain color does not establish conclusively that anything is colored. Perhaps these observations are hallucinations, like Macbeth's, fostering false beliefs; no doubt these beliefs are useful and do indeed track various objective properties and events in the external world, but they are false nonetheless.

Observation reports about the external world are founded upon sense awareness which incorporates, as we have seen, a representative element. I am able to perceive items that are objective and independent through my consciousness of sensory representations that embody information about the objects of perception.

This representative account of sense awareness allows us to

distinguish between what we are directly conscious of and, to use a term of Bertrand Russell's, what we know by 'acquaintance' from other items whose apprehension is indirect, via representations and inferences. There is an argument that what we know by acquaintance constitutes a conclusive reason for thinking that there are colored things. Here is H. H. Price's well-known formulation of this argument:

> When I see a tomato there is much that I can doubt. I can doubt whether it is a tomato that I am seeing, and not a cleverly painted piece of wax. I can doubt whether there is any material thing there at all. Perhaps what I took for a tomato was really a reflection; perhaps I am even the victim of some hallucination. One thing however I cannot doubt: that there exists a red patch of a round and somewhat bulgy shape, standing out from a background of other colour-patches, and having a certain visual depth, and that this whole field of colour is directly present to my consciousness.[14]

When Price says he cannot doubt that there is something red which he is directly conscious of (or acquainted with), he means to assert that it is something he cannot be mistaken about. There is a possibility of error about the nature of this red thing: whether it is mental or physical, whether it is a tomato or a hallucination of a tomato – these are things he can doubt. "But that something is red and round then and there I cannot doubt."[15]

The notion of doubt that enters into Price's argument has a certain ambiguity. It has, on the one hand, a psychological sense: namely, that Price cannot bring himself to believe that there is nothing red "then and there." But more importantly as far as the argument is concerned, the notion functions as a term of *epistemic* (or cognitive) evaluation. Price is not only saying that he cannot do anything to bring about the psychological state of disbelieving the existence of something red; he is also claiming that error cannot occur in this case. But why not? If error can occur with respect to his belief that what he is seeing is a tomato, why can it not occur with respect to his belief that there is something red there?

The reason for this exclusion of the possibility of error is that one cannot be in error about things one is directly conscious of.

But again, why not? I have a striped necktie that I like quite well, and I have always thought that some of the stripes are black. One day my wife asked me why I was wearing a tie with dark green stripes with a red shirt. "Dark green? No, dear, black." "I beg your pardon, dark green." We inspected the tie in a good light and still disagreed. One of us was wrong, and I suspect it was me. But I still do not see the green. The point is that many sensory qualities are borderline cases, and therefore, error is possible. I may be directly conscious of a dark green patch while judging it to be black.

We can even explain the possibility of error in such cases by noting the distinction between direct consciousness and the judgments based on it. Direct consciousness, or acquaintance, is not itself a cognitive state. It is not a state of belief or knowledge. It is just a state in which something is given; it is a sensory event. In the judgments that attempt to describe and classify items of direct consciousness, a concept is applied to a datum. Thus, in Price's example the concept 'red' is applied to the patch he is acquainted with when he takes it to be red. Since the occurrence of the sensory event and the subsequent judgment are distinct, logically independent items, there is no logical impossibility in supposing that the wrong concept has been applied. Perhaps there is less room for error than in other cases, but there is room nevertheless, and as the necktie example illustrates, errors do occur.

Be that as it may, this way in which error may occur is not relevant to the issue we are discussing. Even if Price might have erred with respect to the identity of the color he was acquainted with, could he have been mistaken about whether there is something there of some color or other? How could he have been mistaken in his belief that there is something there that is colored? Of course, the sensory event and the judgment that something is colored there and then are logically independent items, so there remains a logical possibility of error. But, Price may argue, the likelihood of error is so negligible that it need not be taken into account.

However, there is a further consideration that tends to show that even in this case, Price is mistaken in thinking that there exists something colored that he is directly conscious of. It has to do with the status of images. Let us turn to this issue.

5. Images

If you look at a bright light for a short time and then stare at a blank wall or screen, you will very likely see an after-image. The image is ephemeral and disappears very quickly. Suppose, now, that I see an image of a reddish color; it is something of which I am directly conscious. My apprehension of it is not reached by inference or by any introspectible intellectual process. It is present in my visual field for direct inspection. According to Price's argument, the experience of seeing a reddish after-image establishes that something red exists: namely, the image.

Do we want to say, then, that after-images actually exist? What can that mean? They do not occupy physical space even though they appear to be located upon the surfaces on which they are projected. Someone else scrutinizing the place on the screen where the image seems to be located will find nothing there, and no physical instruments will detect it. The argument in section 3 above established that the image does not exist 'in' the mind. Some philosophers have postulated the existence of an inner, or private, space – what Kant called a 'form of sensibility' – as the locus of the direct objects of visual awareness. But the status of private space is as problematic and puzzling as the status of the images themselves.

The ontology that has been assumed in the preceding discussion of sense awareness and color is this: there is an external physical world consisting of material things, their primary qualities, and the spatial and temporal relations among them. Among these material things are the bodies of animal organisms. Connected to some of these animal bodies in ways that we do not yet understand are mental states, among which are sensory events. These mental states may belong to a mental substance, as Descartes thought, or they may be identical with brain states, or they may simply be in causal interaction with brain states. There is no room for after-images in this ontology. Although after-image sensations of reddish spots exist, it doesn't follow that the reddish spots themselves exist.

The feeling that there must be something really there that we are seeing may be just a product of the language we use to report such experiences. For example, consider the sentence: "I see a reddish image." How can one see something that isn't really there? Philosophers have pointed out that the word 'see' is an achievement verb.[16] Unlike the verb 'looks', which represents an activity, 'see' indicates a success. For example, after looking for my watch, I see it on the kitchen table. The watch's being on the kitchen table is a state of affairs whose existence I am now assured of, and I express that assurance by using the word 'see'. Some philosophers have concluded, therefore, that the existence of something seen follows from the fact that it is seen.

However, we frequently use 'see' in cases where we know that the items seen do not exist. For example, we say that the drunkard sees pink rats or that a person sees the railroad tracks converge in the distance, though he knows quite well that they are parallel. We tend to use 'see' not merely when we are assured that there really is something to be seen, but also when the sense experiences involve relatively stable, clearly delineated images. Perhaps when we are operating within the original understanding without the benefit of scientific theory or philosophical reflection, we have no well-defined view about the ontological status of images and related phenomena, so the use of 'see' does not seem inappropriate in these cases.

It is likely that Price uses "directly conscious" to represent an achievement, as does Russell in his use of "acquaintance." Given this usage, it does follow that what someone is directly conscious of or acquainted with exists. But we cannot resolve the issue just by examining the semantic properties of these verbs. The question is whether or not we are justified in using them in these cases. Only if a round red patch actually exists is Price justified in asserting that he is directly conscious of one.

It is well known that some verbs reporting our states of mind do have existential implications, and others do not. For example, it does not follow from the fact that I am imagining a unicorn that any unicorns exist, although this *would* follow from the statement that I am touching a unicorn. The verb 'see' is used sometimes with and sometimes without such an implication. Thus the fact that we are inclined to say that we see a reddish after-image does not settle the ontological question. If we think that there are no such things, we could just as well say that it *seems* as if there is a reddish image, and this way of putting the matter is ontologically neutral.

Let us return to Price's "tomato" argument. The one thing he cannot doubt, he says, is "that there exists a red patch of a round and somewhat bulgy shape." However, he was easily able to doubt the existence of a tomato; perhaps it is just a painted piece of wax. He could report his doubt by saying that although it seems as if there is a tomato there, there may possibly not be a tomato there. He could have said something similar about the red patch: namely, that although it seems as if there is a red patch of a round and somewhat bulgy shape, there may not actually be a red, round, bulgy patch there. He does not show why the sense experience of there being a red patch should be treated any differently from the sense experience of there being a tomato. Both sense experiences (they are actually the same, though described differently) convey information that one is surely inclined to accept: namely, that there is a tomato there and that there is something red there. But the fact that we are inclined to accept it shows neither that it is true nor that we are immune to error if we should accept it. So his argument fails to demonstrate that color skepticism is mistaken.

There is, nevertheless, a legitimate worry that may overtake us. Doesn't the evidence of the senses count for something? Moreover, there is this objection: my argument for color skepticism leaves our noncolor perceptual beliefs intact; I may have argued that nothing has color, but I have not argued that there are no tomatoes or that nothing is round and bulgy; so I am willing to accept the evidence of the senses in some cases, though not in others. How much weight should we give to the evidence of the senses? Let us now turn to this issue.

6. The Evidence of the Senses

Even if the appeal to the evidence of the senses does not provide a conclusive refutation of color skepticism, it certainly shows that we have quite a good reason for thinking that there are colored objects. Here is a red tomato. I see it; you see it; anyone can see it just by looking at it. What better reason can anyone have for establishing the existence of something?

Before we can address the issue, it is necessary to become clear about what the evidence of the senses consists in. On one conception, it consists in those objects, events, and states of affairs that we see or hear or otherwise apprehend through sense awareness; we then make use of such knowledge of the external world as the basis for our further knowledge of nature. On this conception, the evidence of the senses consists in observations of what is really there, together with the true observation reports which record these achievements of sense awareness. Locke calls this conception 'sensitive knowledge'.[17]

However, this is not the conception that is pertinent to our present discussion. At issue is the question of color skepticism, and we want to know whether or not in some particular case we actually have sensitive knowledge of the existence of colored things. When Price looks into his pantry, does he acquire sensitive knowledge of the existence of a red tomato there? That is the question. Given that it looks to him as if there is a red tomato there, and given that it looks to anyone else who happens to glance in that direction as if there is a red tomato there, does it follow that they know that there is a red tomato there? The evidence of the senses that is pertinent is the occurrence of those sense experiences, those sensations of color, that lead us to believe that there are colored objects in the world. How accurate are these sensory representations? Do they provide the foundation and basis of sensitive knowledge? Can I reasonably conclude that there is a red tomato there just because it looks to me to be there?

When do the appearances provide evidence, or good reasons, for how things really are? Suppose I am confronted with some item – call it X – that I take as evidence for the existence of some other item – call it Y. Then my knowledge of the existence of X is evidence for the existence of Y when X is one of a class of similar items which usually occur only when an item that resembles Y occurs. For example, the existence of the smoke that I see is evidence for the existence of a fire that is out of my view, because smoke is usually accompanied by fire. In such cases, X functions as the sort of representation that we call a '*sign*'. This smoke is a sign of that fire. When X is a sign of Y, then for any person who knows that when items resembling X occur, usually items resembling Y occur, X carries the information that Y probably exists.

For anyone who knows that smoke is usually accompanied by fire, the particular smoke he sees carries the information that it is likely that there is a fire in the vicinity.

Are our sensory representations signs of objects and states of affairs in the external world? In particular, is the fact that it looks to me as if there is something red there a sign that there really is something red there? If the answer is "Yes," then the occurrence of a sensation of red provides quite a good reason for believing in the existence of a red object, and thus quite a good reason for rejecting color skepticism.

The sensation is a sign only if it is usually accompanied by a red object. That this tomato looks red is a sign that it is red only if sensations of red are usually accompanied or caused by things that really are red. So we cannot establish that color sensations are signs of colored things unless we first have reason to believe that color skepticism is false. Therefore, we cannot use facts about the colors which objects look to have as an argument against color skepticism, because such facts function as good reasons for believing in the existence of colored objects only if we already have good reason for rejecting color skepticism.

The judgments we make on the basis of sensory experience are usually involuntary. When I look at a tomato, my experience triggers the belief that it is red; I have no choice in the matter. Even if I should accept the argument for color skepticism, I will still believe that the tomato is red. Let us call such involuntary beliefs triggered by the use of our faculties when we operate within the original understanding 'natural beliefs'. Though involuntary, natural beliefs are not beyond rational criticism even within the original understanding. Further experiences or the contrary reports of others may lead me to change my mind. The beliefs that replace those that are natural are 'instructed beliefs'.

Because natural beliefs are triggered by sense experiences and constitute efforts to extract information from them, they constitute interpretations of those experiences. In every moment of our waking lives, we are interpreting the data of the senses to gain information about the external world. In a famous passage, Kant wrote:

Thoughts without content are empty, intuitions without concepts are blind. It is, therefore, just as necessary to make our concepts sensible, that is, to add the object to them in intuition, as to make our intuitions intelligible, that is, to bring them under concepts. These two powers or capacities cannot exchange their functions. The understanding can intuit nothing, the senses can think nothing. Only through their union can knowledge arise.[18]

One of the points that Kant makes so eloquently here is that our sense experience has no meaning for us unless it is interpreted in the light of concepts already in our possession. We need to subsume our intuitions – that is, our experiences in which an object is given – under concepts, in order for experience to be intelligible to us.

Let me now introduce the term '*conceptual framework*' to indicate a fundamental system of concepts and beliefs that underlies efforts to render our experience intelligible. The conceptual framework of an individual incorporates the basic ontological commitments that are presupposed in his or her efforts to make sense of the ways things appear. There is a conceptual framework that underlies our original understanding. This framework is, in the words of P. F. Strawson, "the actual structure of our thought about the world." He goes on to characterize the conceptual framework of the original understanding in these words:

For there is a massive core of human thinking which has no history – or none recorded in histories of thought; there are categories and concepts which, in their most fundamental character, change not at all. Obviously these are not the specialties of the most refined thinking. They are the commonplaces of the least refined thinking; and are yet the indispensable core of the conceptual achievement of the most sophisticated human beings.[19]

Our natural beliefs are the products of the conceptual framework of the original understanding when applied to our sense experiences. Within that conceptual framework of thought is the claim that there are material objects, and that those objects large enough to be seen have colors. What we already think as a result of our conceptual scheme is that there are colored objects. No wonder we cannot help thinking that the tomato is red when we look at it. That it is red is an instance of an ingrained way of thinking, a way of thinking that is likely to be the result of human evolution and that may very well be either innate or so deeply ingrained as to be ineliminable. Even if I convince myself that there are no colored objects, I will be unable to cease believing that tomatoes are red, lemons yellow, and snow white.

However, we are capable of transcending our entrenched, inherited framework of thought in the following way. We can first make it an object of thought; we can reflect upon it, make it explicit, and develop its implications. We can also wonder how much of it is true and attempt to criticize it. Thus the arguments for color skepticism can be understood as constituting a criticism of a fragment of the conceptual scheme of the original understanding. Wilfrid Sellars, who argues for a version of color skepticism, says: "Although the framework of perceptible objects, the manifest framework of everyday life, is adequate for the everyday purposes of life, it is ultimately inadequate and should not be accepted as an account of what there is *all things considered*."[20] We are able to stand outside the framework to some extent, to comment on it, and to point out that this or that fragment of it may very well be false. Thus, although our judgments of color are involuntary, we can say about them in our moments of philosophical reflection: "These judgments are false, each and every one of them." When I return to the original understanding, I can also bring my criticisms of its framework with me. At the time I judge that the tomato is red, I can whisper to myself: "It really isn't."

The content of the framework of the original understanding was probably constituted, in part at least, by the pressures of natural selection. It is a practical product of the human struggle for existence. It is not a product of philosophical thought or reflection. It is not a product of reasoning, in which we take account of the totality of things that may be said for it and against it. Thus there is no way of providing prior assurance that any particular fragment will survive criticism when, as Sellars says, all things are considered. Thus I cannot agree with Strawson's claim that the commonplaces of our conceptual scheme are "the indispensable core of the conceptual equipment of the most sophisticated human beings." Those parts of it that fail to survive criticism are not indispensable. Our most sophisticated thoughts about nature, about mind, and about human life are not totally constrained by the original understanding. In Plato's terms, we are capable of moving from the dark cave, in which the only things we can apprehend are the illusory reflections of our commonsense picture of reality, into the sunlight, in which those illusions are overcome.

Further Readings

C. L. Hardin, *Color for Philosophers* (Indianapolis: Hackett, 1988).

Immanuel Kant, *Prolegomena to any Future Metaphysics.*

Charles Landesman, *Color and Consciousness: An Essay in Metaphysics* (Philadelphia: Temple University Press, 1989).

John Locke, *An Essay Concerning Human Understanding*, Bk II, ch. viii.

Arthur Lovejoy, *The Revolt against Dualism* (La Salle, Ill.: Open Court, 1929).

Barry Maund, *Colors: Their Nature and Representation* (Cambridge: Cambridge University Press, 1995).

Wilfrid Sellars, "Philosophy and the Scientific Image of Man," in *Science, Perception and Reality* (London: Routledge and Kegan Paul, 1963), pp. 1–40.

3

Skepticism

1. Skepticism with Regard to the Senses

The title of this section echoes the title Hume gave to one of the sections of his *Treatise of Human Nature*. With reference to the skeptic and the belief in the existence of body, he asserts:

> Nature has not left this to his choice, and has doubtless esteem'd it an affair of too great importance to be trusted to our uncertain reasonings and speculations. We may well ask, *What causes induce us to believe in the existence of body?* but 'tis in vain to ask, *Whether there be body or not?* That is a point, which we must take for granted in all our reasonings.[1]

According to Hume, that there are bodies cannot be proved without begging the question, because we assume there are "in all our reasonings." The only question left concerns the psychology of the belief: how we arrive at it. Hume divides the question in two: "Why we attribute a CONTINU'D existence to objects, even when they are not present to the senses; and why we suppose them to have an existence DISTINCT from the mind and perception."[2] We believe that bodies have a continued, distinct existence. Call this belief 'realism'. We are all realists, even the skeptics among us, since we cannot help believing that there is a natural world which transcends our sense experience, which contains material things that have an objective, independent existence and that continue to exist even when no one is experiencing them.

Hume's pessimism about the possibility of providing a philosophical argument sufficient to establish the truth of realism was an outcome of almost a century of intense reflection on the question that began with Descartes's *Meditations on First Philosophy*. Although Descartes was not himself a skeptic and even thought that he had provided a conclusive proof of realism, nevertheless, in the very first of the *Meditations*, he provided a reason for doubting the existence of the external world that was so provocative that the question of realism and the issues that surround it became the central topic on the philosophical agenda.

The discussion of color skepticism in chapter 2 provides a starting point for thinking about Descartes's more radical skepticism. If nothing has color, then all the beliefs we have that say that a particular object has a color are false, even though everyone is convinced that almost all of them are true. This leads us to wonder what other things we are firmly convinced of are also false or, at least, lack adequate foundations. We recognize that others have beliefs which we would classify as prejudices, and if we are honest, we will admit that some of our own beliefs are likely to be prejudices as well. This is the point that Descartes had arrived at when he began to compose his *Meditations*: "Some years ago I was struck by the large number of falsehoods that I had accepted as true in my childhood, and by the highly doubtful nature of the whole edifice that I had subsequently based upon them."[3]

His whole system of beliefs, then, was placed under a cloud of suspicion. He had arrived at a time of life when he had the maturity and leisure necessary to step back from his conceptual framework and the variety of beliefs that it had led him to endorse, to wonder which of them were true, which false. He was not interested in initiating an inquiry into any one belief or any limited group of beliefs, such as whether or not the sun revolved around the earth. This was a task that belonged to the special sciences, and although in the past he himself had conducted scientific investigations into many particular matters, what he was now interested in was the question of the legitimacy of the framework within which he had pursued these inquiries. Realism is a central principle of this framework, so it was inevitable that the question of realism would arise.

He decided that he would pursue the method of doubting all

those "opinions which are not completely certain and indubitable."[4] He would examine various classes of opinions within his belief system, and if he could find reasons to doubt them, then that would show that they lacked a satisfactory foundation, and his assent to them would be suspended until an adequate foundation could be discovered. Of this method of doubt, Descartes said that "its greatest benefit lies in freeing us from all our preconceived opinions, and providing the easiest route by which the mind may be led away from the senses."[5] The method, he thought, would enable us to identify those framework assumptions and classes of beliefs which are merely prejudices, including those which have been acquired by means of sense awareness.

The first class of beliefs to which he applied the method of doubt were those based on sense awareness. Descartes knew very well that "the senses occasionally deceive us with respect to objects which are very small or in the distance."[6] But this is not sufficient to allow us to doubt all our perceptual judgments, since many of them concern objects that are not very small and not far away. For example, how can he bring himself to doubt that "I am here, sitting by the fire, wearing a winter dressing-gown, holding this piece of paper in my hands"?[7]

At this point Descartes turns to the fact that when he sleeps, he dreams, and in his dreams he is convinced that certain things are taking place which in fact have not occurred. "How often, asleep at night, am I convinced of just such familiar events – that I am here in my dressing-gown, sitting by the fire – when in fact I am lying undressed in bed."[8] He also notices that anything he could do to convince himself that he is not dreaming, such as pinching himself, is also something that he could very well dream he was doing. He concludes that "there are never any sure signs by means of which being awake can be distinguished from being asleep,"[9] and that is sufficient to show that his perceptual judgments are not indubitable but are capable of being doubted.

Let us examine more carefully what this appeal to dreams amounts to. In a dream, he thinks, we have various experiences that trigger judgments and beliefs about events we think are occurring in the external world. These experiences resemble those in our waking lives that would trigger similar beliefs. The example of dreams illustrates the general point that the occurrence of an experience *by itself* does not conclusively prove the reality which it persuades us of. The experience might, logically, occur in the absence of that reality. Moreover, there is no feature internal to an experience, taken by itself, that proves that it is veridical, that the information embedded in it is true.

The account of sense awareness provided in the previous chapters supports this view. Sense awareness is an indirect, representative affair. We suppose that the external world impinges upon our sense organs and causes us to experience sensory events. But the sensory event is one thing, and the external object of which we take it to be a sign is another. They are logically independent of one another; one can occur without the other. Thus, the sensory event provides no logical guarantee that the information we extract from it is correct.

The result is that Descartes is now justified in temporarily excluding from his system of beliefs all those opinions that are grounded in sense awareness. These include not merely his beliefs in the existence of material things (including his own body), but, since his conviction that there are other persons as well as himself is founded upon the perception of their bodies, his belief in the existence of others as well. The framework principle of realism that there exist bodies that have a distinct, continued existence is itself thrown into doubt, along with every instance of it. Whereas color skepticism does not lead us to question realism, and, indeed, the arguments for it presuppose realism, Descartes's method of doubt starts us on the road to a much more radical skeptical position.

The term 'empiricism' has come to be used to denote the view that all our substantive knowledge of matters of fact is based upon experience. At the outset of his philosophical reflections, Descartes was inclined to be an empiricist, for he thought that "whatever I have up till now accepted as most true I have acquired either from the senses or through the senses."[10] One of the first consequences of his application of the method of doubt is to throw empiricism into question. For if empiricism claims that the occurrence of our sensory representations is sufficient to justify our perceptual judgments, then, it would appear, that claim is mistaken. We need, rather, some story about our mind and its interaction with the world that would justify our taking the information embedded in sense experience to be correct. There is no guarantee that the story we arrive at would be consistent with empiricist principles or could be justified on empiricist grounds. Hume was an empiricist, but as a result of attempting to apply the empiricist point of view consistently, he was driven to skepticism. Remember his claim that it is vain to ask for a proof of the existence of body. But more of that later.

By the arguments in the first of his *Meditations*, Descartes was able to convince himself "that there is absolutely nothing in the world, no sky, no earth, no minds, no bodies."[11] At this point, he was able to bring his doubts to an end. There is one thing that he cannot bring himself to doubt: namely, that he himself exists. This he cannot doubt. For should he try to doubt it, the very fact of *his* doubting it establishes that he, the one who is doubting, exists. Even if "there is a deceiver of supreme power and cunning who is deliberately and constantly deceiving me, in that case I too undoubtedly exist, if he is deceiving me . . . I must finally conclude that this proposition, *I am, I exist*, is necessarily true whenever it is put forward by me or conceived in my mind."[12]

At this stage in his argument, Descartes is a *solipsist*. He thinks that nothing in the external world exists. He is sure of his own reality, but, for all he knows, there is nothing else besides himself. If each of us were to follow his argument carefully and agree with the reasoning that underlies it, each of us would, at this point, be a solipsist too. Now, it may very well be psychologically impossible for any normal human being actually to be a solipsist in the sense of doubting the reality of others and acting in accord with that doubt. But the doubt that Descartes recommends has no such practical consequences. His method of doubt encourages us to raise questions about the epistemic status of our system of beliefs during the time we are engaged in philosophical reflection on it. But when we cease reflecting and return to the activities of everyday life, we put our doubts aside and act in accordance with our beliefs. So the solipsism we have arrived at is a theoretical affair. But it is not, for all that, trivial and uninteresting, as long as we are intent upon distinguishing those beliefs that are mere prejudices from those that are well founded.

We shall now look more deeply into Descartes's argument and the question of realism.

2. Realism and Skepticism

'Realism' is the view that nature exists independently of mind, that the world of material things has an objective, independent existence. For the realist, if there were no minds at all in the universe, matter would, or could, still exist. Some realists go even further and claim that minds have evolved out of matter and depend upon the material world for their continued existence. Let us call such a view 'naturalism'. Some naturalists take a further step still and argue that mind is reducible to matter, that mental states and events are nothing but physical states, perhaps states of the brain. This view is 'materialism'.

Descartes was neither a naturalist nor a materialist, but he was a realist. The material world exists independently of the sensory experiences and the perceptual judgments whereby we represent it to ourselves. But, since it is possible to doubt the existence of a material world while being quite sure of one's own existence, the problem he faced was how to move from the skepticism of the first of the *Meditations* back to realism. Can the existence of the external world be proved?

Descartes understood the problem in the following way. One can be certain of one's own existence (at least while one is actually thinking) as well as the existence of whatever is going on within one's own mind, such as one's sensations and thoughts. In order to establish that anything else exists and that we actually have knowledge of the external world through our mental representations of it, it is necessary to construct an argument to that effect taking as its premises only the data available in one's own mind. For these are the only data to which one has access once one has applied the method of doubt and arrived at solipsism.

I shall give only a bare sketch of Descartes's way out. One of the ideas he found within his own mind was the idea of God, a perfect being. He then found that using only methods of inference that he could be sure of because they are self-evidently valid, he was able to prove that God is not just an idea in his mind, but actually exists in reality. Since God is perfectly good, we can be sure that he would not deceive us, because deception would be a sign of imperfection. Since God created everything, including our own minds and faculty of judgment, we can be sure that there is nothing intrinsically deceptive in our cognitive faculties and that, provided we take care in the exercise of judgment, we can trust our faculties to provide us with knowledge. This is an outline of his proof of the external world.

You can see that Descartes was not an empiricist. Our knowledge of the external world does not rest just on sense experience, but requires nonempirical, or a priori, principles to validate it. To prove the existence of the external world, it is necessary to make use of principles and ideas that are independent of sense experience. Our sensory representations are not self-validating. Although, for example, my belief that I am seeing a tomato may be triggered by the sensations I am now having, that these sensations are reliable and that this belief is true find no basis within sense experience itself. Because it relies on what Leibniz (1646–1716) called "truths of reason," it is customary to classify Descartes's theory of knowledge as a form of *rationalism*.

Descartes's way out aroused great interest, but almost no support in the epistemological debates in modern philosophy. Hume's reaction is quite typical:

> Descartes . . . recommends an universal doubt, not only of all our former opinions and principles, but also of our very faculties; of whose veracity . . . we must assure ourselves, by a chain of reasoning, deduced from some original principle, which cannot possibly be fallacious or deceitful. But neither is there any such original principle, which has a prerogative above others, that are self-evident and convincing: Or if there were, could we advance a step beyond it, but by the use of those very faculties, of which we are supposed to be already diffident. The CARTESIAN doubt, therefore, were it ever possible to be attained by any human creature (as it plainly is not) would be entirely incurable; and no reasoning could ever bring us to a state of assurance and conviction upon any subject.[13]

Hume does not think that we have access to any self-evident a priori principles that are convincing beyond a reasonable doubt and capable of overcoming radical skepticism. In addition, he finds that Descartes's argument is circular. The effort to prove God's existence makes use of the very cognitive capacities whose reliability we have been led to doubt. So the argument assumes their reliability, even though this is a point that needs to be proved. In addition, "if the external world be once called in question, we shall be at a loss to find any arguments, by which we may prove the existence of that Being [God] or any of his attributes."[14] Hume thinks that there are no sound a priori arguments for God's existence. The only argument that has any chance of success is the empirical argument from design based upon the order and harmony of nature. But Descartes is prohibited from using that argument since he has been led to doubt the reality of nature. Hume tried to show in his *Dialogues Concerning Natural Religion* that even the design argument is defective. He thinks that Descartes's appeal "to the veracity of the supreme Being in order to prove the veracity of our senses, is surely making a very unexpected circuit."[15] Not only is it unexpected, it is fruitless.

Hume makes no effort to offer a better proof, one that is not vulnerable to these criticisms. As we have seen, he thinks that "'tis in vain to ask, *Whether there be body or not?*" As a philosopher, he is a skeptic about the existence of the external world, although, like Descartes, he does not carry his doubts into practical life.

> I dine, I play a game of back-gammon, I converse, and am merry with my friends; and when after three or four hours' amusement, I wou'd return to these speculations, they appear so cold, and strain'd, and ridiculous, that I cannot find in my heart to enter into them any farther. Here then I find myself absolutely and necessarily determin'd to live, and talk, and act like other people in the common affairs of life. . . . In this blind submission, I shew most perfectly my sceptical disposition and principles.[16]

Hume shows how we can combine skepticism with realism. "In the common affairs of life," he is a realist like everyone else. That there is a world whose existence transcends his sense impressions he does not doubt when he leaves off his philosophical researches and reenters the framework of the original understanding necessary for practical life. But when, as a philosopher, he considers the doubts about the existence of the external world such as those that Descartes offered, he finds that he cannot answer them. His realism is founded upon natural instinct, rather than rational argument.

Hume's skeptical response to Descartes's arguments was by no means greeted with enthusiasm in the philosophical world. For example, Kant, who knew and respected Hume's writings, asserted:

> It still remains a scandal to philosophy and to human reason in general that the existence of things outside us (from which we derive the whole material of knowledge, even for our inner sense) must be accepted merely on *faith*, and that if anyone thinks good to doubt their existence, we are unable to counter his doubts by any satisfactory proof.[17]

Kant suggests a particular reason why the absence of a proof of the external world "remains a scandal to philosophy." We derive, he says, "the whole material of knowledge" from "the existence of things outside us." Therefore, the absence of a proof undermines all human knowledge. Although we think that science provides us with reliable knowledge of nature, although we trust the beliefs of everyday life in navigating the perils of the world, in the absence of a proof, we have no reason to assert that any of this constitutes genuine knowledge. Each of us frequently asserts things we think we know; in the absence of a proof, Kant suggests, every one of these assertions lacks a rational foundation.

Let us now examine some of the attempts to remove this "scandal to philosophy."

3. Realism and Idealism

We have thus far considered two versions of realism: direct and representative. There is a division within representative realism that is implicit in much that has been said, but it has not been formulated explicitly. One may be convinced by the powerful arguments against direct realism that in sense awareness we are acquainted not with things in themselves but with our mental representations of them, and yet still believe that the fundamental features of things in themselves – that objective and independent system of objects we call nature – is just as we represent it to be. Our commonsense understanding of nature is basically correct. Let us call this position 'commonsense representative realism'.

Locke's distinction between primary and secondary qualities challenged this form of representationalism. According to Locke, nature is quite different from what it seems to be. It bears no resemblance to our representation of it with respect to the secondary qualities. The real essences of material objects, to the extent to which they are knowable at all, are more accurately represented by the hypotheses of what he calls "natural philosophy" – what we today describe as the "physical sciences." The name we shall adopt for the version of representative realism which says, first, that the physical sciences provide us with the most accurate understanding of nature as it is in itself, independently of its effects upon the human sensory apparatus, and second, that, so understood, things in themselves bear only a slight resemblance to our prescientific conception of them is 'scientific realism' (to be discussed in chapter 5, section 7).

Both versions of representative realism are vulnerable to the skeptical arguments propounded by Descartes. If one agrees with Hume and other skeptics that there is no rational procedure by which we can prove the existence of the external world and that the only things we can be sure of are the existence of ourselves and the contents of our minds, one might search for an alternative to skepticism which says that there is no need to transcend the contents of our minds, because all we mean by an external world is a certain arrangement of these very contents. This is the view that has come to be called 'idealism'.

A number of philosophers are customarily classified as idealists, such as Kant and Schopenhauer. However, the interpretations which justify this classification are controversial, so I shall discuss here the views of George Berkeley (1685–1753) as reflecting the purest form of idealism in the history of Western thought. Berkeley called his own system 'immaterialism'; the term 'idealism' was not then in use. For Berkeley I is the same as

Berkeley offered a number of powerful arguments against realism, but I shall focus here upon one strand of his thought that he presents in two paragraphs of his *Treatise Concerning the Principles of Human Knowledge* (paragraphs 18 and 19). Given that we are directly acquainted only with our sensations, how are we able to know about the existence of a transcendent material world? Berkeley points out that such knowledge cannot be based upon our senses alone, because the data they provide are all subjective and dependent. These data are, in his terms, ideas in the mind, and they exist only when they are perceived. Knowledge of bodies, he thinks, can be founded only by "inferring their existence from what is immediately perceived by sense."

The inference must be one of two kinds. It is either a necessary inference, whereby, given some phenomenon X, we conclude that there must also exist something else, call it Y, or a probable inference, whereby we infer that Y probably exists given that X exists. But it cannot be a necessary inference because, as Descartes pointed out in his dream argument, it is possible for our sense experience to be what it is even though nothing in the external world should correspond to it. "It is possible we might be affected with all the ideas we have now, though no bodies existed without, resembling them." When it looks to me as if I am seeing a tomato, although I can be sure that I am having this experience, it does not follow conclusively that there actually is a tomato there. I may be dreaming or hallucinating, or being deceived in some way or other. These are all possibilities consistent with my having this experience.

Perhaps the most we are entitled to say is that it is probable that there is a tomato there. But Berkeley does not agree that we can say even that, if by a tomato we mean an independent object that affects our senses. The reason is this. The philosophers against whom Berkeley was arguing, Locke and Descartes in particular, were dualists in their view of the nature of the relation between the mind and the body. They saw the mind as a substance distinct from the body. Both Locke and Descartes believed, as we saw, that the mind and the body are capable of interacting with one another in order to produce both sense experience and action. But if you asked them how it is possible for things so different to interact, how an extended object can cause changes in an unextended one and vice versa, their answer would be that this cannot be explained. God made the world so that they do interact, but the fact of their interaction cannot be rendered intelligible to

us. It is just a brute fact; that is the way the world is. We learn
that some physical events in our brain and nervous system are
capable of bringing about certain mental events, and that certain
mental events are capable of bringing about certain physical
changes. But how it happens that, for example, my decision to
raise my arm brings about those events in my brain, nerves, and
muscles that cause my arm to move is beyond our understanding.

Berkeley says of Descartes and Locke that "they own themselves unable to comprehend in what manner body can act upon
spirit, or how it is possible it should imprint any idea in the
mind." Instead of agreeing with them that body does act upon
spirit, even though we do not understand how, Berkeley concludes that "it is evident the production of ideas or sensations in
our minds, can be no reason why we should suppose matter or
corporeal substances, since that is acknowledged to remain equally
inexplicable with, or without this supposition." Since we cannot
comprehend how a tomato can produce the appearance of a tomato in our minds, we have no reason to suppose that there is a
tomato there as something represented by the tomato appearance.
The appearance of the tomato does not even make it probable that
there is a tomato there.

Underlying Berkeley's argument that there is no valid probable
inference from an appearance to a physical reality that causes it is
an assumption that is not easy to formulate, since he himself did
not formulate it. Perhaps it could be put like this: a necessary
condition for the acceptability of a hypothesis that X causes Y is
that it is intelligible how X causes Y. Let us call this the 'principle
of causal intelligibility' (PCI). I shall return to it shortly.

The basic ontological commitments in the philosophical systems of Descartes and Locke are these: there exist minds and their
mental contents (including sense experiences), bodies and their
primary qualities and spatiotemporal relations to one another, and
God. Berkeley's immaterialism drops the commitment to bodies
and their qualities and relationships. The only things that exist are
minds (or spirits) and their contents (or ideas). God is the mind
or spirit that is responsible for all the rest.

Berkeley rejected skepticism; he did not think that he was
rejecting the existence of bodies as they are understood by common sense. Bodies are merely collections of sensible qualities that
are directly perceived. The red color we see, the bulgy shape we

see, the way the tomato feels, tastes, and smells – that is all there is to the tomato. Berkeley is, in effect, defending our original understanding against the scientific realism of Descartes and Locke. The bodies that he excluded from his system of immaterialism are not the familiar things of common sense that we see and touch, but the transcendent material substances that we are not directly acquainted with in sense awareness. There is no inference which is capable of establishing, with either certainty or probability, the existence of matter so understood, the matter of the philosophers.

Berkeley did not reject transcendent inference altogether, for that would have left him trapped in the solipsism of Descartes's first *Meditation*. He thought that one could validly infer the existence of other minds resembling one's own and the existence of God. When I perceive another body act like mine, I justifiably assume that there exists a mind like mine causing those actions. And the existence of God is justified on the grounds that bodies that are not perceived by any human nevertheless continue to exist (as we all think), and therefore they must be perceived by some other spirit, whom Berkeley identifies with God.

The external world is not really external after all, since it has an ideal, or mental, existence. The materialist thinks that if matter did not exist, mind would not exist either. But idealism asserts the contrary: if mind did not exist, matter would not exist. Mind and its contents are things that are intelligible and that we are directly acquainted with, so there can be no doubts about them. But an independently existing material world has no intrinsic intelligibility at all and must be excluded from any plausible ontology.

Idealism makes use of skeptical arguments to dispose of realism and then provides an understanding of the nature of matter to dispose of skepticism. But can material nature be understood as the idealist supposes?

4. Idealism and Constructivism

In his *Life of Samuel Johnson*, James Boswell recounts this anecdote about Johnson, which occurred in 1763:

After we came out of the church, we stood talking for some time together of Bishop Berkeley's ingenious sophistry to prove the non-existence of matter, and that every thing in the universe is merely ideal. I observed, that though we are satisfied his doctrine is not true, it is impossible to refute it. I shall never forget the alacrity with which Johnson answered, striking his foot with mighty force against a large stone, till he rebounded from it, – "I refute it *thus*."[18]

At first glance, Johnson seems merely to have misunderstood Berkeley's proof of the nonexistence of matter. Berkeley did not deny the reality of material things as understood by common sense. The fact that Johnson was able to kick the stone would be sufficient to establish, on Berkeley's grounds, the existence of the stone. Berkeley did not intend to deny the existence of matter as interpreted within the original understanding; what he did reject was the claim of the philosophers that material objects exist independently of mind. After all, everything that Johnson knows of the stone is based on his experience of it: his seeing it, his touching it, his feeling it. An analysis of these forms of sense awareness shows that the things that are immediately perceived exist only when perceived. Locke and Descartes agree with this. And we saw in the preceding section that, for Berkeley, there is no valid inference from the things we immediately perceive to the existence of transcendent bodies that are not immediately perceived and that exist independently of our sense awareness of them.

But further reflection makes us wonder whether the stone that Johnson kicked is susceptible of the interpretation that Berkeley would impose upon it. After all, we think that after Johnson and Boswell departed from the vicinity of the church, the stone continued to lie there. We do not think that it requires the attention of Dr Johnson for it to continue to exist. That is part of our commonsense understanding of the matter, and Berkeley presented himself as a staunch defender of common sense against the supposed sophistries of the philosophers.

Berkeley accepted the proposition that common sense ascribes a continued existence to bodies when they are not being perceived. The way he undertook to make his system compatible with common sense was to bring God into the picture. Things continue to exist independently of our human perception, he claimed, because, when they are not perceived by us, they are perceived by God.

However, Berkeley's attempt to reconcile his immaterialism with common sense fails to appreciate the radical character of the skeptical starting point of the argument. Berkeley considers his system to be a way out of the skepticism of Descartes's first *Meditation*. Let us place ourselves within the solipsistic consciousness that the method of doubt presses upon us, in order to determine whether idealism succeeds in carrying us back to the world of common sense that we have temporarily surrendered.

The solipsistic position tells that the things we are acquainted with in sense awareness are subjective, dependent features of our consciousness. These things do not exist independently of our perception of them. The color I see when I look at a tomato has no independent existence; it continues to exist just so long as I remain conscious of it. The tomato as I apprehend it is just a bundle of subjective contents of my consciousness. Since, according to Berkeley's way of thinking, our understanding of the nature and activities of God is modeled on the nature and activities of our own minds, for we have nothing else to go on, God's perception of the tomato consists of a bundle of subjective contents of *his* consciousness. My tomato perception may very well resemble God's, but it cannot be identical with it. So, when I cease perceiving the tomato, it does go out of existence, even if God continues to perceive something resembling it. Thus it seems unlikely that Berkeley can reconcile his Cartesian and Lockean account of immediate perception with his commitment to common sense. Dr Johnson had a point.

Let us remain within the solipsistic point of view for a few more moments. If you remember, Descartes thought he could justify his belief in an independently existing material world by an inference backed by an assortment of a priori principles and premises. Berkeley, to the contrary, thinks that no such inference can be justified. Putting aside the question of the validity of the inference, let us consider the question of how someone confined within a solipsistic consciousness could even think of, never mind come to believe in, the existence of matter. This is a question Hume thought he could answer, even though he maintained that "'tis vain to ask, *Whether there be body or not?*"

His answer, given in the chapter "Of Scepticism with regard to the Senses" in his *Treatise of Human Nature*, is too complex to be discussed fully here. But part of his account is summarized in these words:

> Our memory presents us with a vast number of instances of perceptions perfectly resembling each other, that return at different distances of time, and after considerable interruptions. This resemblance gives us a propension to consider these interrupted perceptions as the same; and also a propension to connect them by a continu'd existence, in order to justify this identity, and avoid the contradiction, in which the interrupted appearance of these perceptions seems necessarily to involve us. Here then we have a propensity to feign the continu'd existence of all sensible objects; and as this propensity arises from some lively impressions of the memory, it bestows a vivacity on that fiction; or in other words, makes us believe the continu'd existence of body.[19]

Hume here speaks of a fiction produced by the mind that is motivated by certain mental propensities. When, for example, I look at a tomato on several different occasions interrupted by a passage of time, the sense impressions I am conscious of are not actually the same, but resemble one another rather closely. But my mind possesses a tendency to identify the similar impressions, and it succeeds in doing so by pretending that there is an object that continues to exist, even when no one is perceiving it. In the chapter, Hume undertakes to identify the various mental mechanisms we use to produce "the fiction of continu'd existence . . . That fiction, as well as the identity, is really false, as is acknowledg'd by all philosophers, and has no other effect than to remedy the interruption of our perceptions."[20]

Hume's answer to the question of how we arrive at our belief in the existence of an external material world is the product of a kind of armchair psychology whereby he attempts to show that certain features of our sense impressions, when combined with certain innate propensities of the mind, cause us to construct material objects out of the contents of our own minds. The external world is a mental construction. For this reason, we can use the term 'constructivism' as a label for such a position. Constructivism

in general says that "the world we experience is, and must be, as
it is, because *we* have put it together in that way."[21] It is a view
that is the product of skeptical despair regarding the possibility of proving the existence of a transcendent reality and the realization that our sense impressions are too scattered, diffuse, and
ephemeral to constitute the world of our original understanding
and the world of scientific theory. It claims that the human mind
is constituted so as to compensate for the deficiencies of our sense
experience by using principles of its own to create the world
within which we dwell.

But should we yield so quickly to the despair of skepticism?
Berkeley attempted to show that the skeptic is right in denying
the validity of the inference from sense impression to objective
reality. Let us examine his argument more closely.

5. Idealism and Causal Relations

Berkeley is certainly correct in thinking that the inference from
our sense impressions to independently existing material things
that correspond to them is not a necessary one, because it is logically possible for the impression to exist, even though there is no
corresponding object. Descartes's example of the dream and
Macbeth's hallucination of the bloody dagger illustrate this point.
The question I wish to pursue here is whether the inference could
be defended as being probable. Even if I cannot be absolutely
certain that I am seeing a tomato on the basis of the fact that it
looks to me as if I am, even if I cannot *know* that I am seeing a
tomato, perhaps it is more probable than not that there is a tomato there.

Berkeley objects to this inference for the reason that it is supposed to be grounded in causal relations, and the supposition that
matter is capable of causing changes in the mind is unintelligible.
He thinks of the inference in the following way: I am now having
a sense impression of a tomato; in my present circumstances, the
most probable explanation for the occurrence of the sense impression is that there really is a tomato out there affecting my sense
organs; therefore, it is probable that there really is a tomato out
there. But, according to the dualistic way of thinking characteristic

of Berkeley's philosophical predecessors, in order for the tomato to cause the impression, it must then be true that an extended physical thing can bring about changes in an unextended thinking thing. Berkeley thinks that this is unintelligible and cannot occur.

One way to get around Berkeley's argument would be to reject the dualism, adopt a materialistic position, and deny that there are any unextended mental substances. Berkeley, however, would not consider materialism to be any more intelligible than dualism. He would see it as no more intelligible that a brain process is identical with a conscious state, such as a sense experience, than that a brain process can cause a conscious state.

There is, however, another reason for objecting to Berkeley's idealism. Berkeley supposes that whereas the interaction of matter upon mind is unintelligible and therefore cannot exist, the action of mind upon mind and of mind upon its own contents are intelligible. But are they? Suppose I shut my eyes and imagine a red, round tomato. I form, as we say, a mental image. How did I do it? To be honest, I have no idea. I know that I am capable of forming vivid mental images at will, but I have no explanation of this ability, nor is any such explanation available. It is just a fact that I can do it.

In general, when we want to explain how one event, X, is able to bring about another event, Y, we try to discover a series of events that are intermediaries between X and Y. Thus, if X causes M and M causes N and N causes O and O causes Y, then we understand how X is able to bring about Y. The intelligibility of a causal connection depends upon there being intervening events which provide us with a picture of the various steps by which one event leads to another.

When there is no chain of intervening events, this way of rendering causal connections intelligible is not available. Is there any other way? In his famous discussion of causality in *A Treatise of Human Nature*, Hume argued that no causal relations are intrinsically intelligible, that ultimately it is just a brute fact that this causes that, whatever this and that happen to be. He writes:

We are never sensible of any connexion betwixt causes and effects, and . . . 'tis only by our experience of their constant conjunction, we can arrive at any knowledge of this relation.

> Now as all objects, which are not contrary, are susceptible of
> a constant conjunction, and as no real objects are contrary; I
> have inferr'd from these principles, that to consider the matter
> *a priori*, any thing may produce any thing, and that we shall
> never discover a reason, why any object may or may not be
> the cause of any other, however great, or however little the
> resemblance may be betwixt them.[22]

We are only able to determine that X causes Y, thinks Hume,
when we have established a correlation between the classes of
events to which they belong. We observe fire and then observe
smoke. To assert then and there that the fire is responsible for the
smoke would be an example of the fallacy of *post hoc, ergo propter
hoc*, the fallacy of supposing that just because Y follows upon X,
X must be the cause of Y. That the fire caused the smoke can only
be ascertained, Hume thinks, by noticing that other cases of smoke
are accompanied by fire. There is nothing in the nature of fire and
smoke considered separately that justifies us in thinking that the
one must be the cause of the other. A priori, anything can cause
anything.

Hume directly applies his analysis to the mind–body case. "For
tho' there appear no manner of connexion betwixt motion or
thought, the case is the same with all other causes and effects."[23]
He agrees with Berkeley that the relation between mind and body
lacks intrinsic intelligibility and then denies that there is any intrinsic intelligibility in any causal relation. And he is correct on
this point. If my decision to form a mental image of a tomato is
followed immediately by my producing that image, I can ascer-
tain no intervening events between them. And if there are no
intervening events, then there is no further account of how the
image was brought about. The world is so constituted as to allow
certain of its inhabitants to form mental images at will.

But suppose there were intervening events; perhaps we will
discover that immediately after I decided to produce the image, a
series of events occurred in my brain, the last of which, Z, caused
the imagining of the tomato. Berkeley would say that because the
alleged connection between Z and the imagining of the tomato is
unintelligible, it cannot occur. Hume says that since *all* causal
relations are equally unintelligible, this is no bar to their occurring.

So Berkeley's argument against the probable inference of an object corresponding to a sense impression fails. But there is another, more powerful argument. Return, now, to our solipsistic starting point. By analogy with the smoke–fire example, the inference from the sense impression to the tomato depends upon the truth of the premise that such sense impressions are frequently accompanied by the occurrence of a tomato. We can go from the existence of X to the likelihood that Y exists on the basis of a high frequency of cases of X-like events being followed by Y-like events. But how can the solipsist be sure that this premise is true? The only items to which he has direct access are his own mental contents. He knows of the sense impressions, but the accompanying tomatoes are available only as a result of an inference based on his sense impressions. It is that inference which is now in question. There seems to be no way out for the solipsist. Despite Berkeley's efforts to defend common sense, the scandal to philosophy remains.

Are there any other remedies for it?

6. A Proof of the External World

In his paper, "Proof of an External World," G. E. Moore (1873–1958) attempted to remove the scandal by providing a proof. In fact, he thought he could provide many proofs of an external world, and that there was no difficulty at all in finding such proofs.

Here is the passage in which he presents his proof:

> I can now give a large number of different proofs, each of which is a perfectly rigorous proof; and . . . at many other times I have been in a position to give many others. I can now prove, for instance, that two human hands exist. How? By holding up my two hands, and saying, as I make a certain gesture with the right hand, 'Here is one hand', and adding, as I make a certain gesture with the left, 'and here is another'.[24]

If one has followed the arguments pertaining to skepticism with regard to the senses that have been offered by Descartes, Berkeley,

Hume, and many others, and if one has concluded that it is difficult to reason one's way out of solipsism to a realistic point of
view, one's first reaction to this "proof" is to dismiss it with
contempt. After all, the issue, one might suppose, is to find an
inference that is valid and sound and that arrives at the conclusion
that there exist external material things (such as Moore's hands)
on the basis of premises about one's sense impressions and about
anything else one can be sure of. But Moore makes no attempt to
do anything of the kind. He just waves his hands to get the job
done and thinks that this move is sufficient to remove the scandal
to philosophy.

Moore, however, thinks that "the proof which I gave was a
perfectly rigorous one; and that it is perhaps impossible to give a
better or more rigorous proof of anything whatever."[25] To try to
determine whether Moore is right, let us take a closer look at the
proof. As Moore uses the term, a 'proof' is an argument consisting of a premise or premises from which we can validly argue to
a conclusion and in which we are able to come to know the truth
of the conclusion. A proof is a way of conclusively establishing
that we have knowledge about something. A proof, then, is not
just a valid argument. For example, from the premises "All tomatoes are carrots" and "All carrots are oranges" I can validly deduce
"All tomatoes are oranges"; but clearly this deduction does not
bring it about that I know that all tomatoes are oranges. In order
for a valid argument to constitute a proof, the premises must be
true, and in addition they must be known to be true by the person
who is using the proof to establish that he has knowledge of the
conclusion. A proof transmits knowledge of the conclusion from
knowledge of the premises by a series of steps which show that
the conclusion follows from the premises.

A further condition which Moore thinks an argument must
satisfy if it is to constitute a proof is that the premises must be
different from the conclusion. He claims that his proof satisfies
this condition when he says:

The premiss which I adduced in proof was quite certainly
different from the conclusion, for the conclusion was merely
'Two human hands exist at this moment'; but the premiss
was something far more specific than this – something which

I expressed by showing you my hands, making certain gestures, and saying the words 'Here is one hand, and here is another'. It is quite obvious that the two were different, because it is quite obvious that the conclusion might have been true, even if the premiss had been false. In asserting the premiss I was asserting much more than I was asserting in asserting the conclusion.[26]

The reason why this argument with this premise and conclusion constitutes a proof of an external world is that human hands are among the things that count as external material objects, so that from the conclusion "Two human hands exist at this moment," the further conclusion follows that two external objects exist at this moment. And since human hands are the sort of things that can exist even though no one is experiencing them, his proof constitutes a refutation of solipsism. His proof is a proof that something else exists besides himself and the contents of his own mind. Moore thinks that "nothing is easier than to prove the existence of external objects."[27] If one thinks that Moore is successful in his efforts to provide a proof, then one might come to believe that the real scandal to philosophy is that philosophers have thought there ever was a deep, difficult problem of proving the existence of the external world and refuting solipsism.

Moore recognizes that "many philosophers will still feel that I have not given any satisfactory proof of the point in question."[28] One reason is that these philosophers would expect a proof of an external world to include, in addition to, or instead of, the proof that Moore has given, a proof of the premise. After all, the premise, which consists of his waving both his hands and uttering certain words, was not something which he even undertook to prove, and many philosophers think that it is that premise which is the point in question.

But Moore thinks that a proof of the premise cannot be given.

If this is what is meant by proof of the existence of external things, I do not believe than any proof of the existence of external things is possible. . . . How am I to prove now that "Here is one hand, and here's another"? I do not believe that I can do it. In order to do it, I should need to prove for one

thing, as Descartes pointed out, that I am not now dreaming. But how can I prove that I am not? I have, no doubt,
conclusive reasons for asserting that I am not now dreaming;
I have conclusive evidence that I am awake: but that is a very
different thing from being able to prove it. I could not tell
you what all my evidence is; and I should require to do this
at least, in order to give a proof.[29]

Moore does not think that the fact that he is unable to provide
a proof of the premise is a reason for thinking that he has not
given a proof of an external world. He does not think that the
proof he has given is incomplete or requires supplementation.
Just as it stands, it is a complete, rigorous proof in his view.
Nothing more is needed.

However, the skeptic might argue as follows: "In order for
your argument to constitute a proof, it must transmit your knowledge of the premise to the conclusion. In order to do that, it is
perfectly obvious that you must have knowledge of the premise.
But if you cannot prove the premise, how can you say that you
know it to be true? Thus your proof is woefully incomplete."

Moore is well aware of this skeptical response and provides an
answer to it:

I can know things, which I cannot prove; and among things
which I certainly did know, even if (as I think) I could not
prove them, were the premisses of my . . . proofs. I should
say, therefore, that those, if any, who are dissatisfied with
these proofs merely on the ground that I did not know their
premises, have no good reason for their dissatisfaction.[30]

The crucial point here is that one can know things without
proof. In fact, there is a very powerful argument according to
which one must be able to know things without proof, provided
one has knowledge of things based upon a proof. For suppose one
has knowledge of something based upon a proof. Then one must
have knowledge of the premise of that proof. But if one cannot
have knowledge of things without proof, then one must possess
a proof of that premise too. But, similarly, one must possess a
proof of the premise of the second proof, *ad infinitum*. But since

human beings are incapable of completing an infinite series of proofs, if there were nothing we knew without proof, then there would be nothing we knew at all.

We can illustrate the force of this infinite regress by recalling Descartes's proof of his own existence: *Cogito, ergo sum* – I think, therefore I am. Even if he thinks that he does not exist, it still follows that he does exist. We can represent Descartes's *cogito* as an argument with the premise "I am thinking that I do not exist," which entails the conclusion "I exist." Is this a proof of his own existence? Only if he has knowledge of the premise. Can he prove that he has knowledge of the premise? Descartes would not think so. That he is here and now thinking of something is a fact about the contents of his own mind of which he is certain without proof or argument or any reasoning whatsoever. If he did not know something of that sort without argument, he would be unable to establish by means of a proof that he himself exists.

So the fact that Moore has not provided a proof of the premise, and even thinks that one cannot be provided, is not a reason for thinking that he has not provided a proof of the external world. But doubts remain. Could it really be so easy to prove the existence of the external world? Hume asserted that "'tis vain to ask, *Whether there be body or not?*" Moore does not think it vain to ask this question; not only can the question be definitively, categorically, answered; nothing is easier than to answer it. Let us cast a critical eye on Moore's alleged proof.

7. Conceptual Frameworks and Material Objects

In the discussion of color skepticism, I introduced the notion of a conceptual framework and argued that the original understanding that incorporates, and is structured by, the conceptual framework of our commonsense view of the world should not be accepted as an adequate understanding of what there really is in the world, all things considered. Wilfrid Sellars applies this insight not merely to the issue of color, but to perceptible objects generally. He uses the term 'manifest image' much as I have used 'original understanding', and he says:

If a physical object is *in a strict sense* a system of imperceptible particles, then it cannot as a whole have the perceptible qualities characteristic of physical objects in the manifest image . . . Manifest physical objects are 'appearances' to *human perceivers* of systems of imperceptible particles.[31]

We have seen that if we adopt the point of view of scientific realism and make use of the explanatory apparatus of the physical sciences to explain our sense experiences, then color skepticism is a plausible outcome. Sellars adopts the more radical view that there are no perceptible physical objects at all, that the objects we think we perceive and therefore believe exist do not really exist. It just seems to us as if they existed. What really exist in nature are systems of imperceptible particles whose characteristics it is the job of physics to reveal. These systems of particles affect our sensory apparatus in regular ways, making us think that what in fact are appearances and hence have a subjective, dependent existence are independent, objective realities. We are so constituted as to project our subjective impressions onto the objective world. But the world of the original understanding is a construction and has no objective reality. Sellars's view is constructivist as far as the manifest image is concerned. Yet he is a realist when it comes to the framework of the physical sciences.

We can make Sellars's extended skepticism about the commonsense view of nature plausible by recalling a point that Locke made. Locke said that whereas our sense impressions provide an inaccurate representation of physical things with respect to the secondary qualities, they are mostly accurate with respect to the primary ones. Although the appearances fail to resemble physical things with respect to color, they do resemble them with respect to shape. But that is quite implausible. After all, if a tomato is a system of imperceptible particles, it cannot have the smooth, sharp boundaries that our sense impressions represent it as having. Visible shape is an appearance whose relation to the real shape of the object is so imprecise as to provide us with a distorted picture of the world that exists independently of our senses. Things in themselves are not adequately pictured by our sensory representations. So inadequate are our sense impressions that we are entitled, thinks Sellars, to say that the tomato, that perceptible thing with that color and shape and size and position, doesn't really exist.

Sellars thinks, therefore, that the type of argument offered by Moore to prove the existence of the external world fails. In fact, Moore has not proved that he has hands, because the systems of particles that constitute his physical reality are so unlike what he seems to himself to be that we cannot even say that those systems which cause his sense impressions of hands are hands. Nevertheless, Sellars asks us to be cautious here. It would be a mistake to say, without qualification, that Moore doesn't really have hands; if we heard that, we might well be puzzled. Were his hands amputated? Was he born without hands? But these questions are not at all to the point. Sellars suggests that we understand the issue in these terms:

> Properly understood, the claim that physical objects do not really have perceptible qualities is not analogous to the claim that something generally believed to be true about a certain kind of thing is actually false. It is not the denial of a belief *within a framework*, but a challenge to the framework.[32]

I interpret this remark of Sellars to imply that we should not question the premises of Moore's proof on the grounds that they fail to satisfy the criteria specified by the conceptual framework of common sense for determining the existence of something. That Moore has two hands is a proposition that satisfies these criteria quite well, and according to these criteria, Moore is entitled to claim that he knows that he has hands, that he is quite certain he has hands. The way to challenge the proof is to challenge the conceptual framework itself. This means that even though the criteria within the framework for his having hands are satisfied, they fail to provide sufficient conditions for establishing the existence of anything when all things are considered. Since we operate within the commonsense framework most of the time and accept its criteria for determining our ontological commitments, it seems absurd to deny the reality of Moore's hands, just as it seems absurd to deny the reality of colored objects. Our doubts about perceptible objects, then, are doubts *about* the framework and should not be interpreted as doubts *within* the framework.

Our commonsense conceptual framework allows us to conduct ourselves quite successfully in the affairs of daily life. Is that not a reason for giving some credence to its criteria of ontological commitment? This is a pragmatic argument, which attempts to support the truth and acceptability of a system of thought by reference to its practical success. Sellars, however, does not think that pragmatism in defense of the manifest image is cogent: "The success of living, thinking, and acting in terms of the manifest framework can be accounted for by the framework which proposes to replace it, by showing that there are sufficient structural similarities between manifest objects and their scientific counterparts to account for this success."[33] The framework of the physical sciences is not, Sellars thinks, just an extension of the commonsense framework. Rather, it replaces the latter, because it is able to provide better explanations than the manifest image of a wide variety of phenomena. This is a type of pragmatic justification as well, but it satisfies the prescription that *all* things should be considered, not just the comparatively narrow range of considerations legitimated by the commonsense framework.

Has Sellars succeeded in undermining Moore's proof of an external world? I do not think so. His argument against Moore's proof seems convincing only against the background of scientific realism and the various considerations it suggests. Later (in chapter 5, section 7) I shall argue that his argument is not persuasive, even if scientific realism is accepted. But the standpoint from which Moore's proof became pertinent was the standpoint of solipsism. From that standpoint, scientific realism is not yet an option. The solipsist apparently has reasons to doubt the reliability of science, as well as the reliability of our everyday system of beliefs. So we cannot appeal to the type of argument that Sellars offers to show that the premise of Moore's proof is false. Once scientific realism is available, it becomes legitimate to use it, as does Sellars, to argue against the framework of the original understanding.

Yet doubts about Moore's proof have not been answered. Even if we know some things without proof, is the premise of Moore's proof one of those things?

8. Knowledge of the External World

Moore pointed out in response to the criticism that he failed to provide a proof of the premise of his proof that such a proof is unnecessary, since there are some things that one can know without proof. But that reply is incomplete, because what he needs to show is that the premise is one of those things that are known without proof. This gap in his argument is one of the reasons, I think, why so many of his readers feel that something is missing, even if they cannot say what it is.

He does not attempt to show that he knows the premise even in the absence of proof. Can it be done? Recall from the first chapter that knowing that something is true includes both the acceptance of a proposition as being true (what we have classified as a judgment and belief) and its actually being true. So in order for Moore to *know* that the premise of his proof is true, he needs first of all to accept it, and in addition it must be true. But these two requirements are not themselves sufficient. What more is required?

This is a question that has been much discussed in recent philosophy. What more is necessary for knowledge than just true belief? What must be added to true belief in order for one to have knowledge? The various cases that philosophers have invented to illustrate the fact that you can have true belief, yet not have knowledge, seem to me to have one thing in common: namely, that the true belief has been arrived at accidentally. For example, I may make a lucky guess or conjecture; I have a feeling that this horse will win the race and it does win the race, but although I believed what is true, I didn't actually know it to be true. Other examples point out that one can hit upon a true belief by inferring it from propositions that are false or irrelevant. Bertrand Russell gives the following example:

> If a man believes that the late Prime Minister's last name began with a B, he believes what is true, since the late Prime Minister was Sir Henry Campbell Bannerman. But if he believes that Mr. Balfour was the late Prime Minister, he will still believe that the late Prime Minister's last name began with a B, yet this belief, though true, would not be thought to constitute knowledge.[34]

In this case, a true proposition is inferred from a false one.

A common suggestion is that a true proposition is known to be true only if it is, or can be, justified. This has also been criticized as not being enough.[35] But it is not clear what justification consists of. A plausible view is that a person is justified in accepting a proposition if and only if he can give good reasons for thinking that it is true. This is an *internalist* account of justification, because it lays down the requirement that whatever it is that does the justifying is accessible to, and known to, the person. But Moore's admission that he cannot provide a proof of his premise and that he cannot provide good reasons for it means that an internalist justification is not available. So if we insisted on internalism, then Moore would not know the premise to be true.

We can weaken the conception of justification by dropping the requirement that the person be able to say, or to formulate, what his good reasons are. Instead, he will be justified provided he *has* good reasons, even if he doesn't know that he has them, and even if he hasn't the foggiest notion as to what they are. I now think that even this weak conception is too strong.[36] Suppose I remember something that happened to me in the past. I know that it happened, and I know that I remember that it happened. But do I have anything that can be called a reason? You ask me: "Do you remember so-and-so?" Immediately, without any thought or research, I answer: "Of course." What reasons could there be? Undoubtedly, there is an explanation of my ability to remember this and other things. The explanation would show how events that happened to me in the past affected me and left their traces, to be activated in the present. It would mention what those traces consist of; perhaps they are changes in certain neurons in my brain. But none of the stages of this explanatory story gives reasons that I actually have for this belief. Not every sequence of events that explains how a person acquires a belief includes factors that count as reasons. The concept of having a good reason is an internalist concept, it seems to me. Even if the person does not know what the reason actually is, it must, to count as a reason, at least be accessible to him in some way or another; he must, with further reflection and research, be in a position to give the reason.

But doesn't Moore have a good reason, even in this weak sense? After all, if he is asked how he knows what he knows when he holds up his hands and says "Here is a hand and here is another," he could answer that he *sees* them. That one sees something is very often a good and sufficient reason for thinking that one knows something.

However, although that answer might satisfy a philosopher of common sense like Moore, it would not diminish the dissatisfaction of the skeptic. Even if Moore were to prove the premise "Here is one hand and here is another" by inferring it from "I see one hand and I see another," the skeptic would simply focus his attention upon the new premise and ask: How do you know that you are seeing anything? It is very difficult to understand what one could say in answer to that question. The process of giving reasons is finite, and sooner or later it comes to an end. Sometimes it comes to an end when we have satisfied our interlocutor, even though there is more we could say. At other times it comes to an end when we have said everything we can say, whether or not it satisfies our interlocutor. If we have knowledge even when there is nothing more we can say, then the notions of justification and the having of good reasons are not indispensable conditions of knowing that something is true. Does Moore have knowledge of his premise?

In his essay "The Fixation of Belief," Charles Sanders Peirce (1839–1914), the founder of American pragmatism, argued that certain methods of forming beliefs are unsatisfactory because they produce beliefs on grounds that are incidental or irrelevant to their truth. An example he has in mind is when a government imposes an ideological dogma upon its citizens: for example, "If you do not believe in God, you will be burned at the stake." If the dogma becomes entrenched by this use of authority, then although people believe it, even if it should turn out to be true, their belief is simply an accident. There is nothing about the way they have arrived at it to suggest that it is true.

To remove this accidental character, Peirce suggests that "it is necessary that a method should be found by which our beliefs may be determined by nothing human, but by some external permanency – by something upon which our thinking has no effect."[37] Peirce wants to say that thinking does not make it so, that somehow the very fact that we claim to know enters into the fixing of our belief if, indeed, we do know it. However, in reflecting on the variety of things we know – things we perceive or remember or predict or prove or hypothesize, and so on – there is no single way in which our minds are so connected to the facts as to make our belief nonaccidental. So we shall simply say that a person knows that a proposition P is true only if it is true, and he accepts it as true, and if he has arrived at his belief by a process that is nonaccidental with regard to what he claims to know. Robert Nozick formulates a similar idea in these words: "To know is to have a belief that tracks the truth. Knowledge is a particular way of being connected to the world, having a specific real factual connection to the world: tracking it."[38]

So the question now is whether Moore's acceptance of his premise is nonaccidental. That depends upon the process by which he arrived at this belief. We have seen in the early sections of this book that the question of the nature of the process by which we arrive at those of our beliefs founded upon sense awareness is controversial. According to direct realism, the fact stated in Moore's premise is directly present to his consciousness; he merely has to recognize what is already there and read it off from what is given in his visual field. He is nonaccidentally connected to this state of affairs, in view of the fact that it is directly present to his consciousness.

Representative realism says, however, that the process is much more complex and indirect than that. What we are directly conscious of, our sense impressions, are subjective and dependent. So this method of tracking the truth is not sufficient to establish an objective external reality; it does not give us what Locke called "sensitive knowledge." In sense awareness, we track the truth only when the state of affairs – in this case what is asserted by Moore in "Here is one hand and here is another" – causes a sense impression which we can characterize as a case of that state of affairs visually appearing to us in a way in which we can discriminate it and distinguish it from others, and when the sense impression triggers the belief in that state of affairs. On the supposition that in this case the sense impression and the belief would not have occurred if the state of affairs had not been among the causes of their occurrence, then this process makes it certain that the belief is true.

The question as to whether Moore knows the premise of his proof, then, can be answered in the affirmative, provided that this is the way the sense impression and belief were caused to occur. Note that it is not necessary that Moore himself agree with this account of the process, or that he know about it, or that he can state what it is. Remember, we have rejected internalist accounts of knowledge. Perhaps Moore has nothing at all to say in explanation of how he arrived at his premise. Nevertheless, he knows it to be true provided this process actually occurred. If it occurred, he knows it, and skepticism with regard to the senses is mistaken.

This discussion has, I think, supported Moore's proof of an external world to the extent that it has shown how it is possible for him to acquire knowledge of its premise even without proof. This is a step forward. But an even greater step forward has been taken, because these considerations imply that the skeptic's arguments to the effect that Moore does not know the premise are mistaken. Recall that the skeptic's main argument says that it is logically possible that his sense impressions as of his having two hands could occur even if there were no hands there. This is the point of Descartes's dream argument. This is why Moore says that he could only give a proof of the premise if he could show that he is not dreaming. Although the skeptic is correct about this logical possibility, we are now in a position to understand that it is irrelevant to the question of whether Moore knows the truth of his premise. For despite this possibility, he knows its truth provided the process just described actually occurred. The skeptic's point is compatible with his having knowledge. Moreover, Hume is mistaken when he says that "we may well ask *What causes induce us to believe in the existence of body?* but 'tis vain to ask, *Whether there be body or not?*" He fails to recognize that an account of the causes that induce this belief would contribute to answering the question of whether there be body or not, and that, therefore, it is not vain to ask the question.

There is a further point to mention that pertains to the question of solipsism. Our earlier discussion of the topic made it appear as if the only way out of solipsism is to find a means of justifying an inference from our sense impressions to the existence of an external world, making use of anything we know about the contents of our own minds and anything we are a priori certain of. But we are now in a position to see that this is not the only way out. For we may very well know that there is an external world even if we are unable to justify such an inference, because such knowledge need not rest upon any justification whatever.

The skeptic may, however, shift the focus of his attack. He may argue as follows: "Even if I have not succeeded in showing that Moore lacks knowledge of his premise, you have not succeeded in showing that he has knowledge of it. You will agree, I am sure, that from the fact that Moore says he knows it, it does not follow that he does.[39] Moreover, Moore is not infallible because from the fact that he thinks he has two hands, it does not follow that he does. Even if I accept your account of what knowledge is and of the conditions under which Moore would know the truth of his premise, I have no reason whatsoever to believe that these conditions are satisfied; nor do you. After all, one of the conditions that you mentioned is that Moore's hands be among the causes of certain of his sense impressions. But whether that obtains is the very point at issue."

I interpret this complaint of the skeptic to imply that even if Moore does know the truth of the premise, there is no non-question-begging way of showing that he has this knowledge, because, in order to show this, he would have to appeal to beliefs that, in the solipsistic predicament, he is not entitled to appeal to. I think the skeptic is correct on this point. Moore, if we place him within solipsism, is not able to *show* that he knows the premise of his proof. Perhaps we can even go so far as to say that he does not even know that he knows it. In a way, Moore conceded these points when he said that he was unable to provide a proof of the premise. But none of this supports the skeptic's claim that Moore does not know it. And should he know it, we have a way to escape from the solipsistic predicament.

9. Doubts about the Method of Doubt

The role of doubt in Descartes's philosophy was not to engender indefeasible skepticism, but to assist him in his quest for certainty. What can we be sure of? What can we know? Consider the totality of beliefs of any given individual, their belief system. Some will be true, and some false. Some will be backed by good reasons, frequently represented by other beliefs in the system, and some not. Some are things they feel quite sure of, whereas others they are uncertain of. Some are things they know, whereas others are merely opinions. The method of doubt is a method of reforming a system of beliefs by placing it upon a firm foundation, assuming that there is such a thing. The reformation consists, first, in identifying those beliefs which the person is entitled to feel quite sure of, and that are not themselves grounded upon, or justified in terms of, other beliefs. These beliefs have passed the test of doubt, and are certain. Examples in Descartes's scheme of things are beliefs about the contents of one's own mind such as that one is thinking about such and such ("I am thinking that I do not exist"). Let us call these 'basic beliefs'.

Having identified which beliefs are basic, Descartes's next step is to specify which beliefs can be justified by deriving them through various intellectual processes from those that are basic. These beliefs are 'derived'. For example, "I exist" is derived from "I am thinking that I do not exist," and "God exists" is derived from "I have an idea of God" among other propositions. The particular intellectual process by which "I exist" is justified in term of "I am thinking I do not exist" is 'intellectual intuition'. We just "see" that the former follows necessarily from the latter, so that, since we are sure of the latter, we are entitled to feel sure of the former. Our certainty is transmitted from premise to conclusion. This is the sort of thing that qualifies as a proof according to Moore's conception.

Beliefs that are either basic or derived are justified. Beliefs that are neither basic nor derived are unjustified and should be given up, for there are no good reasons to accept them. For Descartes, doubting is a reflective procedure that may lead us to revise our system of beliefs in various ways. We cannot tell without applying the method how radical our revisions will be. Descartes himself thought that most of our commonsense beliefs would survive, as well as belief in God.

We can see that, according to Descartes, the philosophical study of human knowledge – epistemology, as we now call it – has normative implications. It does not merely describe the human cognitive predicament; it claims to improve our cognitive situation by showing which of our beliefs are true and which are false and uncertain. If we adopt the epistemic rule "Believe only those propositions that are basic or are derived from those that are basic," then epistemology becomes an instrument for intellectual reform, and, to the extent to which what we do depends upon what we think, broad cultural and institutional reform as well.

In his essay "Some Consequences of Four Incapacities," Charles Sanders Peirce launched a brilliant assault on Cartesian epistemology. One of his main points concerns the method of doubt:

> We cannot begin with complete doubt. We must begin with all the prejudices which we actually have when we enter upon the study of philosophy. These prejudices are not to be dispelled by a maxim, for they are things which it does not occur to us *can* be questioned. Hence this initial skepticism will be a mere self-deception, and not real doubt; and no one who follows the Cartesian method will ever be satisfied until he has formally recovered all those beliefs which in form he has given up. It is, therefore, as useless a preliminary as going to the North Pole would be in order to get to Constantinople by coming down regularly upon a meridian. A person may, it is true, in the course of his studies, find reason to doubt what he began by believing; but in that case he doubts because he has a positive reason for it, and not on account of the Cartesian maxim. Let us not pretend to doubt in philosophy what we do not doubt in our hearts.[40]

The maxim Peirce refers to here is the resolution that Descartes announces in his first *Meditation*, which constitutes his understanding of the method of doubt:

> Reason now leads me to think that I should hold back my assent from opinions which are not completely certain and indubitable just as carefully as I do from those which are patently false. So, for the purpose of rejecting all my opinions, it will be enough if I find in each of them at least some reason for doubt.[41]

Peirce claims that this resolve is unable to produce real doubt, that Descartes is merely pretending to doubt. In his essay "The Fixation of Belief," Peirce pointed out that our beliefs guide our conduct, and that doubt tends to make us suspend our actions in order to undertake an inquiry into the truth of our belief.[42] But Descartes's doubt has nothing to do with how we act; while engaged upon his project, Descartes acted no differently from before. This means that he did not actually suspend his believing attitudes, and that he did not really doubt.

For Peirce, Descartes's wholesale doubt is a psychological impossibility. Specific reasons can lead us to doubt specific beliefs. Someone might, for example, point out a fallacy in an argument for God's existence that I had previously thought to be sound. Further reflection may lead me to give up my belief as a mere prejudice or to find better reasons for it. But in that case, the doubt was directed at a particular belief, for reasons that are germane to that belief and no other. For Peirce, doubt is context-specific; it can only be generated by local considerations. And the considerations that produce it must not be mere abstract possibilities such as the fact that it is logically possible that my belief that here is one hand and here is another is false; they must refer to actual difficulties in the local situation.

On Peirce's view it is futile to engage in the sort of project that Descartes was engaged in to discover, once and for all, the foundations of human knowledge by identifying our basic beliefs and those that can be justified in terms of them. We can only start out with our belief system as it is actually constituted, with all the prejudices that it includes. We can reform it only gradually, when specific experiences provide us with reasons for questioning specific beliefs. Peirce called himself a "fallibilist"; this means that no beliefs are absolutely certain.[43] We cannot rule out a priori the possibility that certain parts of our belief system will be revised by subsequent experience. There are no unshakable foundations for human knowledge, and the quest for them is fruitless.[44]

Descartes was not only a foundationalist in his epistemology, he was an individualist as well. The project he attempted to carry through in his *Meditations* is one in which he, as an isolated individual, constructs secure foundations for the whole edifice of human knowledge. For Peirce, on the other hand, inquiry, or the search for truth, is a public affair; it is conducted within a community of inquirers and is terminated when agreement is reached. "We individually cannot reasonably hope to attain the ultimate philosophy which we pursue; we can only seek it, therefore, for the *community* of philosophers."[45]

For Peirce, there is no genuine problem of solipsism, because the line of reasoning that is supposed to get us into the predicament of not knowing that there is an external world and not knowing that there are minds other than our own cannot even get started. I cannot actually doubt that here is one hand and here is another. If I should wave my hands before a crowd of people, they would all agree that here is one hand and here is another. It would never occur to them to doubt this, and even if it did, they could not bring themselves to do it.

Peirce's profound criticisms are not, however, sufficient to make us completely shelve Descartes's project. For we may reformulate his project without bringing the concept of doubt into play. It is true that I cannot actually doubt Moore's premise, especially when it is my own hands that I am waving. And I do not think that a person who sincerely believes in God, whose belief is deeply entrenched by long years of experience and reflection, will actually come to doubt God's existence just on the grounds of Descartes's maxim. However, long ago, Aristotle (384–322 BCE) pointed out that "it is owing to their wonder that men both now begin and at first began to philosophize. . . . Since they philosophized in order to escape from ignorance, evidently they were pursuing science in order to know, and not for any utilitarian end."[46] One of the things we may wonder about is human knowledge itself, and whether we actually know what we think we know. This does not mean that we actually doubt our system of beliefs in a wholesale manner. But we may want to know about the grounds for various of our beliefs and what makes them grounds. We may recall from our study of the history of the sciences, of philosophy, and of religion the wide variety of conflicting beliefs that people have held at various times and places. We recognize that others have been just as sure of their beliefs as we are of ours, even when ours contradict theirs. I may recognize that those who disagree with me are frequently just as intelligent and informed as I am. This may lead me to wonder about the cogency of my own belief system. Although this is not living doubt as Peirce understands it, it is a kind of doubt: the awareness of human disagreement may rob us of some of our confidence in what we believe. We are not as sure as we were before we adopted the reflective standpoint of philosophical wonder about the epistemic status of our beliefs.

As I pointed out earlier, we are capable of stepping back from our conceptual framework and making it an object of inquiry. We can examine its structure and how we use it to substantiate the beliefs within our system. We can examine what evidence consists of, what it means to know and to believe, what the difference between certainty and probability amounts to. We can wonder whether and how our belief system is in contact with the realities it claims to inform us of. Although none of this implies that we are actually doubting any of our beliefs, we cannot exclude a priori the possibility that we may come to find some of them wanting in the light of the standards of evidence and justification that we make explicit. Thus, my defense of color skepticism led to finding a whole collection of our most deeply entrenched beliefs to be false.

So Peirce's argument is not a reason for giving up epistemological inquiry of the Cartesian sort. However, it does lead us to rethink what exactly we are doing when we reflect upon human knowledge. Descartes's method of doubt is one way of formulating the task of epistemology. But the failure of the method does not establish that other formulations cannot do the job.

Further Readings

George Berkeley, *A Treatise Concerning the Principles of Human Knowledge*.
René Descartes, *Meditations on First Philosophy*.
John Dewey, *The Quest for Certainty* (New York: Minton, Balch, and Co., 1929).
David Hume, *A Treatise of Human Nature*, Bk I, Pt iv, sect. 2: "Of Scepticism with Regard to the Senses."
G. E. Moore, "A Defence of Common Sense" and "Proof of an External World," in *Philosophical Papers* (New York: Collier Books, 1962), pp. 32–59, 126–48.
Barry Stroud, *The Significance of Philosophical Scepticism* (Oxford: Clarendon Press, 1987).
Ludwig Wittgenstein, *Philosophical Investigations* (Oxford: Blackwell, 1953).

4

Self-Knowledge

1. Beyond Sensitive Knowledge

'Sensitive knowledge' is the term Locke used to designate those of our beliefs that accurately record the information that sense awareness delivers. That this is a tomato, that that is a piece of paper, that there is a tulip tree in my garden are examples of sensitive knowledge; these are all things that I know to be true just by using my senses, just by looking around and finding out what is there. In the discussion of Moore's proof of an external world, we saw that the skeptic failed to show that there is no sensitive knowledge. What the skeptic *could* establish is that if we were try to prove the existence of external objects on the basis of an inference from our sense impressions, then we do not have enough internally validated principles and data to demonstrate its soundness. But we have seen that an internalist justification is unnecessary; we may very well have knowledge of the external world, even though we are not able to prove that we do. Let us continue this discussion on the assumption that we have knowledge of the external world in the manner explained.

At this point I wish to emphasize the relevance of Peirce's fallibilism. Nothing is immune to revision, in the sense that no matter how absolutely sure we may feel about something, there are no guarantees that future experience and reflection will not lead us to give up our belief. I have attempted to illustrate this point in the discussion of color. Nothing has color, I have argued, even though we all believe in the reality of countless colored objects. It follows that in countless cases in which we think we are in possession of sensitive knowledge, we are not. Our internal feelings of conviction are not infallible guides to what is really there in the world. Our cognitive apparatus is capable of projecting features upon the world that nothing actually exemplifies.[1] So fallibilism even extends to our claims to be in possession of particular bits of sensitive knowledge.

How do these points bear upon the organization of our system of beliefs? There are derived beliefs, those that we have inferred from others and that we hope are justified by such an inference. What about basic beliefs? The cases of sensitive knowledge that we actually have qualify as being basic, because they are not derived from others. Sense awareness triggers certain judgments and beliefs that articulate information transmitted by the physical and sensory processes that underlie it. The judgments are, in that way, based upon sense awareness, but they are not inferred from other beliefs. When such a judgment has the status of knowledge, because it is true and caused by the right objects in the right way, then it is basic in the strongest sense. It is something we know without inference or argument. Because we have rejected internalist accounts of sensitive knowledge, we cannot say that such basic beliefs are justified. Justification, I argued, is an internalist notion. But we know them; we have a right to believe them.

Consider now the claim that there is a red tomato that I am seeing. I have a sense impression as of a red tomato, and this triggers the belief. But, if color skepticism is true, this belief is false; there is nothing red there (even though there is a tomato there). There is nothing unusual in judgments triggered by sense awareness turning out to be false. They are just not cases of sensitive knowledge. We may, however, feel that even though they are false, even though they do not qualify as basic beliefs in the strongest sense, nevertheless, the way we have arrived at them entitles us to accept them. For at the moment we make the judgment, we have done as well as could be expected.

Consider the red tomato again. Suppose I know nothing about color skepticism, nothing about skepticism with regard to the senses. I look carefully at the tomato in broad daylight and pronounce it to be red. I am, as far as I can tell, in an excellent position to make an accurate judgment about what I see. I have no reason to think that there is anything wrong with my eyes or that my faculties are tending to mislead me. My belief that it is red is, as far as I can tell, as firmly based in sense awareness as my belief that it is a tomato. I feel that I have as much right to believe that it is red as I have to believe anything.

When I reflect upon my system of beliefs, I am inclined to think that I have not done anything wrong in judging that it is red, because I have done as well as I can. Of course, I have made a mistake, since in making that judgment, I have come to believe something that isn't true. But that judgment was one that I had an epistemic right to make because, from within, it was no different from many judgments that count as sensitive knowledge. Therefore, I am entitled to use that belief in forming other beliefs I may hold.

In light of these considerations, I will classify as *basic* any belief (or judgment) that, first, is not actually derived from other beliefs or judgments and, second, we have an epistemic right to have. Not only does my sensitive knowledge that this is a tomato count as basic; so does my belief that it is red. Since both of them are triggered by sense awareness, I shall call them 'perceptual beliefs'. Perceptual beliefs are among those that are basic. Though not derived in the technical sense of being inferred from other beliefs, perceptual beliefs are *grounded* in sense awareness. The notion of grounding refers to a type of conscious process that tends to produce belief in a noninferential way. Sense awareness, then, is one example of a process by which beliefs are grounded.

A perceptual judgment is an act grounded in sense awareness of accepting a proposition as true. Propositions that we have come to accept in this way are usually preserved in us as memories in which the information they embody is stored. These are perceptual beliefs, relatively permanent traces which have cognitive import. Those of us whose memories are unimpaired have ready access to them. Some of them may be easily forgotten; that I saw a tomato yesterday will not be remembered next week. It has gone out of storage; it has disappeared completely. Others remain in storage although they may be difficult to remember; we may then have to "search our memory" to find them. The memory of events that we have previously perceived is not a condition that is the source of the right to believe in them; rather, memory is a way of storing beliefs to which we may already have an epistemic right.

'Foundationalism' is a normative theory of how we gain our epistemic rights to believe. It says, first, that we have a right to some of our beliefs because they are basic. It also says that any beliefs that are not basic to which we have a right must be derived from those that are basic in such a way as to transmit the right to believe from the basic to the nonbasic. Beliefs that are neither basic nor derived are mere prejudices; we have no epistemic right to believe them at all.

Traditional foundationalism of the sort one finds in Descartes, Locke, Hume, and many others tends to identify two classes of beliefs as basic: those grounded in sense awareness and those that are self-evidently true or known by some sort of intellectual intuition. Foundationalists also distinguish two sorts of inferences by means of which the right to believe is transmitted: those that are deductive, or demonstrative, and those that provide nondeductive support to their conclusions. The latter are sometimes called 'inductive'; however, I shall use the term 'inductive' more narrowly in what follows.

It has frequently been thought that skepticism is the only alternative to foundationalism. If human belief lacks firm foundations connecting it to the realities which it asserts to exist, then our belief in those realities is thought to be unwarranted. We do not have any knowledge, or rational opinion, at all.

In recent years, however, foundationalism has been criticized by a number of philosophers who are not skeptics. Dewey and pragmatists generally, Wittgenstein, Quine, and many others reject the foundationalist model of human knowledge. Some of them (for example, Rorty) have even gone so far as to reject epistemology entirely, as a project tainted by the failure of Descartes's search for secure foundations. In the following chapters, we shall examine some of the issues involved. However, one general point needs to be made at this juncture.

The type of foundation that Descartes thought he was in need of is one that provides absolute, unshakable certainty. For Descartes, knowledge is a condition in which one is not merely not mistaken, but one in which one could not be mistaken, or at least one in which the possibility of error is reduced to an absolute minimum. But this conception bumps up against Peirce's fallibilism. That nothing is immune to revision is an idea that has become deeply entrenched in recent philosophy.

Moreover, it is widely believed that fallibilism is incompatible with foundationalism: that if nothing is immune to revision, there are no foundations for human knowledge. However, this claim is correct only for certain versions of foundationalism, not for the general idea of it. A basic belief need not be known with absolute certainty; it need not even be known at all; further, it could very well be false and still be basic. That we have a right to believe something is compatible with our later discovering that we were mistaken, that what we believe probably isn't true, and that we need to revise our belief system accordingly.

In fact, the idea that nothing is immune to revision does not exhaust the content of fallibilism. It also includes the idea that the fact that I think that I know something to be true does not prove that I actually know it to be true. My claim to be in possession of knowledge may, logically, be mistaken.[2] I am capable of having excessive confidence in what I think. However, suppose that in fact I know some proposition, P, to be true. If nothing is immune to revision, then it is possible that future experience may make it reasonable for me to reject P. It may be reasonable for me to move from knowledge to error, as well as from error to knowledge. I may be rationally required to reject what I should have had confidence in. There is no way of guaranteeing that knowledge will always stand fast.

2. The *Cogito* and the Problem of Self-Knowledge

Among the items that each of us thinks he has knowledge of are the very persons who claim to know. I know, or think I know, not only items of the external world, of the world beyond myself; I also think that I have a multitude of correct beliefs about myself. In this and subsequent sections, I shall pursue the question of how our knowledge of ourselves fits into our system of beliefs.

Descartes, you remember, brought his radical skepticism to an end and began the constructive portion of his philosophy with his *cogito*: "I think, therefore I am." The first part, "I think," is known to be true, because it describes the contents of the mind of the thinker, something, according to Descartes, one cannot be mistaken about. The second part, "I am," is entailed by the first; the existence of the thinker is necessarily implied by the fact of *his* thinking; that he exists follows from the fact of there *being* someone, namely himself, doing the thinking.

What, then, is this self whose existence is thus proved? Descartes believed that the basic clue to its nature is contained in the very *cogito* itself. In speaking of the skepticism of the first *Meditation*, he says in one of his letters:

> Thus I would have accustomed the reader to detach his thought from things that are perceived by the senses, and then I would have shown that a man who thus doubts everything material cannot for all that have any doubt about his own existence. From this it follows that he, that is to say the soul, is a being or substance which is not at all corporeal, whose nature is solely to think, and that it is the first thing one can know with certainty.[3]

The self is a thinking thing, not a corporeal thing. That is the first result of the inquiry founded upon the *cogito*. In presenting his argument, Descartes makes use of the notion of doubt, a use which we have found, following Peirce, to be problematic. But his point can be made in another way. In the process of examining our system of beliefs, we make a discovery about our *concept* of the self. We find that the thing we refer to by means of the first-person pronoun 'I' can, logically, exist independently of the existence of the human body which is connected to it. There is no contradiction in supposing that I have a body different from the one I now inhabit or that I have no body at all. Whatever we think of the question of the truth of the doctrine of the immortality of the soul, such immortality cannot be excluded on purely conceptual grounds; there is no contradiction in it. To the question, What then is the nature of this self whose essence can be specified independently of its bodily existence?, Descartes answers: Its nature is to be a thinking thing, a thing capable of thinking.

Our concept of the self, therefore, is not the concept of a material extended thing. This is what we learn from the *cogito*, and on this point Descartes is quite correct. I shall label this view 'conceptual dualism'. According to conceptual dualism, it is logically possible for the self to exist even though the physical body in which it is embodied ceases to exist. There is no strong logical connection between self and body. It follows, I think, that the self cannot be identical with a physical body, since what makes it a self is not the same as what constitutes a human body. However, there is another claim he makes that is problematic. He thinks that the concept of the self is incompatible with the concept of an extended thing, so no actual self can be realized in an extended thing. Let us call this 'substance dualism'. Conceptual dualism does not directly entail substance dualism; but the fact that the two concepts are independent does not of itself establish that they are incompatible.

When something actually exists that is an instance of a concept, let us call that thing a 'realization' of the concept. Thus, for example, that particular physical thing on which I am writing these sentences is a realization of the concept of a computer. It is quite possible for a certain type of entity to be realized in many different ways. A poem, for example, can be written or spoken in many different ways and in different media. There is a 'type', and there are many different 'tokens' of the type.

Descartes's substance dualism entails that there cannot be any physical realization of the self.[4] The self can be realized only in a nonextended substance; if you ask what is the nature of this substance in addition to the absence of any physical or material properties, Descartes answers that its positive nature is that it is capable of thinking; the self is a thinking substance. With respect to any physical substance, we can ask what it is made of. I am now holding a small white stone in my hand. If I wish to know what it is made of, I can take it to a geologist who is competent to satisfy my curiosity. If we ask what the self-substance is made of, however, there is no obvious answer forthcoming other than that it is not made of any material stuff. We can give a name to the stuff that composes it – call it 'mind stuff'. All we know of it is that it is something or other capable of supporting the capacity to think.

Why should anyone accept substance dualism? One reason frequently given is that it enables us to understand how survival after death is possible. If each of us is identical to a nonphysical substance, then the decay of our bodies does not necessarily threaten our existence. But immortality does not require a thing composed of mind stuff. Some religious traditions speak of the resurrection of the body. Concept dualism allows the possibility that, after death, the same self will be realized in another body. After all, if God is capable of creating everything that exists from nothing, then, it would appear, he is capable of creating another vehicle in which the self could be realized.

The best reason I know in favor of substance dualism is that we do not now understand how thinking and other mental functions can be realized in a physical medium. We do not, it would appear, know how an act of thought or a sensation can actually consist of electrical impulses in the brain. We do not understand how the physical descriptions we give of the brain or nervous system can apply to the same system of changes as do the descriptions appropriate to acts of thought. Here is an example of such an expression of disbelief:

> We speak of an idea as clear or confused, as apposite or inapposite, as witty or dull. Are such terms intelligible when applied to those motions of electrons, atoms, molecules, or muscles . . . ? Can a motion be clear, or cogent, or witty? . . . These adjectives are perfectly in order when applied to ideas; they become at once absurd when applied to movements in muscle or nerve. . . . On the other side, movements have attributes which are unthinkable as applied to ideas. Movements have velocity; what is the average velocity of one's ideas on a protective tariff? Movements have direction; would there be any sense in talking of the north-easterly direction of one's thought on the morality of revenge?[5]

But is this really absurd? After all, we express ourselves in language, in which the thoughts we entertain are physically realized. A series of ink marks with a certain molecular and atomic constitution can be used to indicate what one thinks of a protective tariff. There are great uncertainties about how we accomplish this, about how a physical medium can be used for expressions of thought and feeling. Controversies within philosophy abound as to how meaning gets into linguistic tokens. But there is no doubt that meaning does get into linguistic tokens, so there is no absurdity here. That we do not have a sure grasp on how our thoughts may be realized in various physical systems does not prove that they cannot and are not so realized. So the best argument for substance dualism does not, I conclude, have much force.

Thus far, we have been assuming the soundness of the *cogito*. There is a very interesting challenge to its soundness in Nietzsche's (1844–1900) *Beyond Good and Evil* (section 17). An argument is sound provided its premise is true and the conclusion actually does follow from it. It is difficult to deny that "I exist" follows from "I think," but Nietzsche raised questions about the truth of "I think":

> A thought comes when 'it' wishes, and not when 'I' wish, so that it is a falsification of the facts of the case to say that the subject 'I' is the condition of the predicate 'think'. *It* thinks; but that this 'it' is precisely the famous old 'ego' is, to put it mildly, only a supposition, an assertion, and assuredly not an 'immediate certainty'. After all, one has even gone too far with this 'it thinks' – even the 'it' contains an *interpretation* of the process, and does not belong to the process itself. One infers here according to the grammatical habit: 'Thinking is an activity; every activity requires an agent; consequently' . . . Perhaps some day we shall accustom ourselves . . . to get along without the little 'it' (which is all that is left of the honest little old ego).[6]

Nietzsche thinks that the "I think" is a product of grammatical habit, not a reflection of metaphysical reality.

His critique of the *cogito* is an instance of his wholesale rejection of Descartes's quest for certainty. "But that 'immediate certainty', as well as 'absolute knowledge' and the 'thing in itself', involve a *contradictio in adjecto*, I shall repeat a hundred times; we really ought to free ourselves from the seduction of words!"[7] The "I think" is not, says Nietzsche, something we are absolutely certain of. It is a product of interpretations in which we take many things for granted.

When I analyze the process that is expressed in the sentence, 'I think', I find a whole series of daring assertions that would be difficult, perhaps impossible, to prove; for example, that it is *I* who think, that there must necessarily be something that thinks, that thinking is an activity and operation of the part of a being who is thought of as a cause, that there is an 'ego', and, finally, that it is already determined what is to be designated by thinking – that I *know* what thinking is.[8]

But do I not *know* what thinking is? Nietzsche answers:

For if I had not already decided within myself what it is, by what standard could I determine whether that which is just happening is not perhaps 'willing' or 'feeling'? In short, the assertion 'I think' assumes that I *compare* my state at the present moment with other states of myself which I know, in order to determine what it is; on account of this retrospective connection with further 'knowledge', it has, at any rate, no immediate certainty for me.[9]

Even if the "I think" is not immediately certain, do I not have an epistemic right to it? Do I not have knowledge, or at least justified belief, about the contents of my own mind? Descartes's skepticism in the first *Meditation* came to a halt with his mind; but his skepticism seems modest when compared with that of Nietzsche, who is inclined to go all the way. Nietzsche cannot even stop at solipsism, for that says: "I know of nothing besides myself." The solipsist at least admits the self. But Nietzsche is intent on throwing doubt even upon this. What can we say about knowledge of ourselves?

3. The Disappearance of the Self

The self whose existence Descartes thought he had proved by means of the *cogito* is not only a *nonphysical* substance; it is a *substance*. This means, first, that it is an entity that endures through time; it is not something momentary like a flash of lightning. Second, it is relatively independent of other things; it is capable of preserving its integrity despite changes in its environment. Third, it possesses agency, the capacity to act and to cause changes on its own. Fourth, it possesses a nature that explains the way it is capable of exercising its agency: given its nature as a thinking thing, a person or self or mind acts by exercising its powers of thought. Finally, even though it consists of distinct parts or powers, a substance possesses a definite unity; it is not just a scattered object, such as one of the stellar constellations or a large university; the parts hang together in a unified way. This unity is both simultaneous – the parts hang together at any given time – and historical – they hang together through the passage of time. Since the self is something mental, the unity is mental as well; it consists of manners of connection constituted by thought.

An important point in Nietzsche's criticism of the *cogito* is that this conception of the self goes beyond anything that can be obtained by reflecting upon "I think." The only unity expressed by the 'I' in "I think" is the grammatical unity of the word itself. The substantial self of Descartes is, for Nietzsche, a philosophical fiction suggested by an uncritical inference from the characteristics of a verbal expression to a supposed reality represented by it. Descartes is merely interpreting the "I think" according to his own prejudices. The self as he understands it is not something he has found; it is a myth he has created.

Nietzsche's criticism of the self as substance comes at the end of a line of thought initiated in modern philosophy by Hume.[10] As an empiricist, Hume claimed that all ideas that pertain to the external world are traceable to sense impressions. "We have therefore no idea of substance distinct from a collection of particular qualities, nor have we any other meaning when we either talk or reason concerning it."[11] A substance, then, is a collection, not a real unity. Talk of its underlying nature makes no sense. Agency consists of just one thing following another. This happens, and then that happens. Substances have no greater causal efficacy than anything else. Consider our old friend the tomato. List the qualities you perceive it to have: its color, shape, size, taste, odor, and so forth. That bundle of qualities is all there is to it, according to Hume.

No matter how hard he looks, Hume cannot find the substantial self in whose reality Descartes believed. When he looks within himself, he finds just a flux of various impressions.

But self or person is not any one impression, but [as the Cartesians think] that to which our several impressions and ideas are supposed to have a reference. If any impression gives rise to the idea of self, that impression must continue invariably the same, thro' the whole course of our lives; since self is suppos'd to exist after that manner. But there is no impression constant and invariable.[12]

In a famous pair of sentences, Hume casts away the Cartesian self: "For my part, when I enter most intimately into what I call *myself*, I always stumble on some particular perception or other, of heat or cold, light or shade, love or hatred, pain or pleasure. I never can catch *myself* at any time without a perception, and never can observe any thing but the perception."[13] What then is the self? Hume answers:

They [selves] are nothing but a bundle or collection of different perceptions, which succeed each other with an inconceivable rapidity, and are in a perpetual flux and movement. . . . The mind is a kind of theatre, where several perceptions successively make their appearance; pass, re-pass, glide away, and mingle in an infinite variety of postures and situations. There is properly no *simplicity* in it at one time, nor *identity* in different.[14]

Hume's bundle theory of the self is the outcome of reflecting upon Descartes's view of the self as a mental substance, using an empiricist test of existence. Experience consists of a flux of impressions. The various items we apprehend are ephemeral and transitory; all connections and modes of unity are external and accidental. Any philosophical claim about the existence of some object must be tested by seeing whether we can find that object within the flux of impressions. If we find it there, its existence is verified. If we cannot find it there, it is at best a philosophical fiction.

Bertrand Russell had an interesting argument against Hume. Suppose I am perceiving the sun. Then, according to the representative theory of sense awareness, I am directly aware of (or in Russell's terms, acquainted with) a sense impression (or sense-datum) that represents the sun. So there exists a certain fact that consists of my being acquainted with a certain sense-datum. Now, that fact is itself something I can be acquainted with, for how else could I learn about it?

> Thus, when I am acquainted with my seeing the sun, the whole fact with which I am acquainted is 'Self-acquainted-with-sense-datum'. Further, we know the truth 'I am acquainted with this sense-datum'. It is hard to see how we could know this truth, or even understand what is meant by it, unless we were acquainted with something we call 'I'. It does not seem necessary to suppose that we are acquainted with a more or less permanent person, the same today as yesterday, but it does seem as though we must be acquainted with that thing, whatever its nature, which sees the sun and has acquaintance with sense-data. Thus, in some sense it would seem we must be acquainted with our Selves as opposed to our particular experiences.[15]

Russell's argument has a peculiar character. He does not contradict Hume directly, by claiming that, contrary to what Hume discovered when he attended to the flux of his experience, he, Russell, discovers the self within the flux. That we are acquainted with the self is the conclusion of a line of reasoning, not the outcome of direct experience. We know, thinks Russell, of the existence of facts of the form "I am acquainted with X," where X is some sense impression. We could only know of such facts by acquaintance. Therefore, I am acquainted with facts of the form "I am acquainted with X." But I can be acquainted with a complex entity only by being acquainted with each of its constituents. Therefore I am acquainted with that constituent denoted by "I."

The difficulty here is that if I am acquainted with myself, why do I need an argument to prove it? Whatever I am acquainted with is an object of my consciousness; it is right there, before my very eyes, so to speak. Right now I am looking at a cup on my desk. If I am asked what makes me think there is a cup on my desk, I answer simply that I see it. If, instead, I had to give an argument to prove its existence, I would begin to suspect that I am not acquainted with it at all. On Russell's and Hume's assumptions, the best reason for thinking that something exists is that one is acquainted with it. And the best reason for thinking that an object of acquaintance exists is that it is an object of acquaintance. Yet Russell fails to use this reason. Why? Perhaps because he agrees with Hume that when he looks within himself, he cannot find the self abiding among the flow of impressions. But then it isn't an object of acquaintance.

A different sort of criticism is that Hume presupposes the very proposition that he is denying. Remember Hume saying that he never catches himself without an impression, and that the only things he stumbles upon are his impressions. Roderick Chisholm asks:

> How can he say that he doesn't find himself – if he is correct in saying that he finds himself to be stumbling and, more fully, that he find himself to be stumbling on certain things and not to be stumbling on certain other things? . . . If he finds not only perceptions, but also that *he* finds them and hence that there is *someone* who finds them, how can his premises be used to establish the conclusion that he never observes anything but perceptions?[16]

Even if Chisholm is correct in supposing that Hume's very language assumes that there is a self that is examining its impressions to determine what it will find there, it does not follow that the self which is doing the examining is the self as Descartes understood it, the Cartesian ego. After all, Hume did not deny that the term 'I' represented something. He thought there was a self, but that it was just a bundle of experiences, a stream of consciousness, not a Cartesian ego to which the stream belonged. Moreover, since our determination of what the self is, is a matter of philosophical reasoning rather than of direct acquaintance, our use of 'I' does not assume that we are in possession of a correct theory of the self or of any theory whatever. It is doubtful that we are capable of generating a correct account of the self just by reflecting upon the *cogito*. As Nietzsche pointed out, our language compels us to use 'I', but just because our language requires us to use a substantive, that does not mean we should think there is a substance.

In fact, nothing much hinges upon the use of 'I'. When I need cash, I frequently use the ATM machine at a bank. Occasionally it is out of cash and informs me of this fact by flashing "I cannot give you cash now" on the screen. It uses 'I'. Nothing follows from this fact. It is just a machine, not a person. It is a complex of parts. It produces this sentence on its screen without knowing what it is doing. It has no conception of itself. It cannot find itself or stumble upon itself. Yet it is capable of using language, including the first-person singular pronoun.

Suppose the machine flashed "I think, therefore I exist" on the screen.[17] Has it succeeded in proving to its own satisfaction that it exists? One may wonder whether the "I think" is even true. Is a computer capable of thought? And assuming that we human beings are capable of thought, how are we able to verify "I think"? Nietzsche denies that the "I think" is an immediate certainty; our knowledge of it, whatever that amounts to, is a matter of interpretation.

Hume's argument depends upon an empiricist account of how we verify something's existence. We do not find an impression of the Cartesian ego, so we have reason for thinking that there is no such thing. However, our previous discussion of color skepticism has given us cause to reject this method of determining our ontological commitments. We have sense impressions of color, but this, we saw, was no reason for thinking that anything is colored, not even the sense impression itself. The fact that I am acquainted with something does not prove that it exists. I am acquainted with after-images, but, as we have seen, there is every reason to suppose there are no such things. Moreover, the representative account of sense awareness implies that there are many things that exist that no one is acquainted with – for example, the imperceptible particles of theoretical physics or even Moore's hands and Price's tomato. We can have theoretical reasons for thinking that something does or does not exist, reasons capable of outweighing the evidence of our senses. Thus the fact that Hume was unable to discover the Cartesian ego among his impressions is not a conclusive reason for supposing that there is no such thing. If the existence of a Cartesian ego is presupposed in the best explanation of our mental life, that is a reason in its favor, despite our inability to stumble upon it.

Russell would probably object to the view that acquaintance does not prove the existence of the object of acquaintance by saying that, as he is using the term, its existence does follow. When X is acquainted with Y, then necessarily Y exists, just because of what 'acquainted with' means. So be it. In the previous paragraph, I used acquaintance without this existential presupposition, so, for me, that X is acquainted with Y does not entail the existence of Y. But I can also use 'acquaintance' in Russell's way to make the same point. I would then say that the fact that I seem to be acquainted with something does not entail that I am acquainted with it. So the fact that I seem to be acquainted with an after-image does not prove that I am acquainted with it, hence does not prove that there is any such thing.

4. Reflection

In this section, I shall consider Locke's account of self-knowledge. His empiricism consists of the claim that all our ideas are derived from experience. Experience consists of two distinct forms of observation:

> Our Observation employ'd either about *external, sensible Objects; or about the internal Operations of our Minds, perceived and reflected on by our selves, is that, which supplies our Understanding with all the materials of thinking*. These two are the Fountains of Knowledge, from whence all the *Ideas* we have, or can naturally have, do spring.[18]

The first form of observation he calls "sensation" and is the basis for our sensitive knowledge of the external world. The second he calls "reflection," and it is by means of this that we obtain ideas of our mental operations such as *"Perception, Thinking, Doubting, Believing, Reasoning, Knowing, Willing"* and various passive states such as desire and pain.[19] Once we are in possession of the ideas of various mental operations and states, we are capable of acquiring knowledge of them. Just as sensitive knowledge is acquired by means of sensation, so reflective knowledge is acquired by means of reflection. Today the term 'reflection' is no longer used with this meaning; it is customary to use 'introspection' in its place. Here I shall use both terms interchangeably.

How does reflection compare with sensation? Locke answers that "though it [reflection] be not Sense, as having nothing to do with external Objects; yet it is very like it, and might properly enough be call'd internal Sense."[20] The difference between them is that whereas reflection is directed at internal objects, sensation is directed at those that are external. Otherwise they are so similar that reflection is a kind of internal sense.

However, we cannot be satisfied with Locke's understanding of self-knowledge. In the first place, according to the representative theory of sense awareness, my perceptual consciousness of external objects includes a sensory consciousness of sensations or sense impressions. I learn, for example, that there is cabbage cooking in the kitchen as a result of my sense of smell being affected by the chemicals it gives off. I discover that the stove is hot as a result of the sensation I get in my fingers when I touch it. Sensations are states of the self; they are subjective and dependent. If reflection includes, as it should, the direct consciousness of our inner states, then every act of perceptual consciousness includes a moment of reflection. Thus my olfactory awareness of the cabbage includes a reflective awareness of the sensation of smell with which it affects me.

Second, in our discussion of sense awareness, we found it necessary to distinguish the sense awareness of an object from the judgments and beliefs it triggers. I see a tomato; this is a case of sense awareness, and it includes two forms of consciousness: perceptual consciousness of the tomato and sensory consciousness of the sensations with which it affects me. Then I judge "That is a tomato," and thus acquire sensitive knowledge. We need to make a similar distinction with respect to reflection. There is the reflective consciousness of the sensation in my fingers when I touch the hot stove, and then there is the reflective judgment: "This is a sensation of heat." The reflective, or introspective, judgment is intended to report the nature of the inner state that is the object of introspective awareness.

Third, sense awareness enables us to become conscious of external objects by means of direct acquaintance with the sensations whereby they affect us. But it is doubtful that reflection is mediated in the same way; hence it is questionable whether reflection should be classified as an inner *sense* as Locke thinks. Suppose I believe that the cat is on the mat. According to Locke, my knowledge that I have this belief is gained by reflection, which he thinks is a kind of observation. But there are no sensations specific to belief as there are sensations specific to heat or to smell. The reflective consciousness directed at the inner state of believing is not accompanied by anything like the sensory consciousness that accompanies sense awareness. If a sense is a source of consciousness of an object that operates by means of sensory consciousness, then reflection is not properly termed a sense.

Fourth, many states that we are inclined to classify as states of the self that are subjective and dependent are actually of a mixed sort. Consider my seeing the tomato. An analysis of this fact brings to light that it consists of three constituents: the one who is seeing it, the tomato which is the thing seen, and the act of seeing which is directed at the tomato. The act of seeing includes a part that is subjective and dependent: namely, the visual sensation of color, shape, and so on. But it also includes the tomato itself as a constituent. So when, upon seeing the tomato, I also come to know that I am seeing it, what I know includes both an external object and an internal state. If introspection is restricted to internal states and sense awareness to external objects, then what is the faculty which provides knowledge of these mixed conditions?

There is a lot that needs to be clarified here. Let us make a start by distinguishing between two types of mental states. The first consists of sensations. These include the sensory appearances of objects to us, such as the feelings produced by touch, the sensations produced by taste and smell, the ways things sound characteristic of hearing, and the ways things look characteristic of sight. Some of these sensory appearances are constituted by bodily sensations that are observed to have a specific location on a part of the body; others are sensations that lack a perceived specific location, as in sight and sound. In addition to sensory appearances, there are other bodily sensations, such as pains, tickles, itches, sexual feelings, and so forth, that are not involved in the perception of external objects. Some of these provide information about internal bodily states; for example, a soreness in the throat tells us of an infection; nausea informs us of indigestion. I think we should extend the notion of sense awareness to include consciousness of internal physical states mediated by sensations.

The second type of mental state includes things such as belief, desire, judgment, thoughts of various sorts, and many emotions. All these are marked by the fact that they possess content. More about these later.

When we describe a mental state, we frequently refer to objects external to the state, as the example of seeing the tomato illustrates. Let me use term 'reduction' for the process of eliminating such reference. There is no particular problem here with respect to sensation. For example, we can replace the description "pain in my tooth" by "pain of the toothache sort," where the phrase "toothache sort" is intended to characterize the pain without reference to any actual teeth. We can replace "the way the tomato looks" by "tomato-type visual sensation" and "the smell of cabbage cooking in the kitchen" by "cooked cabbage sensation." The replacement descriptions in these reductions must be interpreted so as to lack reference to any other objects. The terms 'toothache', 'tomato', and 'cooked cabbage' that occur in them simply characterize the type of sensation, without implying anything about the existence or nature of its external cause.

Knowledge of reduced sensory states is founded upon the fact that they are *conscious* states to which we can attend and which we can hence describe (assuming we possess the requisite vocabulary). Because they are conscious states, they manifest themselves directly, without the mediation of other sensations. Our awareness of them is not, therefore, a sensory awareness, as is our awareness of external objects. It is a direct awareness of states that possess the peculiar quality of consciousness. This sort of introspective awareness, then, is not, contrary to Locke, founded upon a sense. Reflective knowledge as expressed in the judgments we make such as "This is a pain of the toothache sort" and "It appears to me as if there is a tomato there," unlike the perception of external objects, is founded upon a direct awareness of the fact that is known. The fact itself is directly present to consciousness. These are cases of basic judgments that are grounded upon sensation; but the grounding is different from that of the basic judgments of sense awareness. In the latter, the sensations contain information about the objects that cause them, information that the judgment extracts. But reflective judgments about sense experience are grounded in virtue of reporting facts directly present to consciousness. There is no transcendent reference here; the reduction guarantees that.

5. Mental Content

According to the representative theory of sense awareness, the sensation which carries the information about the external world has a representative function. For example, the visual sensations caused by Price's tomato represent to the perceiver the tomato as well as it color, shape, size, and position. Representation is a three-termed relation: X (the representation) represents Y (the represented) to Z (the interpreter). I am using the term 'representation' as the most general concept applicable when one thing stands for another thing to someone. This relation occurs in many different forms; such notions as 'sign', 'meaning', and 'reference' are particular cases of representation. Anything that functions as a representation has a content that is specified by what and how it represents. This content is described as being "mental," because something is a representation only to the interpreter; and being an interpreter is a mental function, so the relation of representation is constituted in part by a mental relation. For example, the causal relation between fire and smoke is, in itself, a natural, nonmental relation. But if someone takes smoke as a sign of fire, then the smoke acquires a representative function in virtue of the person interpreting it in that way. The smoke then has the fire as its content, but only in relation to the interpretive actions of the interpreter. Something is a case of mental content relative to the mental acts which bind it to a representation. Philosophers have frequently used the term 'intentional content', as well as mental content, and think of the term 'intentionality' as signifying the representative function.

Let us first consider the representative function of sensations as they occur in the sense awareness of external objects. Our examination of each of the senses in the initial sections of this book justifies the hypothesis that the ground of the ability of a sensation to function as a sign is a causal relation between it and the object that constitutes its content. The sensation in my fingers tells me that the stove is hot, because hot things generally cause that type of sensation. The interpreter is able to extract that information from the sensation in virtue of a regular connection between sign and signified constituted in this case by the causal relation. I do not wish to suggest that the interpreter consciously thinks of the causal relation when he takes the sensation to inform him of a hot object. His interpretive ability sooner or later takes the form of a habit inculcated by early experience.

When the representative function of a representation is founded upon a causal relation or some other natural nonmental relation, I shall classify it as a 'natural sign'. Its intentionality, then, is derivative: it is something it possesses not in its own right, but in virtue of a relation it bears to something else.[21] Since the relation is causal, I shall characterize the type of intentionality of the representation by the term 'causally derived intentionality'.

Language is another intentional phenomenon of great importance, and there are numerous controversies as to how purely physical phenomena such as word and sentence tokens acquire meaning, reference, and illocutionary force.[22] How, for example, does the name "Julius Caesar" acquire the ability to refer to a particular citizen of ancient Rome? In general, we think that the reference and meaning of words and sentences is conventional, rather than natural. It is a product of our usage, rather than being founded upon a relation independent of human thought and action. Locke uses the term 'voluntary imposition' to designate the type of action whereby a word acquires a representative function.[23] Searle has argued that the capacity of sentences to represent "is not intrinsic but is derived from the intentionality of the mind."[24] As a general point, this is quite correct, since usage determines meaning and reference, and usage is just a type of habitual action, and action is a product of intention, and intention is a type of mental function. Ultimately, the representative capacities of linguistic objects are determined by various mental functions, but exactly how that is accomplished is a matter of great controversy, and I shall not pursue it here.

In some cases, it is not usage, but stipulation, which accounts for the intentionality of symbols. For example, suppose I put a rubber band on my wrist to remind me to turn off the computer. I have stipulated that the rubber band on my wrist means "Turn the computer off." I may never do this again, so this is not a case of usage, but of a particular, unrepeated voluntary imposition.

How shall we classify and understand the intentionality and mental content of our mental states, such as belief and desire? There is a definite analogy between thought and language here. When I say "I state that the cat is on the mat," I formulate a proposition – that the cat is on the mat – which I take to be true. When I say "I believe that the cat is on the mat," I formulate the same proposition, and I take it to be true. Just as the sentence in the statement is composed of words put together according to grammatical rules, so it is plausible to suggest that there is a mental sentence in the belief composed of mental words structured according to rules.

But what is the language from which the words and the grammatical rules of the mental sentence are drawn? And from where has this intentionality been derived? Earlier, I drew a distinction between judgment and belief. A judgment is a momentary event, such as my saying to myself that the stove is hot. It may seem that judgments are made in sentences we say to ourselves in the language we normally speak, English or French or whatever. But my believing something is not a momentary event; a belief may last for a long time, even for a whole life. It is a judgment preserved in some way or other, ready to be activated on appropriate occasions. We do not now have knowledge of the medium in which it is preserved. Perhaps our believing things is stored in the brain; perhaps for each belief there is a corresponding trace in the brain.

Is the English language the vehicle of the beliefs of speakers of English? If that were so, the brain traces of English speakers would be different from those of French speakers, and so on. That is certainly possible. But then the intentional content of our mental states would have to be derivative, just like the content of our sentences in natural language. However, the intentionality of these sentences was derived from our mental states, so we cannot, without circularity, explain the origin of the content of mental states by reference to natural language. Further, it seems that animals who lack language entirely possess mental states with content.

This has been denied, most famously by Descartes, who thought that animals are just machines without souls. But the similarity between the behavior of the higher animals and that of humans suggests that both are capable of belief, desire, and intention. If I reach for a banana, I think to myself, "I want this banana." There may be a similar thought in the mind of a monkey who reaches for a banana. The monkey may not classify its object of desire in the way humans do; it may not have the concept 'banana'; but that doesn't mean that it has no mental mode of representing what it wants. The evolutionary continuity between animals and humans suggests that when animals perform actions similar to those which, when performed by humans, are indicative of powers of thought, we are justified in ascribing powers of thought to them as well.

So there is reason to subscribe to the hypothesis that there is a language of thought analogous to human languages in possessing a vocabulary and something like grammatical rules, and that, unlike the spoken languages, is common to human beings generally.[25] It is also unlike any spoken language in that its intentionality is not derived in any way that we can understand, neither by usage nor by stipulation nor by causal relations. Until we have evidence to the contrary, it is reasonable to suppose that the intentional content of the words and sentences in the language of thought is intrinsic, as Searle argues, rather than derived. If thinking and other mental functions are realized in the brain, as materialists argue, then just as the functions of the brain are biological, so is mental content. Since the only interpreters we know of have animal bodies, it is very likely that representation is, ultimately, a biological notion.

What, then, can we say about knowledge of our mental representations? When I believe that the cat is on the mat, I am capable of knowing that I believe it and of knowing what it is I believe. How is this possible?

6. Propositional Attitudes

If I should ask you: "What do you think about protective tariffs? Do you think they are beneficial or harmful?," you may not at first know what to say. You may not have made up your mind; so you begin by considering the reasons for and against thinking that protective tariffs are beneficial. Suppose you decide, in light of the available evidence, that they are beneficial; that is the judgment you retain in your mind. You now actually believe that they are beneficial. If, in the future, you are asked what you think about protective tariffs, you no longer have to consider the reasons for and against them; you have already done that; you have an established belief. You simply say what you think. You say, for example, "Protective tariffs are beneficial." That sentence is an expression of your belief. If I should say to some third party: "He believes that protective tariffs are beneficial," I am then ascribing that belief to you.

If we rely upon the surface structure of sentences that ascribe beliefs to people, then, it would appear, believing something consists of a relation between a person and a proposition. In belief, there is the proposition believed – namely, that protective tariffs are beneficial – and there is the person who believes it; there is also the state of mind of that person directed to the proposition in virtue of which it is something believed. Other states of mind can be directed to propositions as well: doubt, desire, hope, worry, intention, and so forth. These states of mind are called 'propositional attitudes'. The proposition is the intentional content of the attitude.

But we need to go beyond the surface structure in order to expose more clearly the analogy between propositional attitudes and utterances in language. When I say in words, "Protective tariffs are beneficial," the proposition is expressed by means of a particular sentence token which functions in that context as its vehicle. By analogy, the propositional content of the belief has a vehicle as well.

Although much of the information in our possession can be fully expressed in sentences of natural language, not all of it can. For example, I know how a pineapple tastes, but I cannot put it into words. I know how a violin sounds, but I have no words for it. If I should hear something that sounds like a violin, I can say: "A violin sounds like that." But I have pointed at the sound, not described it. In order for me to communicate what I know to you, it is not enough that you understand the sentence; you must also be conscious of the sound to which I am directing you. Not every proposition that I believe is fully expressible in words, although many are. So it is not true that the vehicles for all propositional contents are sentences; they may be stored images or have a different nature entirely.

The structure of a belief, then, involves a person, a proposition, the vehicle that expresses it, which is called a 'mental representation', and the believing attitude. Since belief is one of a large number of propositional attitudes, there is the question as to what it consists of, and how it differs from other attitudes. For example, consider the difference between my believing that the window is open and my wanting it to be open. The same proposition is involved in each case; the difference lies not in the content, but in the attitude towards the content.

There is a difference, but how do we know it? Locke's answer is that we have the power of reflection, and that this power is the capacity to perceive the operations of our own minds. Just as I can become conscious of an external object when it affects my senses, so I can become conscious of my states of mind by turning my glance inward and apprehending what is going on.

Locke, however, is making a certain assumption that is, I think, unjustified. It is the assumption that all basic beliefs must be grounded, and that the grounding consists in some conscious state in which the item known is either directly present to consciousness or is represented by a vehicle that is directly present to consciousness, such as a sensation. But this assumption does not appear to be warranted in this case. If you ask me whether I believe that protective tariffs are beneficial, I can affirm that I believe it right off, without any inward glance or soul searching. Of course, if I have not made up my mind about the issue, then I may do some searching; however, this is not an investigation into some content already fixed in my mind but is, rather, a study of the reasons for and against protective tariffs. Once I have made up my mind, once my belief is fixed, I know without any conscious introspection at all what I believe and that I believe it.

If I were asked how I know that I possess this belief, my honest answer would be that I have no idea. If you ask me how I know there is a tomato there, I will say that I see it. I mention the way the belief is grounded: namely, by a visual experience. But when

I reply that it is my firm, long-standing belief that protective tariffs are beneficial, I am not aware of any experience, sensory or any other kind, that grounds my knowledge. In general, a good deal of our knowledge of our propositional attitudes consists in ungrounded basic beliefs. They are basic, because they are not inferred or justified in terms of other beliefs, and they are ungrounded, in that there is no accompanying conscious experience that gives us the right to believe them.

But if they are ungrounded, what gives us the right to believe them? Only the fact that these beliefs are usually correct. They are the results of processes unknown to us that produce true beliefs more often than false ones. We can speculate about the underlying mechanisms that make it possible for us to report accurately on our propositional attitudes. Perhaps the brain is capable of scanning its own states just as a computer can be made to scan what is on its hard disk. We just do not know the mechanisms that make self-knowledge of our propositional attitudes possible. This is a matter for further empirical research, not for philosophical dogmatizing.

Earlier, I made a distinction between a mental state and its mode of its realization. Just as my statement that protective tariffs are beneficial is realized in a particular sentence token, a series of specific words in a natural language, so, one would suppose, the propositional attitudes are also realized in particular tokens. Although we identify and individuate them by reference to their propositional content and the person in whom they reside, we do not know the nature of the tokens that realize them. Perhaps they are brain states, traces left by the experiences and other events that caused them. We have access to the sentence tokens through which people express their propositional attitudes in public speech, but the manner in which each of us gains knowledge of our own attitudes, knowledge of what we believe or desire or intend leaves us in the dark about the intrinsic nature of their realization. This is another topic for empirical research into mechanisms underlying our mental content.

How, then, do we distinguish between belief and desire? How do I know that I believe the window is open, rather than desire it to be open? Remember, we are referring here to beliefs and desires that have already been fixed. The experiences that triggered them are in the past. Again, nothing seems to tell me. My knowledge of the type of propositional attitude again seems to be ungrounded. Certainly something produces my knowledge, but I do not know what it is.

Of course, we are not completely in the dark about the differences among the attitudes, because we know something about how they are triggered, and we know something about the conduct to which they contribute. I may learn that the window is open when I feel a chill. Or, believing that it is open, I may get up to close it in order to end my shivering. So we are capable of identifying someone's propositional attitudes by examining their previous history and their present conduct and inferring both the type of attitude and its content on this basis. If, for example, I see someone looking at a tomato, I can reasonably suppose that they believe there is a tomato there. If I see them eat it, I can reasonably suppose that they want to eat it. If I know that a certain man has made an appointment to see Madame X at 8:00 p.m. and if at 7:55 p.m. he gets up from his chair and looks in the mirror, I can reasonably infer that he expects Madame X. So it looks as if our conceptions of the propositional attitudes as they occur within our commonsense framework are functional in nature: they are identified and individuated as to both type and content by reference to their antecedents and consequences, including the linguistic tokens that people use to express them. We have no direct access to them via introspection or reflection. In fact, when we say that we know of certain of our own attitudes by introspection, we are just giving a name to something we know nothing about.

In some cases, I may come to know about my own beliefs and desires in the same way as I come to know about the beliefs and desires of others. If they guide my actions, then I may not be able to identify them until I discover how I will act. Do I really want to move to Siberia? I may think I do, but if I keep putting the move off, then there may not really be any desire at all, only an inoperative daydream. This example illustrates the truth of fallibilism as applied to our knowledge of the propositional attitudes. The fact that I think I have or lack a certain attitude does not establish conclusively that what I think is true. One can be mistaken about the contents of one's own mind. Freud argued that much of the contents of our minds is unconscious and out of reach of knowledge. Let us turn to this issue now.

7. Privileged Access

A peculiarity of our self-knowledge is that it frequently involves privileged access. A person has a way of knowing his own states of mind that is direct and unmediated, whereas the access he has to the states of others is indirect, via behavior and speech. For example, that I have a certain pain I can know by feeling it, by being directly conscious of it, by being, to use Russell's term, acquainted with it. No one else has that sort of access. It is a kind of self-observation.

As I pointed out in the last section, we are not acquainted with our own propositional attitudes as such; we do not observe them. But we frequently have an unmediated knowledge of them, not via direct consciousness or a conscious inferential process, but through some mechanism whose nature we do not yet know. For that reason, such knowledge was characterized as ungrounded. By contrast, we have to figure out the attitudes of others on the basis of observing their conduct, situations, and speech.

Freud distinguished between conscious and unconscious mental states. Most of our mental life is unconscious; however, some of the unconscious material is easily available. Although I was not thinking just a few moments ago of my desire to move to Siberia, nevertheless, should the question arise, I could easily report on whether or not I wanted to make that move. Freud called such states of mind "preconscious." But other states of mind are not accessible at all, no matter how hard we try. He speaks "of the frequency and power of impulses of which one knew nothing directly and whose existence had to be inferred like some fact in the external world."[26] This is the unconscious proper, and we have no privileged access to these impulses. It is clear in this passage that the notions of the unconscious and of consciousness are epistemological: these terms refer to the type of access that the person has to his own states of mind.

In some passages, Freud treats consciousness as a quality that can be present or absent,[27] rather than as a kind of access. I think the reason for this is that the term "consciousness" expresses two distinct notions. When I say, for example, that my toothache is a state of consciousness, I may mean that my access to it is direct, that it is not hidden from me, that I know of it in a noninferential manner. But I may mean something entirely different, something that it is difficult to express directly in words, but with which all of us are quite familiar. In this sense, states of consciousness are things that go out of existence, when, for example, we are anesthetized or are in a deep, dreamless sleep or when we are knocked unconscious through a blow to the head. The reason that these two notions are easily confused is that when one is in a conscious state in the quality sense, then this state is also conscious in the epistemological sense. But a state can be conscious in the epistemological sense, yet not conscious in the quality sense, as with my desire to move to Siberia. I shall use the term 'sentience' to refer to consciousness in the quality sense.

Freud thinks that a person can gain access to some of his unconscious mental states through the special technique of psychoanalysis. For example, let us say that Smith has an unconscious incestuous sexual desire for his sister. The analyst may infer this on the basis of various things that Smith has said and may try to convince Smith of its truth. At first, Smith resists admitting this to the analyst, as well as to himself, but at some point he may overcome his resistance and say: "You are right; I now see that I have always wanted to have sexual intercourse with my sister." It is Freud's claim that we can have deferred privileged access to some of our epistemologically unconscious mental states. Of course, these states would then no longer be unconscious.

The question of privileged access is complicated by the fact that many of our mental states are unreduced (in the sense of section 4 above), because they incorporate external objects in their intentional content. My seeing the tomato was taken as an example. My being angry with Jones is another. We saw that in certain cases it is possible to reduce them by eliminating reference to external objects. The process of reduction consists in asking what is left of the state's content if we suppose that there is no such external object at all. In the case of the tomato, what is left is a visual sensation. In the case of anger, what is left if we drop out the object may vary from case to case. For example, when Jones drops out of the picture, perhaps only a visceral sensation remains; perhaps there also remains a thought: "Someone did this to me." As Wittgenstein has frequently pointed out, the inner aspects of our states of mind are not constant from case to case.

We cannot always determine their content a priori by reflecting upon their abstract type.

The case of propositional attitudes is more complicated. Consider, for example, Smith's belief that Jones voted against him. What is left of the belief if Jones drops out of the picture? Suppose there is no such person as Jones, and that Smith is paranoid and demented. We would not then describe Smith's mental state by the words "Smith believes that Jones voted against him," because these words entail that there exists a person who voted against him, and since there is no such person, it is false that Smith believes such a thing. What shall we say of his state of mind? We should attempt to describe it in a manner that does not entail any ontological commitment to the existence of Jones. We could say something like: "Smith believes that there is a person named 'Jones' who voted against him." This sentence represents the reduced representation of Smith's mental state. In fact, that is all there is to his mental state. The original sentence used by Smith describes no mental state at all. There is no such thing as Smith's belief that Jones voted against him, but there is a certain thought that Smith has that he incorrectly describes by the original sentence, and that can be correctly described by the reduced form.

However, suppose instead that Smith is neither paranoid nor demented, and that there really is a person named "Jones" who voted against him, and that he believes it. Since his having this belief entails him believing that there is such a person, the reduced form of the belief is also one of his beliefs. That is, if he believes that Jones voted against him and would express his belief in the sentence "I believe that Jones voted against me," then he believes that there is a person of that name who voted against him. So it is possible in general to isolate the inner mental content of the propositional attitudes in a way that abstracts from the external content.[28]

In certain cases, after we have performed the reduction, the mental state that remains is no longer of the same type as the unreduced state. Consider Smith's anger with Jones for having voted against him. If we eliminate Jones, what is left are certain sensations plus the belief as above that there is such a person who voted against him. But this reduced remnant is no longer the emotion of anger.

To the extent to which our mental states are subject to reduction, to that extent we are capable of having privileged access to them (provided that they are conscious). Our access to the unreduced states that have external objects as part of their content is partly privileged with respect to their reduced form and partly founded upon whatever other mode of access has grounded our knowledge of the existence of the objects.

The fact of privileged access has important implications for the mind–body problem. I shall use the term 'objective understanding of the human reality' (OUHR) to indicate the kind of apprehension we can achieve if we confine ourselves solely to what we can learn about human beings just from observation and scientific inference, without bringing into the picture any interpretations that make use of information acquired by privileged access. Such an understanding consists of knowing human beings only in their guise as material objects. Even if, for example, our OUHR were to produce a complete knowledge of the human brain as a material object, even if it were to produce knowledge of everything going on in some particular brain, we would still have no knowledge whatever of any correlated mental states.

Suppose, for instance, I find in some brain a certain set of neurons that is now firing. Let us suppose that the person whose brain it is, is feeling a toothache as a result of the brain event. If I am forbidden to rely upon that person's privileged access to his toothache or the privileged access of anyone else to their toothaches, including myself, then there is no way that I can identify that brain event as one involving that particular sort of pain. The epistemological limitation that defines OUHR prevents our seeing others as persons with minds, since we have no basis for ascribing mentality to them.

It follows that, on the assumption that our privileged access reports are frequently true, privileged access provides us with knowledge of a domain of fact concealed from OUHR. This domain of fact includes, first, conscious (or sentient) states and, second, propositional attitudes, their types and their intentional contents. So even if mental states are, contrary to what Descartes thought, realized in physical states of the nervous system, privileged access reveals aspects of those states that are not available objectively. This means that the mental is a domain of fact not completely reducible to the physical. Even if mind emerges from matter in the evolutionary process, what emerges is something new, which is not fully understandable in terms of its material basis.[29]

8. Abstract Objects and Mental Content

In our discussion of the reduction of states of mind in order to eliminate reference to objects, the various objects intended were things in the external world such as Price's tomato or Moore's hands or the persons about whom we have beliefs and emotions. But there is another sort of object that enters into our states of mind that cannot be eliminated by reduction, for these objects determine the essential nature of the states of mind themselves. These are abstract objects such as propositions, concepts, and universals, which have been argued about since the origin of philosophical analysis in the writings of Plato.

Let us start with propositions, for these enter into the propositional attitudes as their objects and as specifying their content. Consider, for example, Smith's belief that Lincoln loved his wife Mary. There is a certain fact about Smith – namely, his having this belief – and there is the proposition believed, which is represented by "that Lincoln loved his wife Mary." From the fact that propositions are objects of belief, we can infer that, whatever else they are, they are at least things capable of being true or false; or, to put the same point another way, they are either matters of fact or not. If your belief is true, then what you believe is a fact, so there is an intimate connection between truth and factuality.

In addition, since the same proposition can be expressed by many different vehicles – just consider the variety of languages in which Smith's belief can be expressed – we cannot identify the proposition with the specific vehicle that happens to express it. The sentence "Lincoln loved his wife Mary" is no more to be identified with the proposition whose truth Smith accepts than are those different sentences in French or German or other languages in which others might say the same thing.

Moreover, different people can believe the same thing, so the proposition, that whose truth they accept, is not the private property of any one individual, as Frege (1845–1925) has insisted.[30] Propositions are objective entities, capable of being represented and understood, affirmed and denied, doubted and believed, by thinking beings. But because they are capable of being false as well as true, they cannot be identified with concrete existing objects such as Price's tomato or Moore's hands. For that reason, they are frequently classified as abstract objects, items that do not have a specific spatiotemporal location but that, so Frege thought, are nonetheless real things.

But if they are real things, what kind of things are they? And how can they be known? Frege, for example, did not believe that our access to them was through sense perception. Does the human mind have a special power of grasping them, independently of any sensuous realization? We began by thinking of a propositional attitude as involving a relation between a person and a proposition. Yet, when we think about what sorts of things propositions can be, they turn out to be very puzzling indeed.

Bertrand Russell gave a very powerful argument against supposing that there are any such things at all:

> The necessity of allowing for falsehood makes it impossible to regard belief as a relation of the mind to a single object, which could be said to be what is believed. If belief were so regarded, we should find that . . . it would not admit the opposition of truth and falsehood, but would have to be always true. This may be made clear by examples. Othello believes falsely that Desdemona loves Cassio. We cannot say that this belief consists in a relation to a single object, 'Desdemona's love for Cassio', for if there were such an object, the belief would be true. There is in fact no such object, and therefore Othello cannot have any relation to such an object. Hence his belief cannot possibly consist in a relation to this object.[31]

Let us suppose that Smith's belief is true, so that we may plausibly say that there is or was such a thing as Lincoln's love for Mary. Let us call such a thing a fact. So when a belief is true, there is a fact to which the one who believes it is related. Perhaps we should identify a true proposition with a fact. But that still leaves us with the problem of false propositions. On Russell's view, there are no such things at all; yet we can believe them. How should this be understood?

Let us think about the problem by considering how we identify propositions in the first place. How do we know what Smith believes? Well, he utters the sentence "Lincoln loved Mary." Since we share both Smith's language and his historical knowledge, we are able to interpret the noises he produces as words in English. We also know which persons the proper names 'Lincoln' and 'Mary' are being used to refer to, and we also know what relationship the verb 'loves' stands for. Because of our familiarity with the grammar of English, we also know that the relationship represented by 'loves' is asserted by Smith to go from Lincoln to Mary, not from Mary to Lincoln. As Russell says, relations have a sense or a direction.[32] Moreover, our familiarity with the language allows us to judge that Smith is making an assertion, and thus expressing what he believes, rather than asking a question or expressing a doubt and so on. That is, we are capable of recognizing the type of speech act that he is using these words to produce.

Wittgenstein has warned us over and over again not to be misled by the superficial grammar of a sentence when thinking about our ontological commitments.[33] In the sentence "Smith believes that Lincoln loves Mary" the clause "that Lincoln loves Mary" functions like a singular term; for example, it can function as the subject term in a sentence, as in "That Lincoln loves Mary is what Smith and many others believe." It can be replaced by other terms that function like singular terms, such as "what you believe." But we should not be seduced by the grammatical form that the phrase assumes into thinking that there actually is some entity that it names. After all, it does not follow from Smith's thinking that Lincoln loves Mary that there is any such thing as Lincoln's love for Mary. It is an accident of our language that we indicate the content of our thought by a singular term; but the content could have been represented by other means entirely.

Moreover, the interpretation we gave to Smith's sentence does not lead us to think that there is any such entity as the proposition it expresses. Our interpretation did commit us to the reality of Lincoln and Mary as the people he was talking about and to a certain relationship represented by 'loves', but our understanding of the sentence certainly includes no commitment to that relationship actually holding between Lincoln and Mary. Smith takes it to hold between them; he asserts it to hold. But asserting a relationship to hold is compatible with it not actually holding.

As a result of our understanding of what Smith has asserted, we know what must be the case if what he says is true. We know that there must be persons named by 'Lincoln' and 'Mary' and that they must love one another. We know the 'truth conditions' of the speech act. But such an understanding of truth conditions does not imply that they are realized. What we grasp in our knowledge of the truth conditions is not an actual entity but, in this case, a possible state of affairs, something we can imagine or conceive, something we can represent and speak about and make the object of our attitudes, but which, for all that, might have no actual existence at all.

What about the argument that propositions must have objective reality because they can be apprehended by different minds? But people can imagine the same event or dream the same dream without what they imagine or dream being real, so the same applies to what they assert or believe. Again, we should not be pushed into thinking that because we are using a noun or a noun phrase, there must be some actual entity corresponding to it.

So we do not have to believe in the reality of propositions in our discussion of the propositional attitudes. We can speak as if the attitudes were relations between persons and propositions, provided this is recognized as shorthand for talking about the common content of people's mental states. And there is something we can call 'common content'. Compare "Lincoln loves Mary" with the corresponding sentence in French "Lincoln aime Marie." The semantic interpretation of both commits us to the existence of Lincoln and Mary and to the relationship of one person loving another. So there is a common content, even though what is common is not a proposition. Upon reduction to eliminate external objects from our commitment, we can describe Smith as believing that there are people bearing those names such that the first loves the second. However, even in reduced form, Smith's mental state seems to incorporate reference to objects, not concrete objects such as Lincoln and Mary, but abstract objects such as the item represented by the general term 'loves'. We cannot reduce the mental state further, to eliminate reference to abstract objects, for then the state disappears entirely. It looks as if abstract objects constitute the ineliminable content of the mind.

9. Conceptual Representation

Let us examine our sample belief ascription – "Smith believes that Lincoln loves Mary" – to summarize where we stand at this point. If it is true, then there exists something about Smith that we describe as his having this belief. We can learn that he has it by what he says and, perhaps, by what he does and from his sources of information. We hypothesize that there is a vehicle for his belief, but we know nothing about its nature other than that it bears some analogy to the sentences in Smith's language that he might use to communicate what he believes to others. Our ascription of that belief to Smith commits us to the existence of two actual persons (in addition to Smith himself), Lincoln and Mary, as well as to the relationship that he believes holds between them. It also commits us to there being a possible, perhaps nonactual, state of affairs which would exist if the belief were true. This is the proposition believed, but remember, we need not consider it to be an actual entity, even though the verbal forms in which it is represented occasionally tempt us to do so.

If we were to describe Smith's state of mind independently of a commitment to the existence of objects such as Lincoln and Mary, we would say that what he believes is that there is a person called 'Lincoln' and another person called 'Mary' and that the first loves the second. By reduction, we can eliminate reference to the actual persons in such a way that the ascription of the reduced belief to Smith does not commit us to their existence. But the reduced belief itself possesses a content; in order for it to be Smith's belief, he must possess the concept of one person loving another and the concept of a person bearing a name. In virtue of his possessing and using these concepts, he is able to conceive of the state of affairs that would make his belief true. We cannot reduce this belief further by eliminating reference to the objects of these concepts, because there is no further belief to reduce it to. The end of the road of reduction leaves us with a conceptual content.

This is what is known by introspection when Smith knows what it is that he believes.

Just as the sentence that Smith utters to convey his belief – "Lincoln loves Mary" – expresses content that includes both concepts and objects, so, we hypothesize, does the mental representation that functions as the vehicle for his belief. The next question that arises is how it is possible for such mental vehicles to acquire such a representational capacity. We saw that when this question was asked about language, a plausible answer was that word types acquire their meaning and reference as a result of human social practices and conventions, and that their content is, in this way, imposed upon them in virtue of the communicative intentions of language-users. But this way of looking at the matter presupposes that language-users are capable of possessing states of mind prior to the possession of language. Language presupposes thought. But how, then, is thought possible? What is involved in the production of mental vehicles with intentional content?

This issue was much discussed in seventeenth-century philosophy under the rubric of the "origin of ideas." Descartes and Leibniz claimed that many of our ideas are innate, but Locke argued that all our ideas come from experience. We begin our lives, Locke thought, with a *tabula rasa*, a blank mind, and our mind gradually acquires the ideas of all the things it can think and speak about by means of the experiences delivered by sensation and reflection. Initially, we perceive various objects through our senses and thus acquire ideas of these particular objects and of their particular qualities. By a process that Locke called "abstraction," we are able to consider groups of particulars, to retain what is common to them and eliminate their points of difference, and thus gradually to build up a stock of general ideas. The mind also has the capacity to operate upon the ideas it possesses in various ways, thereby producing more complex ideas without the necessity of further experience. By reflection, the mind becomes aware of these mental operations and thus acquires ideas descriptive of its mental life.

A natural question to ask of this empiricist account of the origin of mental content is: How is it possible that, from the fact that we experience something, we are able to form an idea of it? A child looks at a tomato and at other red things and, as a result of the accumulation of similar experiences, comes to possess the idea of the quality red. Locke quite correctly pointed out that we know nothing of the underlying mechanism by which experience generates mental content. His basic claim is simply that this is what experience is capable of doing to minds such as ours, and his most convincing argument is that we discover that children acquire their conceptual abilities gradually, after being exposed to the objects of these concepts through experience.

Something like Locke's story must be true of many of our concepts. In the case of an adult who is ignorant of something, the easiest way of causing them to acquire the relevant concept is to show them an example. If, for instance, someone from a primitive society lacks an idea of an automobile, all we need to do is to show them one and show them how it works. We do have the power of acquiring ideas from experience. There are countless examples of this. So Locke's empiricist theory of the origin of ideas seems to be the simplest and most plausible account of the acquisition of many of our concepts.

It is doubtful, however, that it can explain the origin of all our ideas. Consider Locke's own problem with the idea of substance. Sensation is capable of furnishing our minds with simple ideas. In this way, we form the ideas of color and shape and size and so on. But we also acquire the habit of thinking of such qualities not as independent actualities in their own right, but as predicable of objects or substances. Along with the ideas of these qualities, we also operate with the idea of substance. "So that if any one will examine himself concerning his *Notion of pure Substance in general*, he will find he has no other *Idea* of it at all, but only a Supposition of he knows not what support of such Qualities, which are capable of producing simple *Ideas* in us; which Qualities are commonly called Accidents."[34]

How do we get into this habit of thinking of these qualities as predicates of an object? Locke cannot say that this habit (which is what he calls the idea of substance) is a result of our sense awareness of the object, because what is given in experience are just the qualities, not that of which they are predicates. There seems to be nothing in the apparatus at Locke's disposal in his account of experience to explain the origin of this habit. Later Kant argued, in *The Critique of Pure Reason*, that certain of our concepts constituted a framework, what Strawson and Sellars and others have called a "conceptual framework," that we use to organize the items that sensation delivers into a spatiotemporal system of objects, and that this framework – Kant described it as the forms of sensibility (space and time) plus a system of categories – cannot originate in experience, because it consists of those powers of the mind that make experience possible.

The system of categories is, according to Kant, a system of fundamental ways of thinking about the sensory manifold that is innate in the human mind. The intentional content that constitutes the basic framework for the deployment of the empirically derived content is not itself derived empirically, for it is part of the apparatus by means of which our other concepts are derived empirically. The debate over what is derived empirically and what is innate continues to this very day. What is there, in the human mind, that makes our learning from experience possible? Whatever it is, it cannot itself be learned from experience. It is unlikely that Locke was correct in thinking of the human mind as originally a *tabula rasa*.[35]

Further Readings

Quassim Cassam (ed.), *Self-Knowledge* (Oxford: Oxford University Press, 1994).

Jerry Fodor, "Methodological Solipsism Considered as a Research Strategy in Cognitive Psychology," in *Representations* (Cambridge, Mass.: MIT Press, 1986), pp. 225–53.

David Hume, *A Treatise of Human Nature*, Bk I, Pt iv, sect. 6: "Of Personal Identity."

Gilbert Ryle, "Self-Knowledge," in *The Concept of Mind* (London: Hutchinson's University Library, 1949), ch. 6.

5
Beyond Basic Belief

1. The Reliability of Basic Beliefs

Our system of beliefs, thoughts, and judgments is structured by a conceptual framework that incorporates both our fundamental ontology and a system of categories. Among our beliefs are those we are entitled to possess, those we have an epistemic right to believe because they are produced by processes that tend toward producing beliefs that are true. Among these are beliefs that are basic – so called because they have been arrived at by a process which does not consist solely of inferring them from other beliefs. That we are entitled to believe them cannot be explained completely by reference to other beliefs that we are entitled to, from which we inferred them. Thus, when I learn that there is a tomato on the table by seeing it there, that is a basic belief. Among the basic beliefs are those that are grounded in conscious experience, such as the one about the tomato, and those that are not.

To the question of why we are entitled to those of our beliefs that are basic, the answer is that they are arrived at by processes that are truth-tending. A belief could be basic even if it turned out to be false, provided it was produced by a process that is reliable. Sense awareness is reliable, because the judgments and beliefs triggered by the impact of physical energies upon our sense organs are more frequently true than not. Sensory consciousness is reliable, because the judgments about bodily sensations and feelings and sensory appearances are more likely to be true than not.

What about our ungrounded basic beliefs? My recall of a past experience need not be grounded in any contemporary item present to my consciousness. Why am I entitled to believe that the event I recall actually happened? The answer is the same: because the process which enables me to remember it, though not a conscious process, is reliable; my memory beliefs about particular events are more likely to be true than not.

There are a number of problems and difficulties with this way of thinking about our basic beliefs. I shall discuss some of them now, and others will be taken up in subsequent discussions of the ethics of belief and the problem of truth.

The first is this. If we are able show that basic beliefs are truth-tending, does this not prove that they are not basic after all? They are justified as being the results of a reliable process; there is some process of reasoning which establishes that they are more likely than not to be true. Isn't this enough to establish that they are derived, rather than basic?

The answer rests on the fact that the distinction between basic and derived beliefs is relative to the belief systems of particular persons. What is basic for one may be derived for another. For example, if I see something and tell you about it, my belief is basic, whereas you are entitled to it on the grounds that my testimony is reliable. Your entitlement is the product of reasoning, mine is not. Similarly, the belief in the existence of the tomato triggered by my sense impressions is not arrived at by reasoning, and thus is basic; but it might have been arrived at by reasoning by another who derives it from his beliefs about the reliability of his impressions. Whether a belief is or is not basic depends upon how it is actually produced, not upon how it might be produced in other circumstances or by other persons. The question of whether or not one is entitled to a basic belief depends upon the *truth* of our theories of the nature of the underlying processes and their reliability, but the person who has the belief need not himself know anything about these theories in order to be entitled to it. It is sufficient that these processes *be* reliable, regardless of whether the individual knows that they are reliable or knows what they are. We trust our memories, even though most of us know nothing about the mechanisms in the brain/mind system that produce and store them. But in fact these mechanisms are reliable, and that entitles us to trust our recollections. There are pathological cases in which the mechanisms are injured or diseased and in which what is recollected is frequently merely an illusion. But in such cases, the recollections would not be basic, because their unreliability would defeat the claim that the person was entitled to these beliefs no matter what he thought.

At this point, it is natural to wonder what justifies me in declaring with such assurance that this process is reliable, that one unreliable. How do I know about these matters? The answer is that we all have plenty of evidence about the reliability of many of the processes underlying the formation of our beliefs, even though we may lack a full understanding of their nature. That your sense awareness is reliable is something I can confirm because I find that the beliefs it triggers are usually true. You say, for example, that you believe there is a tomato on table because you see it; I confirm the truth of what you say by observing the tomato there myself. I find that Smith's memory has become unreliable because, knowing him quite well, I find that most of what he says happened to him didn't really happen at all. We do not have to know much about the underlying mechanisms to have sufficient reason to trust some modes of belief formation and distrust others.

But isn't this circular? If I appeal to the results of sense awareness to confirm its reliability or to the results of memory to determine that memory can be trusted, am I not establishing their credibility by reference to themselves? How can that be reasonable? If I doubt your word because I think that you frequently lie, I would not try to convince myself that you are telling the truth by asking you whether you are. But isn't that what is being done when I convince myself of the reliability of sense awareness or memory by appealing to their deliverances?

What is involved here is not exactly a circle, however. If I confirm the reliability of your sense impressions by reference to what I see and hear, then I am assuming the reliability of mine, not yours. In determining whether someone's beliefs are basic, I do not appeal to those very beliefs. The circle, if there is one, does not pertain to the specific beliefs in question. There is a greater appearance of circularity if the question of reliability is asked not of some particular person's beliefs, but of a certain mode of belief formation in general. Is sense awareness in general reliable? Is memory in general reliable?

However, in assessing the reliability of, say, sense awareness, I do not appeal to sense awareness in general, but to a specific constellation of perceptual beliefs. According to what I and others can determine about people's perceptual judgments, they are more often true than not. This is consistent with some people's judgments being completely deranged. It is an inductive inference. The judgments of people whose accuracy I have checked are usually true, so probably sense awareness in general is a pretty good way to arrive at accurate representations of the external world. With greater information at my disposal, I may qualify my estimate. For example, the arguments for color skepticism show that our judgments of color are almost always mistaken. So, even if I use the beliefs based upon my sense awareness to evaluate sense awareness in general, there is no guarantee that the grade I award will invariably be favorable or favorable in all respects. There is, of course, the skeptical objection that one is not entitled to use the products of sense awareness at all to evaluate its reliability, since we are not entitled to use them until its reliability is first established. With this objection, we have returned to Descartes's problem of how to emerge from solipsism without employing any mode of belief formation whose veracity has been once called into question. I have already dealt with this difficulty in discussing Moore's proof of an external world. We can use our perceptual beliefs not because we have established their reliability without appealing to our perceptual beliefs, but because they have been arrived at by a method that is reliable whether we have established that or not. If Moore knows that there is an external world by his proof, if his senses provide him with such knowledge, then he is entitled to make use of what he knows in any further assessments he may make of the veracity of his perceptual beliefs. The skeptic may, of course, respond that Moore was unable to give a proof that he really knew what he claimed to know. But this second-level skepticism directed at the question of whether one knows that one knows does not undermine our first-level trust in our knowledge-producing faculties. Why should it? Why should our inability to prove that we have the knowledge we claim to have inhibit us from making use of what we claim to know? Skepticism on the second level does not show that there is anything the matter with our first-level claims. It does not show, for example, that we do not know what we claim to know.

2. Derived Belief

Some terminological stipulations are now in order. A belief or opinion that someone is epistemically entitled to have is one that is *warranted* for that person. Some beliefs that are not derived from others may not be warranted; they are, therefore, not basic beliefs, because all these are warranted. Let us call them *basic prejudices*. Among a person's warranted beliefs are those that they have *validly derived* from others that are warranted. One that is derived, but not validly derived, is a *derived prejudice*. Thus warranted beliefs are those that are both basic and validly derived.

We extend the notion of a reliable, or truth-tending, process to derived beliefs as well. These are warranted because they are derived by processes that themselves are truth-tending. In the case of basic beliefs, the processes are physical and psychophysical events by which the organism receives information in a manner that does not involve items having intrinsic mental content. The intention here is to present an objective, realistic conception of warranted belief. Basic beliefs are those that are warranted because the processes that produce them bring the human organism into contact with the facts that they purport to represent more frequently than not. Validly derived beliefs develop and extend in reliable ways the information embodied in those that are basic. A person's total belief system is warranted to the extent that the particular beliefs that comprise it are warranted. Whether a belief is warranted, then, is not a matter of opinion; it does not matter what we think or prefer or hope. The things that make up the world have the features they do quite independently of what we think about them, and we either succeed in representing them accurately in a non-accidental way or we do not. And if we do not, then our belief system incorporates prejudices to some degree or other.

Descartes hoped to eliminate the prejudices that infected his belief system by using the method of doubt to clear his mind of anything that might be a prejudice and then searching for a criterion to distinguish prejudices from warranted beliefs. If we can find a criterion, then we have a way of ascertaining that anything we add to our system of beliefs will also be warranted. His position is an internalist one, because of his insistence on the need for an accessible criterion to enable us to determine with certainty whether a proposition whose acceptance we are considering is warranted for us. His position is also a version of *foundationalism*, because he insists that human knowledge rests upon a foundation of basic beliefs that are in contact with the reality that we aim to know.

However, the view I am developing here is externalist, not internalist, because I do not think that a criterion is always available. In the case of sense awareness, we do not possess a criterion independent of sense awareness in general that would enable us to distinguish veridical sense impressions from those that are not veridical. That is the point of Descartes's dream argument. However, as I argued in the discussion of Moore's proof of an external world, the absence of a criterion does not actually prevent us from having knowledge. Once we have some knowledge or, at least, some warranted belief, we can build on that to find new and reliable ways of adding to our warranted beliefs. This view also belongs to the family of views known as 'foundationalism', because of its acceptance of the notion of basic belief as a ground of warrant.

The conception of reasoning that Peirce developed is the one I shall build upon in what follows. In "The Fixation of Belief," he explains:

> The object of reasoning is to find out, from the consideration of what we already know, something else which we do not know. Consequently, reasoning is good if it be such as to give a true conclusion from true premises, and not otherwise. Thus, the question of validity is purely one of fact and not of thinking. A being the facts stated in the premises and B being that concluded, the question is, whether these facts are really so related that if A were B would generally be. If so, the inference is valid; if not, not. It is not in the least the question whether, when the premises are accepted by the mind, we feel an impulse to accept the conclusion also. . . . The true conclusion would remain true if we had no impulse to accept it; and the false one would remain false, though we could not resist the tendency to believe in it.[1]

Peirce here presents an objective conception of valid reasoning. Whether an argument is valid depends upon whether it be such as to give a true conclusion from true premises, no matter what we happen to think. Not only does thinking something to be true not make it true, but thinking that your reasoning is good does not make it good. Reasoning that is valid or good is truth-tending.

Peirce then introduces another valuable concept, that of a *guiding principle of inference*:

> That which determines us, from given premises, to draw one inference rather than another, is some habit of mind, whether it be constitutional or acquired. The habit is good or otherwise, according as it produces true conclusions from true premises or not; and an inference is regarded as valid or not, without reference to the truth or falsity of its conclusion specially, but according as the habit which determines it is such as to produce true conclusions in general or not. The particular habit of mind which governs this or that inference may be formulated in a proposition whose truth depends on the validity of the inferences which the habit determines; and such a formula is called a *guiding principle* of inference.[2]

When I speak of our system of beliefs, I intend to include in its contents not only the beliefs themselves but the guiding principles or habits of reasoning by means of which new beliefs are derived from old. I also include within the system markers which represent the paths of derivation that connect our beliefs to one another.

Peirce points out that our guiding principles are initially possessed as habits of mind, rather than as explicitly formulated rules. We derive one belief from another without necessarily being able to articulate our underlying rules of derivation. We can, however, step back and ask whether our rules are any good, whether they are such as to enable us generally to derive true conclusions from true premises. We are able to improve our reasoning practices by revising habits that fail to be valid or replacing less reliable habits with those that are more reliable. Logic is the discipline whose purpose is the study of those guiding principles that are topic-neutral, that are applicable to all subject matters, those that Peirce claims are "absolutely essential as guiding principles."[3]

Some of our guiding principles are such as can never fail to produce true conclusions from true premises. These are the logical truths whose study belongs to *deductive logic*. There are others that are reliable, though not perfectly so; they are capable of producing falsehoods from truths, though not usually. In the arguments that they regulate, the premises confirm or support the conclusion to some degree or other. The study of these principles of confirmation belongs to the *logic of evidence*. In some cases, our aim is not to formulate a belief that is warranted, but to arrive at a "good idea," a conjecture or hypothesis that is worth exploring, that may be warranted but needs further investigation before its true value is revealed. The study of methods of arriving at fruitful conjectures is the *logic of heuristics*.

A valid argument or line of reasoning is one that is of a type such that if its premises are true, then usually its conclusion is true as well. So, as we move from the study of basic beliefs to those that are derived, the concept of truth begins to occupy a central role. What, then, is truth?

3. Truth

Three issues are bound up with the question of the nature of truth. How do we manage to know the truth and to distinguish what is true from what is false? is one of them, and is the central topic of this book. A second is: What type of entity is capable of being either true or false, of having truth-value? This is the question of the bearer of truth, and the answer we gave to it (in chapter 4, section 8) is that propositions are truth-bearers. And the third is: What is the nature of truth? What is it that true propositions have that false one's do not have?

The identification of propositions as truth-bearers is somewhat paradoxical, because of their problematic ontological status. Basing our considerations upon Russell's argument, we saw that although true propositions can plausibly be identified with the facts or the existing states of affairs that make them true, false propositions have no reality whatever. How, then, can we plausibly predicate falsehood of them?

We are tempted to say that a proposition is a possible state of affairs, some of which are actual (those that are true), some not (those that are false). However, even that is mistaken. Sometimes our reasoning involves the consideration of impossible states of affairs. For example, in mathematics, it is common to prove the truth of a theorem by a *reductio ad absurdum* argument, in which we assume its falsity and deduce a contradiction. But the falsehood assumed is impossible, and so is the contradiction deduced. So we should identify propositions not with possible states of affairs, but with those that are conceivable or thinkable or supposable.

But if false propositions do not exist, if they are mere thinkable things, how are we justified in predicating falsehood of them? How can a nonexistent thing be in possession of any character whatever? To say of a proposition that it is false is just to say that it does not exist, that it is a state of affairs that fails to be actual. It may be possible, or, failing that, it may be conceivable; but there actually is no such thing at all among existing objects.

If I say that the proposition expressed by "Lincoln loved Mary" is false, am I not referring to it by using the singular term "the proposition expressed by 'Lincoln loved Mary'"? If I refer to it, must it not exist? How can one refer to, and speak about, something that does not exist at all?[4] In recent years, it has become customary to assume that existence is a necessary condition for reference. If in uttering the sentence "Lincoln loved Mary" I have succeeded in referring to Lincoln, it follows, on this assumption, that there actually is such a person. The existence of Lincoln is a necessary condition of the truth of the proposition expressed by the sentence. So, from "Lincoln loved Mary" I can validly infer "There is someone who loved Mary," a mode of inference termed 'existential generalization', named after the existential quantifier "there is."

However, the way we use singular referring terms and the quantifier "there is" in ordinary discourse does not require or presuppose an existence condition.[5] I can say, speaking truly, that Pegasus was a winged horse and that Zeus was a Greek god without supposing that there actually are winged horses and Greek gods. The expression "there is" does not mean the same as "there exists," although we frequently use it to assert existence when we are speaking of entities we believe to exist. But we can also use it to speak of entities that we know do not exist; that there is someone who loved Hamlet is true because Ophelia loved him. We are able to conceive and imagine possibilities that we can make into subjects of discourse and thought quite independently of their falling within the class of actual existents. Our use of "there is" is thus ontologically noncommittal. We commit ourselves ontologically not by saying that there is a such and such, but by saying that there actually exists a such and such.

Lifting the existence condition for reference complicates our notion of truth and falsehood. We can no longer say that a proposition or state of affairs is true only if it actually exists, for "Ophelia loves Hamlet" is true even though neither Ophelia nor Hamlet can be numbered among the existents. I shall distinguish between a state of affairs existing and its being realized in some universe of discourse. That Ophelia loved Hamlet is realized in the universe of discourse constituted by the world Shakespeare imagined in the play *Hamlet*, whereas that Hamlet admired the husband of his mother is not realized in that universe. That Lincoln was elected president is realized in the universe of discourse constituted by the actual world and is realized in that world. A proposition is true if it is realized in the universe of discourse that is intended by the one who thinks it. Some universes of discourse are products of the human imagination and thought; but there is one privileged universe of discourse in both science and everyday life: namely, the actual world, for that is the universe that we have an urgent need to obtain knowledge about. The question of whether or not a certain proposition is true can be answered only if we first specify or presuppose a universe of discourse with respect to which the question of truth is addressed.

The most frequent answer in the history of philosophy to the question of the nature of truth is that a proposition is true if and only if it corresponds to reality or corresponds to fact. The impulse behind this *correspondence theory of truth* is the idea that the truth of what we say or think depends not upon what we happen to believe, but upon the way the world is. What we think is true or false depends upon whether or not there is something in the world that answers to it. Thus the correspondence theory belongs to the tradition of realism which says that there is a world that is independent of thought and belief that we aim to learn about in our inquiries.

The correspondence theory says that there are two things: the bearer of truth and that in the world which is responsible for its being true and to which it corresponds. That Lincoln was elected president is true because there exists the corresponding state of affairs of his being elected president. However, the view of truth put forward in this chapter denies such a duality. When a proposition is true, it is identical with a realized state of affairs. This *identity theory of truth* preserves the realism that lies behind the correspondence theory – what there is determines whether or not a proposition is true. Moreover, the identity theory allows for a certain relation of correspondence. Remember that we express propositions by means of various vehicles such as sentence tokens, mental representations, pictures, and images. So we can say that the vehicle of expression corresponds to fact when the proposition it expresses is true. And we can also say that the vehicle is itself true or false derivatively as the proposition it is used to express is true or false. Thus the identity theory may be understood a particular version of the correspondence theory, a particular way of understanding the nature of correspondence.

The *minimalist conception of truth* attempts to avoid introducing metaphysical considerations into the question of the nature of truth. The version of this conception put forward by Paul Horwich makes use of the intuitive plausibility of the formula (T): The proposition that P is true if and only if P. Every instance of T which we obtain by replacing the same proposition-expressing sentence for each occurrence of "P" is self-evidently true. According to Horwich, the theory of truth consists of nothing more than these instances of T. There is nothing more to know about truth than these instances.[6] After all, if to say that a certain proposition is true is to say no more and no less than what you say just by asserting it, then, it would appear, the concept of truth has no more content than that. If, for, example, the proposition that Lincoln loved Mary is true is no different from the proposition that Lincoln loved Mary, then, it would appear, there is no specific content to the concept of truth that is not captured just by asserting the proposition itself. Our understanding of the term "true" consists, according to Horwich, merely of our disposition to accept any instance of T.[7]

Although the minimalist conception does not attempt to explain truth in terms of correspondence, "it does not deny that truths *do* correspond – in *some* sense – to the facts."[8] Horwich does not deny that the traditional correspondence theories were getting at something interesting: "No doubt one may formulate interesting, plausible schema that relate the concepts of truth, fact and correspondence. But the conjunction of such schematic principles is best viewed as an extension of our theory of truth; it does not provide a tempting alternative."[9] The reason is that the notion of correspondence is not constitutive of our concept of truth but something additional to it. So the notion of correspondence plays no role in the explication of the nature of truth.

It probably is not a matter of great importance whether or not correspondence is an answer to the question of the nature of truth or is merely an extension of the theory of truth to related matters. However, it seems to me that the notion of correspondence is essential to characterizing truth's nature. Consider that many philosophers have doubted whether there are any facts in the world that correspond to ethical statements. The reason they give is that when we say, for instance, that theft is wrong, we are merely expressing our disapproval of theft, not referring to any actual state of affairs that the statement reports. I do not wish to endorse this view. But I am inclined to say that if this view of ethical discourse is correct, then ethical statements can be neither true nor false, because there is nothing to which they are answerable. They are more like explicit expressions of feeling such as "Alas" than like fact-stating bits of discourse.[10] The fact that the instance of T "The proposition that theft is wrong is true if and only if theft is wrong" is grammatically correct is consistent with denying that it expresses a logical equivalence, since it is not composed items capable of having a truth-value. And if a good reason for denying its being an equivalence is that its constituents do not possess a truth-value because there is nothing to which they can correspond or fail to correspond, then it would appear that correspondence of some sort is essential to truth.

In general, we tend not to ascribe any truth-value to sentences or other intentional vehicles when we cannot convince ourselves that our intention in producing tokens of them is to represent some aspect of some universe of discourse, actual or conceivable. The formula T need not be interpreted to establish the vacuity of the concept of truth. It can be understood in a manner that implies the correspondence theory. After all, that the proposition that Lincoln loved Mary is true is itself true if and only if there is something that makes "Lincoln loved Mary" true. The reason we can drop the "is true" and be content with the bare assertion is that the notion of correspondence implied by "is true" is implicit in the bare assertion.

4. Evidence and Inductive Skepticism

Just this morning (October 7, 1994), I read a news story on the front page of the *New York Times* on sex in America. Among the interesting items reported was this: "In the new study, based on surveys of 3,432 men and women 18 to 59 years of age, 85 percent of married women and more than 75 percent of married men said they are faithful to their spouses. And married people have more sex than their single counterparts: 41 percent of all married couples have sex twice a week or more, compared with 23 percent of the singles." One of the authors of the study, John H. Gagnon, was quoted as saying: "Good sense should have told us that most people don't have the time and energy to manage an affair, a job, a family and the Long Island Railroad."

It is clear that Gagnon thinks that responses from the sample of 3,432 people who were surveyed provide sufficient evidence for a generalization about the sexual behavior of all Americans. If 75 percent of the men reported that they are faithful, then this is evidence that about 75 percent of all American men are faithful. What justifies his confidence? The story gives this reason: "The study is considered important because it is one of the first to rely on a randomly selected nationally representative sample. Most previous sex studies . . . relied on information from volunteers, a method that may seriously skew the results, experts say, because those who are interested in sex and are most sexually active tend to participate."

This study is a fairly typical case of inductive inference. *Induction* is a method of fixing belief through sampling the members of a population. If the sampling is conducted properly, we are then inclined to believe that the characteristics of the members of the sample in which we are interested match or are representative of the same characteristics in the whole population. In that case, we think that we have evidence in favor of a statistical generalization about the members of the population to the effect that a certain proportion of them possess the characteristics in question. In certain very special cases, the statistical generalization is universal, and says that all the members of the population exemplify the characteristics.

Inductive inference is not deductive. In a valid deduction, the conclusion follows necessarily from the premise or premises, so it is logically impossible for the premise to be true and the conclusion false. Deduction is a species of necessary inference in which the premise entails the conclusion. But in a valid induction, the evidence does not entail the generalization. That 75 percent of the married men in the sample were faithful does not prove conclusively that 75 percent of all American married men are faithful. The truth of the premise or evidence statement is logically compatible with only 1 percent or less of all American married men being faithful.

David Hume's skepticism about inductive inference is the outcome of the most famous discussion of induction in philosophy. This is the way he formulates the question:

We always presume, when we see like sensible qualities, that they have like secret powers, and expect, that effects, similar to those which we have experienced, will follow from them. If a body of like colour and consistence with that bread, which we have formerly eat, be presented to us, we make no scruple of repeating the experiment, and foresee, with certainty, like nourishment and support. Now this is a process of the mind or thought, of which I would willingly know the foundation. It is allowed on all hands that there is no known connexion between the sensible qualities and the secret powers; and consequently, that the mind is not led to form such a conclusion concerning their constant and regular conjunction, by anything which it knows of their nature. As to past *Experience*, it can be allowed to give *direct* and *certain* information of those precise objects only, and that precise period of time, which fell under its cognizance: But why this experience should be extended to future times, and to other objects, which for aught we know, may be only in appearance similar; this is the main question on which I would insist.[11]

Hume combines his consideration of inductive inference with inference of another sort. It is not unusual to explain the existence of something that we observe by supposing that it is caused to exist by something that we do not observe. For example, we explain why a puddle of rainwater evaporates in the sun by supposing that the water consists of molecules which are too small to see, which move faster and faster as the puddle is heated by the sun. As their velocity increases, they knock against each other with increasing force and, as a result, they are gradually expelled from the puddle. I shall call this style of explanation 'transcendent inference', to indicate that the object whose existence is inferred transcends our powers of observation.

Hume supposes that induction is frequently or usually accompanied by transcendent inference. In the example of the bread, we suppose that it has "secret powers" that explain why it nourishes. This is a case of transcendent inference. In the case of other bread which I am considering eating, I suppose also that it has similar secret powers, and will likewise be nourishing. This is a case of induction in which the character of the sampled bread is used as evidence for the character of other bread in the population of similar breads.

Now Hume finds two difficulties with inductive inference. The first is that he does not think we are entitled to rely upon transcendent inference, because "there is no known connexion between the sensible qualities and the secret powers." (We shall consider transcendent inference in a later section.) The second pertains specifically to induction. Observation informs us only of the items we have actually sampled. Induction purports to tell us about the unsampled items, those that we have not yet observed or perhaps never will observe. But the unsampled members of the population are different from those that have been sampled. It is logically possible that they possess different characteristics from those sampled. So it appears that we are not entitled to infer anything about them. That this bread has been nourishing does not require that future bread will be nourishing. There is no certainty that future bread will be nourishing, no matter how large the sample of breads I have eaten (so long as the sample is less than the whole). So I do not *know* that future bread will be nourishing. Not only does inductive inference fail to produce knowledge, it also fails to produce reasoned belief.

> These two propositions are far from being the same, *I have found that such an object has always been attended with such an effect*, and *I foresee, that other objects, which are, in appearance, similar, will be attended with similar effects*. I shall allow, if you please, that the one proposition may justly be inferred from the other: I know in fact, that it always is inferred. But if you insist, that the inference is made by a chain of reasoning, I desire you to produce that reasoning. The connexion between these propositions is not intuitive. There is required a medium, which may enable the mind to draw such an inference, if it indeed be drawn by reasoning and argument. What that medium is, I must confess, passes my comprehension.[12]

Even if inductive reasoning fails to produce certainty, perhaps the evidence establishes the conclusion with some probability. I cannot know for sure that the next bread I shall eat will be nourishing; but isn't the fact that the breads that I have sampled were nourishing a basis for thinking that it is quite likely that the next bread will be so as well? Hume thinks not. The probability of an induction rests upon the assumption that "the future will be conformable to the past." But this assumption can only be justified, if at all, by induction. "To endeavour, therefore, the proof of this last supposition by probable arguments, or arguments regarding existence, must be evidently going in a circle, and taking that for granted, which is the very point in question."[13]

Hume's skeptical conclusion is that "in all reasonings from experience, there is a step taken by the mind, which is not supported by any argument or process of the understanding."[14] The principle whereby we infer what the future will bring on the basis of past experience is not reason, but custom or habit.

> Custom, then, is the great guide of human life. It is that principle alone, which renders our experience useful to us,

and makes us expect, for the future, a similar train of events with those which have appeared in the past. Without the influence of custom, we should be entirely ignorant of every matter of fact, beyond what is immediately present to the memory and senses.[15]

According to Hume, inductive inference is a practice deeply entrenched in the human mind. We could not live without it. Every one of our expectations of what the future will bring that is based upon past experience is a projection founded upon sampling. And yet there is no noncircular way of establishing that this mode of inference ever provides knowledge or even probable opinion, or that it is reliable to any degree. Even if we have knowledge based upon what we now observe and what we remember observing in the past, we have no knowledge that extends beyond these cases.

The inductive skepticism of Hume resembles that of Descartes about the external world in the first of his *Meditations*. In both cases, a deeply entrenched mode of fixing belief is alleged to provide neither knowledge nor probable opinion. In the case of the external world, we have found that we could explain why Moore's proof does indeed defeat the skeptical argument. Is there any way of defeating skepticism about induction?

5. The Rationale of Induction

In the study of the sexual behavior of Americans discussed in the previous section, the rule of induction that was used to arrive at statistical conclusions about the whole population was as follows: Project the ratio found in the sample onto the population. Thus, if three-quarters of the married men who were surveyed were faithful, then, according to this rule, it is reasonable to suppose that three-quarters of American men generally (in that age-group) are faithful. Let us call this the 'standard rule'. Other rules – an infinity of them in fact – are theoretically possible. We could apply any number of mathematical operations to the observed ratio and project one of these. However, we use the standard rule, so we shall consider the question of its reliability. Do we have any reason to trust it as a way of arriving at truth? Are the inductive projections that it legitimizes epistemically warranted?

Hume thought that when we use induction to predict the future, we are assuming that the future will resemble the past. I assume that the bread which I have not yet had a chance to eat but which resembles samples I have eaten will also be nourishing. If we were to generalize Hume's idea to cover all cases of sampling, it would say that our use of the standard rule assumes that the ratio in the population matches that in the observed sample. Let us call this the '*inductive assumption*'. However, it is far from clear that we actually make such an assumption, because not only is it false, but we *know* it to be false. There are countless cases in which the ratio in a population fails to match that in a sample. Induction frequently produces false conclusions, a result that is not surprising, since it is not a method of necessary inference. And since the inductive assumption is false, it cannot be used to show that inductive inference is sound.

When we project an observed ratio onto a population, we *hope* that the latter approximately matches the former, but we do not necessarily have much confidence that it does. Our acceptance of the inductive conclusion is usually tentative and provisional, and we are not surprised if it turns out to be mistaken, though we may be disappointed. Here again is a point in favor of fallibilism.

The authors of the new survey of the sexual behavior of Americans claim, according to the news story at least, that their inductive projections are more reliable than those of previous surveys, because they relied upon "a randomly selected nationally representative sample," whereas the samples of previous studies failed to be random and representative, because they relied on volunteers. It is supposed that some samples are more reliable indicators of the statistical makeup of the population because they have been selected by a random procedure. Randomness is thought to produce representativeness; a sample is representative when its makeup matches that of the population with respect to the relevant characteristics. Inductive inference is reliable to the extent that the samples on which it is based are representative.

The reason why previous sex surveys were thought to be unreliable is that the samples consisted of volunteers. The reason why such a sample is not random is that people who volunteer for such a survey are more likely than not to think that their sex lives are interesting and thus worth talking about to others; it is quite likely that the frequency of the behavior they report will deviate from the norm and that the makeup of the sample will fail to match that of the population.

This example provides the understanding we need of the notion of randomness. Suppose we are interested in the frequency of occurrence of a characteristic C of a certain population. For example, let C be infidelity among married American males 18 to 59 years of age. Thus our sample will be selected from among this group. A sample will fail to be random if the characteristic D used to select its members influences the occurrence of C. Let us call D a 'biasing characteristic'. A characteristic that is not biasing is impartial. Thus, if D is the characteristic of being a volunteer, then we suppose that more of those who possess D are likely to be unfaithful than those in the population at large. So the use of D will make it unlikely that the sample is representative.

Consider another example. Every swan that I have observed in Europe and America has been white. The use of the standard rule led me to suppose that all swans are white until I learned that there are black swans in Australia. Something's being a swan that I happened to observe in Europe and America is the characteristic that was used to select my sample. If the color of birds is influenced by the climate of their habitats, then this characteristic is biasing, because the place where swans live affects their color.

We want the characteristics we use to select our sample to be impartial, for only then do we have reason to suppose that the sample may be representative. In the examples just discussed, our determination that a characteristic is biasing or impartial is itself a result of information that has been acquired by inductive inference. That being a volunteer in a sex survey makes it more likely that a person is unfaithful or that a temperate climate influences the colors of birds is itself a statistical generalization founded upon an inductive projection that we hope is representative. Therefore, we use induction to assure that our inductive conclusions are based upon randomly selected, hence representative, samples.

But what if we have no knowledge at all of which characteristics are biasing and which impartial? In that case, we have no choice but to use whatever samples happen to be available. We have no reason to suppose that our use of inductive inference in such cases is reliable. However, if we keep using induction over and over again, we will gradually acquire more information about the members of the population; we will then be able to correct our previous conclusions on the basis of sampling that is, we think, more representative. Our hope is that inductive inference is self-correcting and that as we use it to gain more and more information about the world, we can gradually increase its reliability.

How can we be sure that our inductions become more reliable as time goes on? Induction itself can provide such assurances in particular cases. As we learn more and more about birds, for example, we are in a better position to select representative samples of birds than we were before. Our knowledge of human nature based on past inductions helps us to identify impartial characteristics with which to select samples in sex surveys. Induction builds its own support over time. However, this provides no reply to Hume; he would point out that if we are interested in the validity of inductive inference in general, it is a case of fallacious circular reasoning to use induction to prove its validity.

Let us suppose, as Descartes did in his first *Meditation*, that the world is controlled not by a benevolent deity, but by an evil demon bent upon deceiving us. Among the things he does is arrange things so as to falsify our inductive conclusions. Thus, should we conclude that 75 percent of married American males between the ages of 18 and 59 are faithful, he will cause 50 percent of future males to be unfaithful. Should we conclude after sampling swans in all climates that 80 percent are white, he will then cause 60 percent of unobserved swans to be black. Even as we "correct" our inductions in the light of new evidence, the demon acts so as to falsify them. When we come to believe that all bits of matter in the universe obey Newton's law of gravitation, the demon creates new bits that do not obey it. This abstract possibility shows that the world may be such as to defeat the standard rule of inductive inference. We think that induction is a self-correcting procedure that will yield the true ratio if pursued long enough. But the demon possibility shows that there may be no correct ratios, that any ratio we project will be falsified. The world controlled by the demon is extremely unstable.

In an extremely unstable world, inductive inference based upon the standard rule is invalid, because it does not tend to the truth.

The demon defeats any and every trend that we take to be established. In a more stable world, some inductive inferences may be valid, not because they produce truth more frequently than not – perhaps more than half of those we actually make are false – but because they tend to approximate the true ratio; they tend to track the truth. In a very stable world, inductive inference would be quite reliable and trustworthy. Thus the validity of the inferences we make using the standard rule depends upon the nature of the world in which we make them. Our previous inductions appear to establish that the world is stable enough for induction to be reliable. If we assume the validity of induction, then we are in a position to show that induction is reliable in many cases. But the Humean skeptic is quick to point out the circularity involved in this argument.

However, the world may be relatively stable, and if it is, then induction would be reliable and truth-tending. In that case the beliefs we form would be warranted. There might even be some aspects of the world that are so stable that our inductions are completely reliable, providing us not merely with probable opinion, but with knowledge. So the arguments of Hume do not show that inductively based beliefs are not epistemically warranted. At best the skeptic is able to show that we cannot prove that they are warranted. But as in the case of our perceptual beliefs about the external world, the fact that we cannot prove that our beliefs are warranted does not show that they are not warranted. So skepticism is unable to establish its main point: namely, that because we cannot provide a noncircular proof that inductive inference is reliable, it fails to fix beliefs to which we are epistemically entitled. Moreover, we have no more reason to suppose it unreliable than reliable, and we have plenty of inductive reasons to suppose it reliable. Even if our minds have the standard rule as part of their innate program, so that the use of it is a matter of inborn habit and custom, as Hume thinks, we are not totally without good reason for relying upon it.

6. Observation and Transcendent Inference

By means of transcendent inference, we form hypotheses about what is unobservable, often by postulating the existence of unobservables for explanatory purposes. Transcendent inference is not limited to science. A person who believes that God exists on the grounds that the existence of an intelligent designer is the best way to explain the order of nature is making use of transcendent inference. There is, however, a certain ambiguity in the notion of observation that must first be cleared up.

Remember that we distinguished between observation and observation reports or beliefs (chapter 2, section 4). What we observe is what sense awareness reveals to us in the external world; observation reports are our fallible formulations of propositions about what we observe. In one sense, what we observe is just what falls under our senses. But what fall under our senses are events, objects, and states of affairs that are susceptible of multiple descriptions. Observation reports are couched in terms of certain descriptions rather than others. I can say that what I see is a chocolate cake or my dessert or Emily Jayne's favorite dish. Our current interests influence the descriptions we choose, but our background knowledge also plays a role. I have to know something about Emily Jayne's preferences, for example, to characterize the cake as her favorite. So the items that fall under the senses do not uniquely determine the content of our observation reports.

There is a certain ambiguity in the notion of what falls under the senses. When we think of seeing something, we usually have in mind seeing it with our naked eyes. This is seeing in an unqualified sense. However, we frequently use instruments to compensate for the deficiencies of our sensory apparatus. Some things are too small to see with our naked eyes, or too far away, or not in the line of sight. We use spectacles, microscopes, telescopes, periscopes, television sets, and many other instruments to bring objects into our field of vision. This is 'seeing' in a qualified sense. I see a star through a telescope; I witness a football game on television; I read my copy of the *Oxford English Dictionary* using a magnifying glass. All these are cases of 'observation' as I intend to use the term.

Now consider the case of our postulation of the existence of molecules in order to explain evaporation. Since we cannot see them with our naked eyes, the molecules count as unobservable entities. However, their existence might be controversial; we might wish to find a way to prove that they exist, so that they are not merely speculative posits. Let us suppose that we invent a plate coated with chemicals that are sensitive to individual molecules; when a molecule strikes the plate, it makes a mark visible to the naked eye.

Can we say that the molecules are now observed? I think that is what we do say. By making a mark on the plate, they have become visible; of course, we do not see them with our naked eyes; we see them by means of an instrument we have created. And by observing them, we have produced an argument for their existence much stronger than just appealing to their explanatory utility.

One might be inclined to object on the grounds that what we observe are not the molecules themselves but their effects. We observe the marks on the plate and infer that they were made by molecules. This is not seeing the molecules; it is a case of transcendent inference.

This objection is not plausible, because everything we observe in the external world is observed by means of its effects upon something or other. In sense awareness, we are caused to experience events of sensory consciousness which contain the information about the external world that we extract in our perceptual judgments. Even seeing Price's tomato or Moore's hands is a case of something falling under the senses because of its effects upon our eyes and nervous system.

There is another, more serious objection. If everything is observed via its effects, how do we draw the line between observation and inference? When you first saw the water evaporating, you were observing the effects of the molecules that compose it. You didn't observe the molecules in that case, by your own admission, but you now want to say that seeing their marks upon the plate is a case of observing them. How do you tell the difference?

The answer is that there is no sharp distinction between observation reports and inferential conclusions. Observation reports are interpretations of the meaning of the data presented in sense awareness. Usually the meaning includes the causes of the data, so the report is a result of a process of extracting information from a sensory datum. This is an activity of the mind that is as inferential as any other. It involves using background knowledge to arrive at a conclusion. Usually, one of the premises is a datum, rather than a formulated proposition. But our interpretive transition from datum to judgment is mediated by, and based upon, knowledge that we have previously acquired, knowledge that counts as a premise as well. We may not be conscious of all the steps in the process of arriving at observation reports, but that does not defeat the claim than an inferential process actually occurred. We can determine the character and components of the process by reflection, after it has taken place.

This still does not answer the question of why seeing the water evaporate does not count as a case of observing molecules, while seeing certain marks on a plate does. Both are cases of acquiring knowledge of something by observing something else. What is the difference? I suggest that the difference is to be explained in terms of the degree of confidence we are entitled to in each case. Upon observing the evaporation, I invent a hypothesis to explain it; my theory is a pure invention, which rests upon shaky grounds. But after establishing the experimental apparatus and putting it to work, I have much stronger grounds for my belief in molecules. When our belief is shaky, when it is only a conjecture, we are inclined to classify it as a hypothesis that needs further testing. But when the entities in question actually affect the experimental apparatus in the predicted manner, we are inclined to say that we have observed them.

Thus the difference between transcendent inference and observation is relative to what we know and to the stage of the process of confirmation we have reached. The formulation of observation reports relies upon inference. We don't call it transcendent inference when we classify the report as observational. The line between them is not very sharp, however. We can argue about particular cases, but before going too far, we should be sure that the disagreement is not merely verbal. Not much hangs upon whether we call a particular judgment an observation report or the conclusion of a transcendent inference. But there are disagreements that are not necessarily verbal. Someone who denies that I have made an observation may do so because he thinks that my report is mistaken or shaky or based upon inadequate grounds or false information.

What are we to make of Hume's skeptical remark that "there is no known connexion between the sensible qualities and the secret powers"? This seems to be skepticism about transcendent inference in general. Would he be satisfied when we have brought the secret powers under observation by the construction of an experimental apparatus, as in the example of the molecules? Not likely. He would argue that even observation reports are the products of inference from subjective data. The inference is not deductive. There is no way to legitimize it a priori in the manner of Descartes. A priori, anything can cause anything. We are never directly conscious of the entities whose reality we infer. So why should we repose any confidence in the products of transcendent inference?

This argument that I have attributed to Hume is quite similar to the argument in Descartes's first *Meditation* that brought us to solipsism. We have already dealt with solipsism in the discussion of Moore's proof of an external world. There exist the objects of common sense that we can see, such as Price's tomato and Moore's hands. The question is whether we are entitled to infer on the basis of data drawn from sense awareness of the external world the existence of the unobservable entities postulated by science to explain observable phenomena. If Price's tomato is one step removed from the data of which we are directly conscious, then the molecules that make it up and the particles of which the molecules are composed are two steps away. Are we entitled to take the second step? Can we move beyond commonsense representative realism to scientific realism?

7. Scientific Realism

In our previous epistemological ruminations, we distinguished the items in sensory awareness that we are directly conscious of from other items that we are capable of observing, such as Price's tomato and Moore's hands (objects of common sense), and from unobservables postulated for explanatory purposes. Commonsense realism accepts the existence of the objects of common sense. It is challenged in the first place by arguments leading to solipsism, but we turned that challenge aside by the use of Moore's proof of an external world. Another challenge arose from Sellars's claim that the objects of common sense are merely appearances caused by the postulated objects of scientific theory: the puddle of water that I think I see really has no existence at all; there is just a bunch of molecules that affect my senses, producing the sensory phenomena that I incorrectly interpret as being a puddle of water.

An alternative to Sellars's view is that the objects of common sense are literally composed of the imperceptible, postulated objects of science. The puddle of water and the bunch of molecules are identical. An argument for Sellars's view is that the bunch of molecules possesses so few of the qualities that we observe in the water – it is so unlike the puddle – that there is no basis for identifying the two. The argument against it is that there is a sufficient similarity for them to be the same: they occupy the same place, and they are approximately of the same shape and size. There are differences, but they can be demoted to the status of appearances: the bunch of molecules possesses no color, but then neither does the puddle. One might be inclined to side with Sellars if one is impressed with the differences; if, however, one is impressed by the similarities, one would be inclined to retain commonsense realism. Once one has pointed out the similarities and the differences, there is no further fact of the matter that can settle the question. My own inclination is to retain commonsense realism, because rejecting it constitutes a shock to the system that is quite unnecessary. So in what follows, I shall assume commonsense realism, and consider the question of the validity of scientific realism.

But what exactly does scientific realism say? In order to determine that, let us take note of the fact that we are in possession of a variety of theories about the world, theories created by science and by one or another of the various religions, which imply ontological commitments to a variety of unobservable entities. Anyone who accepts such a theory, who believes that it is true or likely to be true or the best candidate for the truth, also commits himself to one degree or another to the existence of these entities. And because he accepts these entities as real and the theories as true, he also accepts the transcendent inferences that generated them as being trustworthy, as being such as to generate true hypotheses. He accepts that he has evidence which supports these theories, and that the formulations of the evidence are premises of trustworthy transcendent inferences.

However, we also know that science (we shall put religion aside here, as complicating the discussion) evolves, and that the theories accepted at one time are frequently rejected in whole or in part at a later time. Moreover, theories themselves evolve; they are modified to take into account new data or new calculations. This means that there is a certain degree of instability in the ontological commitments of science. Entities to which a science is committed at one time may fall out of favor and be replaced by different entities postulated by new theories at a later time. In addition, there may be sustained controversy about the reality of certain entities when there is little confidence among groups of scientists in the theories that refer to them: the Freudian unconscious is a good example.

Scientific realism is a philosophical theory about the scientific enterprise in its historical sweep. As a philosophical claim or set of claims, it is not itself committed to the content of science at any one time. For example, a scientific realist living at the time of Newton who said that his realism consisted in endorsing the imperceptible entities of Newton's cosmology would have found his realism refuted as soon as new and better cosmologies arose that were not committed to the existence of absolute space, time, and motion. Scientific realism is not so easily refutable, and thus it does not consist in accepting the ontological commitments of any particular theories. What, then, does it say?

In the first place, scientific realism is a claim about the aims of scientific inquiry. It says that one of the aims of science is to gain knowledge or, if that is not possible, probable belief about the nature of the world as it exists in itself, a world that exists independently of the human inquirers who are attempting to achieve such knowledge. That is, scientific realism is a form of realism and rejects the various forms of idealism and constructivism which say that the world we are trying to gain knowledge about does not exist independently of the human mind and does not have an independent and objective existence. It also rejects the skepticism which claims that this aim is unrealizable.

This is not all that it says. It points out that, in trying to satisfy our curiosity about the workings of the world, we sooner or later come to realize that the objects of common sense and of our original understanding are unable to provide a sufficient ontological basis for our efforts to understand. The reason is that the commonsense world is just too gappy. Take our puddle of water again. Why did it evaporate? Ordinary observation combined with inductive inference convinces us that the sun's warmth has something to do with it. But not everything warmed by the sun evaporates, and ordinary observation does not tell us why the sun's warmth should have this effect. It seems natural that we should make up a story about the underlying nature of the water and about how the warming effect of the sun modifies that nature, causing the puddle to evaporate. The story brings with it commitments to the existence of unobservables. Sooner or later, we recognize that the story is merely a guess or a conjecture, and that if we are to have any confidence that it is true, we must make further efforts to confirm that indeed the gaps are filled in the way it says they are filled.

Moreover, the fact that we are inclined to seek further confirmation of our explanatory conjectures about unobservable entities implies that we think at the outset that they have some chance of being true, hence we would like to find out how much confidence we are entitled to place in their truth. So the scientific realist says that we should consider the theories of science as statements capable of being either true or false, as representational vehicles purporting to refer to and characterize objects that actually exist.

Finally, scientific realism makes a claim about the likelihood of success of realizing the aim of science to provide knowledge of things as they are in themselves. It says, first, that success is a matter of degree. A theory that experience falsifies may yet approximate to some degree to the truth. It claims, further, that the use of careful observation, ingenious experimentation, and reliable, tested, inferential and confirmatory procedures actually improves our theories and brings them closer to the truth. So scientific inquiry is a self-correcting activity that is progressive: it gradually provides better and better accounts of the ways the world is, and eliminates theories that are epistemically defective. Therefore, the theories that are widely accepted within the various sciences at any given time are worthy of acceptance at that time because they are founded on procedures that provide us with the most likely account of the natures of the objects they refer to and the laws that regulate their behavior.

Realism thus characterized has been subjected to a variety of criticisms. It is time to turn to some of these.

8. The Grounds of Anti-Realism

The main objections to scientific realism are based upon considerations that tend to undermine the claim that our beliefs and theories about nature tend to represent nature as it really is. These are mostly skeptical arguments pointing out that, given the factors that determine which theories are acceptable to the community of inquirers at any given time, there is no reason to suppose that scientifically confirmed beliefs gradually approximate to the way things are in themselves. Kant made essentially this point when he said that we can only know things as they appear to us, not as they are in themselves.

The first anti-realist consideration along these lines is that the best we can say about our best-confirmed theories, the theories we have most confidence in, is that we are epistemically warranted in accepting them in virtue of their being supported by the evidence. But a theory can be warranted, yet false. There is no valid inference from the premise "Theory T is epistemically warranted" to the conclusion "Theory T is true." To say that it is true is to go beyond what we are actually entitled to assert. We are entitled to assert only that T is warranted.

Now one might think that this objection to realism misunderstands the notion of epistemic warrant. In order for a theory to be warranted, it must be arrived at by procedures which are reliable, and in science this means by procedures whose continued application tends, in the long run, to approximate to the truth. So there is a valid inference from the premise to the conclusion; it is not deductively valid, but it is valid in the sense that the truth of the premise is a good reason for accepting the conclusion.

This response provides the anti-realist with the opportunity to clarify his notion of epistemic warrant. He points out that the procedures which we think produce warranted theories are those that have evolved because they produce theories that we have found acceptable for a variety of reasons, but that none of these reasons constitute grounds for thinking that the theories are true in the sense of corresponding to things as they are in themselves. So when someone says that a theory is warranted, all they mean is that it satisfies the current criteria of acceptability within the current community of inquirers. Since we have no reason to suppose that the current criteria are truth-tending, the inference is not valid. The only way in which the inference could be valid is by interpreting the notion of epistemic warrant in the way that the realist insists on; but in that case, says the anti-realist, we have no reason to suppose that the premise is true.

The next set of considerations is intended to show that we have no reason to suppose that the current criteria are truth-tending. In the first place, it is pointed out that in actual fact, the evidence available at any given time never supports just the particular theory we accept on its basis, but any number of theories that are compatible with the data. This feature of theories is called the 'underdetermination' of theories by the evidence. Underdetermination is a logical fact about the relation between evidence and theory which has two sides to it. First, the evidence does not entail the theory, so the evidence never logically coerces us to accept a particular theory. Second, the evidence is entailed by an indefinite number of distinct propositions, so the fact that the theory we accept explains the evidence is compatible with many other theories explaining the evidence as well. The fact of underdetermination raises the question of why we should think that acceptability is a sign of truth.

The next step in the argument for anti-realism is to point out that the actual criteria used to select theories fail to support the realist position. For example, simplicity is one criterion. Pretend you are conducting a scientific experiment whose aim is to determine the relationship between two variables, call one of them x, the other y. Suppose you conduct four trials. In the first you find that one unit of x corresponds to two units of y; in the second, two units of x correspond to four units of y; in the third, three units of x correspond to six units of y; and finally, four units of x correspond to eight units of y. Mark four points on a graph to represent these results. To complete the graphical representation, you would then have to draw a line connecting the points, and the line that you would probably draw is a straight one. If you were asked for the equation that is best supported by the experimental results, you would be likely to say that it is $y = 2x$. The straight line you drew connecting the four points is represented by this equation.

Note, however, that there is an infinity of lines capable of connecting these four points, and thus there is an infinity of equations capable of representing the experimental results just as accurately as $y = 2x$. The data by themselves do not uniquely determine the equation that represents the actual relation between x and y. The straight line goes way beyond the information given in the trials. It is a case of inductive extrapolation. From a purely logical point of view, the evidence supports an infinity of distinct hypotheses. The one you selected happened to be the simplest.

What does simplicity mean in this case? A straight line is relatively simple compared with the enormous variety of curved lines in a visual-aesthetic sense. Further, the equation representing the straight line is easier to calculate with than the alternatives. So aesthetic and practical considerations cooperate to incline you to draw a straight line connecting the points. Of course, future trials may refute $y = 2x$. Suppose on your next trial you find that five units of x correspond not to ten units of y but to twenty. So experience is capable of falsifying even the simplest hypothesis. But that still leaves you with an infinity of alternatives, from which you will again select the simplest available. Although simplicity is a vague criterion and may mean different things in different contexts, it does seem to be operative in our choice of theories.

Moreover, there is no reason to suppose, continues the anti-realist, that simplicity is symptomatic of truth. Our connection to the world, our relation to things as they are in themselves, is constituted by the experimental trials. But these trials do not determine the nature of things as they are in themselves. They must be supplemented by considerations of simplicity. But simplicity is not a further relation to things as they are in themselves. It pertains, rather, to our human interests, needs, and ways of looking at things. The fact that one curve is simpler than another in an aesthetic-visual sense has no bearing whatsoever on whether that curve correctly represents an objective relation among things in themselves. So we have no reason to suppose that the criterion of simplicity is truth-tending and that its use in selecting theories over time causes our theories to approximate ever more closely to the truth.

Thus far we have assumed that at least what counts as evidence for and against a theory can be identified in an objective way. But the anti-realist challenges this assumption. Consider a theory one of whose major parts consists of a proposition of the form "All A are B." Suppose we "observe" an example of A that is not B. Logically speaking, that proves conclusively that "All A are B" is false, and that the theory of which it is a part is seriously in error. But suppose that the theory is well entrenched in the relevant science – it solves a lot of problems, it leads to many verified predictions, it has given rise to many technological accomplishments, and it has no plausible competitors at the present time. We would be unlikely to give up the theory. It would be too inconvenient to do so.

Suppose a purist comes along who insists in a loud voice: "But the theory is false. Not all A are B. So we must give it up." To quiet their consciences, other scientists will point out that perhaps this observation is not really a case of an A that is not a B. Perhaps there was an experimental error. Perhaps the equipment was defective. Perhaps the observer made a mistake. Perhaps the records of the experiment are in error. Perhaps the principle investigator was dishonest. Perhaps, perhaps, perhaps. These possibilities show that we do not have to passively accept observation reports that challenge really useful theories. We can explain them away and continue to use the theory until a better one comes along. Thus it is not true that there is some unique body of data of which we can say that it unequivocally and uncontroversially counts as evidence for or against a particular theory. If a theory is important enough to us, we will find ways to avoid counting the falsifying reports as evidence. Or we may agree that they might be evidence against the theory, but decide to ignore them or put them aside until a better theory is found. Our theories and their role within the contemporary science and technology influence what we take as evidence and how much weight we attach to it. So even the one factor that is supposed to connect us to things as they are in themselves, the observational data, is not independent of considerations and criteria which exemplify no such connection. The belief of the realist that the procedures we use produce epistemically warranted theories that approximate to the truth is totally unjustified. The community of scientific inquirers produce theories that are useful in various ways for a time. But truth in the realistic correspondence sense plays no role in the acceptance or rejection of theories or, more generally, in the evolution of scientific knowledge. At least, this is what the anti-realist claims.

9. Pragmatism and Realism

The basic anti-realist argument is that the grounds on which we accept theories and fix our beliefs about the world do not tend to show that they are true in the sense of corresponding to an independent reality. We want our theories to be empirically adequate; this means that they should be consistent with the empirical data. But we have seen that empirical adequacy is not indispensable; we have ways of dealing with falsifying observations of theories that are well entrenched and useful. We want our theories to solve problems better than the theories they replace; we want them to enable us to make predictions about the future in order to help us control the course of experience to our advantage; we want them to aid us in finding ways of acting in the world to better our lives and to defend ourselves against perils: this is the use of theories that we classify under technology.

Let us summarize these points by saying that it is the utility of theories that constitutes the basis for their acceptability, and that utility is not a reliable mark of truth as the realist understands it. I shall adopt the term 'pragmatism' as the name for this epistemological point of view. This term was invented by Charles Sanders Peirce to designate a certain aspect of his epistemology, and in the writings of William James and John Dewey it became entrenched as the name of a family of epistemologies which emphasize utility, rather than truth, as the basis of acceptance. Pragmatism claims that an examination of the various utilities that justify acceptance provides no argument in favor of scientific realism. Some pragmatists say that we should discard the concept of truth completely and replace it with the notion of justified acceptance (or, in Dewey's terms, warranted assertability). Others insist that the concept of truth should be defined in terms of justified acceptance: to say that a statement is true just means that we are warranted in asserting it, that it satisfies the assertability criteria. However the view is formulated, the various versions of pragmatism hold that the realist conception of truth plays no valid role in the epistemology of scientific knowledge.

One of the main arguments in favor of scientific realism is that the commonsense world revealed in the original understanding is too gappy to include all the items that are needed to explain the course of our experience. This is also an argument in favor of commonsense realism. Within the solipsistic position, the sense impressions that constitute the basic data are also gappy with respect to the objects of common sense. The tomato endures for a while, though we have only infrequent glimpses of it. For a solipsist, Price's belief in his tomato and Moore's belief in his hands can be interpreted as hypotheses to explain the course of their experiences. So a consistent pragmatism should adopt the same attitude toward commonsense realism as it does toward scientific realism: there is no reason to suppose that either is true; the hypotheses that constitute our commitment to the world of common sense, as well as those that constitute our commitment to the objects of science, should be accepted because they are useful, rather than true. That there is a puddle of water there that I see, as well as that it is composed of molecules, are hypotheses that are used to explain our sense impressions and that are justified by their overall utility in enabling us to cope with the world. Our beliefs function, says the pragmatist, not to mirror nature but to enable us to cope with it.[16] Quine has pointed out that common sense is continuous with science.

> Physical objects are conceptually imported into the situation as convenient intermediaries – not by definition in terms of experience, but simply as irreducible posits comparable, epistemologically, to the gods of Homer. . . . Positing does not stop with macroscopic physical objects. Objects at the atomic level are posited to make the laws of macroscopic objects, and ultimately the laws of experience, simpler and more manageable. . . . Science is a continuation of common sense, and it continues the commonsense expedient of swelling ontology to simplify theory.[17]

But it only *seems* as if pragmatism involves a swelling of ontology. Since pragmatism rejects realism, it cannot accept the reality of either the imperceptible objects of science or the objects of common sense. Thus, when a pragmatist speaks of accepting a theory, the theory is accepted not as a truth but only as something that possesses warranted assertability. Yet what can it mean to say that a theory is warranted if not that one is warranted in asserting that it is true? But if we are warranted in asserting as a truth that the puddle of water is composed of molecules, then we are thereby committed to an ontology that includes molecules – just what the scientific realist claims. Thus a consistent pragmatist must insist that when one accepts a theory, one does not claim that it is true or that one is warranted in thinking it true, but only that it is useful. Acceptance for pragmatism is simply the claim that this is the theory that enables us to cope better than any other available theory with our problems.

Thus a consistent pragmatism moves towards a phenomenalist ontology: its only ontological commitments are to the sense impressions that trigger our beliefs. It must even surrender the notion that in science and in common sense we attempt to explain anything. How can mere fictions, like molecules, explain an actual event such as evaporation? Can a nothing explain a something? But we have not reached the end of the matter. A consistent pragmatism moves also toward solipsism. As far as I am concerned, you, dear reader, are merely a convenient intermediary; I posit you to simplify my experience. But, for the pragmatist, my posits of unobservables bring with them no ontological commitments; they are only useful fictions. So goodbye, dear reader.

There is more to come. Even if the theories that are accepted are not accepted as true, the pragmatist still *claims* that the theories that are accepted are not accepted as true. And that, as it stands, is a contradiction, because a claim is merely the assertion of something as being true. Moreover, a pragmatist cannot do without the very notion of truth that he says he is rejecting. After all, one of the major utilities of a theory consists in its ability to predict the future. Using physical theory, an astronomer can predict the next eclipse of the sun. But what is the status of this prediction? Isn't it the claim that a certain event will occur? And isn't this the assertion of a truth? Even if the pragmatist retreats towards phenomenalism, isn't the prediction equivalent to the claim that certain sense impressions will occur? And if they do occur as predicted, doesn't his statement correspond to some observed reality? What makes a prediction useful is that if it is true and if we know it is true, we will be able to act more successfully than if we knew nothing of what is to come.

A consistent pragmatism should have no ontological commitments whatsoever, not even to the reality of sense impressions, in its retreat toward phenomenalism. But such a theory, if we may call it that, is a theory with no subject matter, a theory that says nothing about nothing. Thus a consistent pragmatism tends to disappear in the course of reflecting upon its implications.

This argument against pragmatism does not show us how to avoid the problems of scientific realism surveyed in the previous section. Why is scientific realism so convincing to so many scientists and laymen? First and foremost, I think, the success of technology persuades us of the plausibility of realism. The fact that our theories enable us to make so many extraordinary interventions in nature, that they enable us to invent so many marvelous machines, that they have transformed (not always for the better) our civilization and our lives, convinces us that it is no accident that the advance of science has had these results. How shall we explain the extraordinary success of applied science except by supposing that the theories on which it is based are approximately true, and that the entities that it posits approximate to the entities that really exist? If the success of applied science is no accident, then it is plausible to suppose that our theories capture at least some aspects of reality to some extent.

Freud once claimed that his conception of the mind must be true because only if it is true can one explain the success of psychotherapy. With reference to a patient undergoing therapy, Freud insisted that "his conflicts will only be successfully solved and his resistances overcome if the anticipatory ideas he is given tally with what is real in him."[18] In criticism of this claim, Adolf Grünbaum has argued that for all we know, the patient is cured not because the theory that directs the actions of the therapist is true, but because of the powers of suggestion.[19] It is the placebo effect that produces the cure. Freud claims that the successful application of his theories shows that they are true and that the mental mechanisms they posit actually exist. Grünbaum produces an alternative account of their success, whereby we are not required to accept the existence of the mechanisms. However, physical nature is not vulnerable to the placebo effect. One cannot appeal to it to provide an alternative account of the success of the applied sciences. The success is no accident. There do not seem to be any explanations of its nonaccidental character other than the one offered by scientific realism. It must be, then, that the evidence that shows that our theories are warranted actually establishes that they mirror nature in an approximate, if provisional way. Of course, we cannot be absolutely certain of this. Perhaps a more plausible alternative account of scientific success will be forthcoming. But, as matters now stand, scientific realism has the better argument.

Further Readings

Pierre Duhem, *The Aim and Structure of Physical Theory* (Princeton, NJ: Princeton University Press, 1954).

Roy Harrod, *Foundations of Inductive Logic* (London: Macmillan, 1956).

David Hume, *An Enquiry Concerning Human Understwanding*, sects iv–vii.

Jarrett Leplin (ed.), *Scientific Realism* (Berkeley: University of California Press. 1984).

John Stuart Mill, *A System of Logic*, Bk III: "Of Induction."

Karl Popper, *Objective Knowledge: An Evolutionary Approach* (Oxford: Clarendon Press, 1972).

Richard Rorty, *Philosophy and the Mirror of Nature* (Princeton, NJ: Princeton University Press, 1979).

6

A Priori Knowledge

1. Intuitive Knowledge

The basic beliefs that we have been considering until now have been those founded upon sense awareness and those that convey self-knowledge. We now turn to another epistemological issue: the question of a priori knowledge. From the time of Plato to the present, many philosophers have recognized a fundamental duality in human knowledge and have attempted to explain and account for it. Leibniz marked this duality with his distinction between truths of fact and truths of reason. The former are grounded in sense awareness, whereas the latter are in some sense independent of experience. We get to know about truths of reason in a way that does not depend upon our senses; they are founded, rather, upon a kind of rational insight into abstract objects and structures. They are a priori, rather than empirical or a posteriori. In this chapter we shall consider the issues surrounding the claim that there is such a thing as a priori knowledge.

Let us begin by thinking about the sort of geometrical system that we are all familiar with, the system known as Euclidean geometry. The method of establishing truths within this system consists in providing proofs of various propositions using deductive or demonstrative reasoning. A proposition that is proved is called a 'theorem'. If we are asked how we know that the theorems are true, the best answer is that they are known because we have constructed a proof of them. In that event, our knowledge of the theorems depends upon our knowledge of the premises or the givens of the proofs. These are either previously proved theorems or axioms, or postulates, of the system. The very notion of an axiom, or postulate, implies that these are not themselves propositions that are proved within the system, but rather, the ultimate premises of all the proofs.

The question about our knowledge of the theorems leads to two further questions. The first is: How do we obtain knowledge of the axioms? The second is: Assuming that we do have knowledge of the axioms, how is this knowledge transmitted to the theorems by means of deductive reasoning?

An answer to the first question which has been given frequently in the history of epistemology is that we have noninferential, nonsensory knowledge of certain propositions acquired by a kind of direct intellectual insight. The kind of knowledge thus obtained has often been labeled 'intuitive knowledge', and I shall continue to use this term. Other terms that have been used to characterize it are 'self-evident knowledge' and 'clear and distinct perceptions'. The rationalist epistemologies that agree to there being such a thing as intuitive knowledge belong to the foundationalist tradition. Just as sense awareness is one way we are in contact with the world and is one source of basic beliefs, so intellectual insight is another way and constitutes another source of basic beliefs. This sort of rationalism is now quite unfashionable, for reasons I shall discuss later, but I will attempt to defend it here. The question, then, is: Is there such a thing as intuitive knowledge, and if there is, how is it possible?

The rationalist tradition has thought it obvious that there must be intuitive knowledge on the basis of the familiar infinite regress argument characteristically employed by foundationalists. Not all knowledge acquired through proofs can be founded upon knowledge acquired through still other proofs. For if the premises of our proofs could themselves be known only if we have first proved them, then we would require an unending series of proofs to establish any theorem. And since we are incapable of constructing an infinite number of proofs, there would be no knowledge of the theorems. But since there *is* knowledge of theorems, then we must know some propositions without proof.

An empiricist in the tradition of foundationalism would agree that this argument establishes that we must have some sort of

noninferential knowledge but would claim that it is sense awareness, not intellectual insight, that provides the grounds. However,
the rationalist would reply that there are certain sorts of non-
inferentially known propositions that cannot plausibly be con-
strued as empirical, for the reason that they are necessarily true
or "true in all possible worlds," to use an expression introduced
by Leibniz. Whereas sense experience informs us of truths about
this world, the actual world, it is powerless to tell us of what is
true of necessity, of what holds for all possibilities. That a square
has four sides, for example, doesn't just happen to be true; it is
something that couldn't possibly be false. It is a necessary, rather
than a contingent, truth, whose necessity transcends the deliverances of sense awareness. So our knowledge of it must be a priori.

Let us accept this rationalist response for the moment, and consider the question of how we can possibly know a priori and non-
inferentially that a square has four sides. Early modern philosophers
such as Descartes and Locke spoke of ideas in the mind. Let me
use instead the notion of a concept, rather than an idea. Possession
of a concept consists in a certain sort of knowledge: namely, knowledge of what something is. A person has the concept 'square', for
example, if he knows what a square is. This knowledge can be
demonstrated in many different ways: for example, by recognizing square objects, by being able to draw a square or to form a
visual image of one at will, or by knowing how to use the word
'square' or its equivalents in other languages correctly. Our knowledge of the concept 'square' grows gradually; the child begins by
learning what things described by 'square' look like; he may then
learn how to draw a square or how to use 'square' to describe new
objects of experience. At a later stage, the child may realize that
the shapes of the objects he describes as square are usually not
exactly square, because their sides are not absolutely straight or
their interior angles are not exactly 90 degrees. He may then be
able to provide a definition of the term that characterizes not the
visible things that he has been calling square, but an idealized
notion, an abstract idea of the "perfect" square.

Once a person is in possession of the concept 'square', they can
then determine explicitly how many sides a square has just by
reflecting upon the content of their concept. The person will then
realize that contained in the very concept 'square' is the concept

of having four sides: having four sides is necessary for something to be square; it couldn't be square if it didn't have four sides. In this conceptual reflection, there is no need to consult the deliverances of sense awareness any further. By virtue of being in possession of the concept, the person already has in their possession all the information they need to determine how many sides a square has. So the knowledge that has been attained is a priori; it is independent of experience in the sense that its verification is performed exclusively within the "space" of the concept itself. The person need only extract the relevant information from the content that constitutes the concept 'square'. Of course, the individual's being in possession of this concept owes something to sense awareness; perhaps if they had never seen objects with approximately square surfaces, they would never have been able to learn what a square is. But that is beside the point. Once someone has acquired the concept, nothing further is required than insight into its content. This insight produces the intuitive knowledge.

Intuitive knowledge is possible because human beings have certain mental powers and capacities: they can acquire and be in possession of concepts; they can reflect upon their contents; and they can formulate propositions that make these contents explicit. However, that a square has four sides does not seem to be a very substantive truth; it doesn't tell us anything about the world, but is merely a consequence, one might argue, of our verbal conventions. It is, as Locke would say, a trifling proposition. But there is more here than meets the eye.

2. Trifling, or Analytic, Propositions

That a square has four sides is among the propositions that Locke classified as "trifling," rather than "instructive."

> Another sort of Trifling Proposition is, *when a part of the complex* Idea *is predicated of the Name of the whole*; a part of the Definition of the Word defined. Such are all Propositions wherein the *Genus* is predicated of the *Species*, or more comprehensive of less comprehensive Terms: for what

Information, what Knowledge carries this Proposition in it, *viz. Lead is Metal*, to a Man, who knows the complex *Idea* the name *Lead* stands for. All the simple *Ideas* that go to the complex one signified by the Term *Metal*, being nothing but what he before comprehended, and signified by the name *Lead*.[1]

According to Locke, trifling propositions, "though they be certainly true, yet they add no Light to our Understandings, bring no increase to our Knowledge."[2] That lead has a certain atomic weight would be instructive, because its weight is not included in the very idea of lead. But it is part of the definition or concept of lead that it is a metal, so the addition of the predicate brings no information not already included in the subject. Thus a person who possesses the idea of lead or the concept of lead does not add to their knowledge of lead by extracting the concept 'metal' from the concept 'lead'. All they have done in asserting the proposition that lead is a metal is to make explicit information that is already in their possession.

Kant used the term 'analytic' where Locke used 'trifling', and 'synthetic' in place of Locke's 'instructive'. "Either the predicate B belongs to the subject A, as something which is (covertly) contained in this concept A; or B lies outside the concept A, although it does indeed stand in connection with it. In the one case I entitle the judgment analytic, in the other synthetic."[3] Kant's terminology has become standard, so I use it in what follows. Locke's term 'trifling', however, makes an epistemological point: namely, that such propositions do not add to our knowledge.

We find in Locke the germ of contemporary conventionalist accounts of the a priori. Trifling propositions "carry no Knowledge with them, but of the Signification of Words."[4] Or if there is knowledge, it is merely "*verbal*."[5] On this view, when someone says that a square has four sides, what they are communicating pertains to the meaning of the words 'square' and 'four sides': namely, that the meaning of the latter is included in the meaning of the former. Analytic propositions are true by virtue of their meaning. For Locke, the relation between a word and its meaning is not by a "natural connexion, that there is between particular articulate Sounds and certain *Ideas*, for then there would be but one Language amongst Men; but by a voluntary imposition, whereby such a Word is made arbitrarily the Mark of such an *Idea*."[6]

Many twentieth-century empiricists have agreed with traditional rationalism that there are truths that can be known a priori. In order to adjust this concession to the empiricist epistemology, they have insisted that the objects of a priori knowledge are analytic propositions in which nothing instructive is contained about the world but whose truth is just a consequence of those very linguistic conventions or semantic rules that we have imposed upon "particular articulate sounds." Thus A. J. Ayer says that an analytic proposition merely "records our determination" to use words with a certain meaning. Our assertion of an analytic proposition merely indicates "the convention" which governs our use of words. The truth of an analytic proposition "depends solely on the definitions of the symbols it contains." It tells us "only what we may be said to know already. . . . It does not provide me with any new knowledge."[7]

The conventionalist position hinted at by Locke's theory of trifling propositions and developed by Ayer and the logical positivist tradition contains two major confusions. First, the appeal to linguistic conventions is intended to suggest that because these are our own creations, a priori knowledge simply consists of insight into truths which we ourselves have created in creating language. Thus they tell us nothing about the world; they are not synthetic, or instructive, or factual. But then they cannot be necessary truths as Kant insisted when he argued that necessity is the mark of the a priori. They are not necessary, because a semantic convention or linguistic rule is something optional and arbitrary. That having four sides is part of the meaning of 'square' is a consequence of a decision of the community of English speakers in creating the English language and might have been different.

But if they are not necessary, then they are contingent and, though true, might have been false. Moreover, if the only "facts" they express are those pertaining to our conventions, and if the fact that "the particular articulate sounds" of our language are governed by these conventions rather than some others is a fact that can be determined by *observing* the usage of speakers of our language, then the so-called analytic propositions are really just empirical truths and not analytic at all. So the conventionalist theory of the a priori is not consistent with the existence of a priori knowledge.

Second, the conventionalist theory is based upon a confusion between a sentence and the proposition it expresses. That the word 'square' is used to represent the concept 'square' is determined by a rule of language that might have been different. Connections between words and the items they are used to represent are, in Locke's terms, "voluntary impositions," produced and sustained by the usage of the speech community. That the sentence "A square has four sides" expresses the proposition that a square has four sides is a product of the semantic and syntactic rules of English. If the rules were different, it might have expressed a different proposition. Thus, whether or not a sentence is true depends upon whether or not the proposition it expresses is true. The truth-value of sentences, if we may speak of their being true or false at all, is derived from the truth-value of the propositions they express. But propositions are not linguistic entities; they are not composed of words, although they are expressed and formulated in words. That the property of having four sides is included in what it is to be a square, that being a metal is included in what it is to be lead, are not themselves linguistic facts. So the truth-value of these analytic propositions is not due to any conventions, linguistic or otherwise. It is a matter of one concept being contained within another.

In his profound critique of conventionalism along these lines, C. I. Lewis makes the essential point in these words:

> It is neither the linguistic symbolisms nor their conventionally determined relations to other symbolisms nor the conventions of syntax, which determine analytic truth. These determine only the manner of the expression of it; it is *what is expressed* which is analytically true or not.[8]

But what of instructive, or synthetic, propositions? Is there a priori knowledge of these? Is there a synthetic a priori, as Kant thought?

3. Instructive, or Synthetic, Propositions

Locke thought that there are a priori instructive propositions. "We can know the Truth, and so may be *certain* in Propositions, which affirm something of another, which is a necessary consequence of its precise complex *Idea*, but not contained in it."[9] Kant thought so too, and offered "Everything which happens has its cause" as an example, one that is by no means uncontroversial.[10]

In another place, Locke formulated a general characterization of a host of synthetic a priori propositions.

> For a Man cannot conceive himself capable of a greater Certainty, than to know that any *Idea* in his Mind is such, as he perceives it to be; and that two *Ideas*, wherein he perceives a difference, are different, and not precisely the same. He that demands a greater Certainty than this, demands he knows not what.[11]

Locke's thought is based on his view that an individual has direct access to the contents of the concepts in his possession; hence he attains noninferential intuitive knowledge of propositions that declare certain relations among the contents. In fact, these are among the propositions that are entitled to be classified as knowledge. "*Knowledge* then seems to me to be nothing but *the perception of the connexion and agreement, or disagreement and repugnancy of any of our Ideas.*"[12] When I recognize, for instance, that white is not black or that red is not green or that a square is not a triangle, I have arrived at propositions that I know to be true with maximum certainty.

These cases of knowledge are not to be classified as analytic or trifling by the criterion of conceptual containment that Locke and Kant both accepted. And they are as good candidates for being a priori as any others; once one is in possession of the concepts 'white' and 'black', 'red' and 'green', 'square' and 'triangle', nothing more is needed to recognize these propositions as true than to reflect on them. There is no need to go beyond the concepts to consult experience. The concepts are, moreover, invulnerable to empirical falsification. No experience can present us with any data that would provide a reason for thinking that they might not be true.

It would be implausible to suppose that "Red is not green" is a case of conceptual containment. Being other than green is not part of the content of the concept 'red'. We can see this by recognizing that there is a possible world that contains red things but no green things and that people with our conceptual capacities in that world could acquire the concept 'red'. Thus they can come to know what 'red' is without being in possession of the concept 'green', something that would not be possible if being other than green were part of the content of the concept 'red'.

Propositions such as these seem relatively unimportant, even though they are not trifling by Locke's standards. Why, then, have the logical positivists been so anxious to deny the existence of the synthetic a priori? After all, if we possess the capacity to determine that the content of one concept is contained within the content of another and to formulate that information as an analytic proposition, it would seem that the determination that the content of one concept is *not* included within the content of another is an exercise of the same capacity of mind, even though such propositions are synthetic. That was clearly Locke's view, and in that he was correct.

The reason for the anxiety over the a priori within modern empiricism is that certain scientifically important propositions were conceded by the logical positivists to be a priori, and it would be incompatible with the program of empiricism and the fundamental principles of its epistemology to concede that they are also synthetic. Chief among these are the propositions of mathematics. If one cannot make out the case that these are analytic, then classical rationalism has established its main contention: namely, that there are factually informative a priori truths.

Kant provided an argument that has become quite famous: that "$7 + 5 = 12$" is synthetic as well as a priori:

> The concept of the sum of 7 and 5 contains nothing save the union of the two numbers into one, and in this no thought is being taken as to what that single number may be which combines both. The concept of 12 is by no means already thought in merely thinking this union of 7 and 5; and I may

analyze my concept of such a possible sum as long as I please, still I shall never find the 12 in it.[13]

Kant claims that the concept '12' is not contained in the concept '7 + 5'. His argument has been criticized by A. J. Ayer on the grounds that he uses a "psychological" criterion of conceptual containment, rather than the logical one that Ayer prefers.[14]

I shall discuss the logical criterion in the next section. But I can see no objection to a criterion with a psychological aspect to it. After all, the fact that a person possesses a certain concept and is able to scrutinize its content to extract its various constituents is a fact about certain of our mental powers; it is a psychological fact. And if Kant cannot find the concept '12' within the concept '7 + 5', that certainly is reason for supposing that it isn't there. Perhaps neither Kant nor Locke are entitled to suppose that such findings are absolutely certain; perhaps fallibilism applies to the realm of the a priori as well as to that of the a posteriori. But the fact that error is possible in such cases does not establish that a psychological criterion cannot supply us with good reasons for belief.

There is another argument in favor of Kant's position. The concept '7 + 5' includes the idea of the operation of adding 7 to 5. The concept '12' does not include the idea of an operation; in fact, 12 is a value for an infinite number of different operations, of which $14 - 2$, $120/10$, $6 + 6$, $7 + 82 - 77$ are a few examples. It is implausible to suppose that these cases, which are infinite in number, are all constituents of 12; thus it is implausible to suppose that any are, unless one thinks that the gods of arithmetic play favorites. Of course, it is a necessary truth that adding 7 to 5 gives 12 and that any collection with 12 members also has 7 + 5 members, but that is not enough to demonstrate that "7 + 5 = 12" is analytic, since synthetic a priori propositions are necessary as well.

Another example that is much discussed in the philosophical literature pertains to the concept 'cube'. We all know what a cube is, having observed many objects that are approximate cubes. The correct answer to the question, How many edges does a cube have? is 12. Most of us acquire the concept 'cube' without having learned the number of edges of a cube. I have found that when a person is asked the question, they usually discover that 12 is the right answer by forming a mental image of a cube, rotating it, and counting the edges as they pass. They are usually satisfied that their answer holds not only for the imagined cube but for any cube whatever. They have discovered a necessary truth about cubes.

Clearly, contingent truths cannot be verified by such an act of the imagination. For example, you could not discover how many teeth George Washington lost before his fifty-fifth birthday in this way. The fact that you can form a mental image which you take to be of Washington's teeth at a certain age has no tendency to show that the image carries correct information. An act of the imagination must be distinguished from a memory; if I am not sure whether I had a bagel for breakfast, I might conjure up a memory image of the meal and determine the right answer by inspecting it. And memory enters into the cube example. It is because I remember what cubes look like that I am able to form a mental image of one in the first place; perhaps the fact that the image has 12 edges is due to a veridical memory of some actual cube that I am now imagining; but that having 12 edges is true of every actual and possible cube at all times and all places cannot be extracted from my memory of a particular cube. The memory image is a vehicle of a universal necessary truth whose range of applicability extends far beyond the particular memory.

One might argue that not everything that is contained analytically within a particular concept must be apprehensible simply by inspection. Locke argued that frequently the agreement or disagreement between two ideas can be known only by reasoning. Perhaps we can show by reasoning that having 12 edges is a constituent of the concept 'cube'. One way in which this can be done is by deducing "A cube has 12 edges" as a theorem in Euclidean geometry. But even if such a proof can be constructed, it would not tend to show that the statement is analytic. The reason is that one can show that a proposition is analytic through a proof only by showing that the premises of the proof are themselves analytic and that every step in the proof is a case of analytic (rather than synthetic) entailment. But no one knows how to do that.

The current tendency is to bypass these considerations by appealing to the fact that there are alternative geometries, that the solid geometry of Euclidean tradition which investigates the geometrical structures of cubes is only one among many other possible geometries, and that the determination of which geometry is true of actual space is an empirical matter. The thought here is that the geometry that can be known to be true cannot be known by a priori procedures and that pure geometries which are constructed independently of empirical considerations have, in themselves, no truth-value; they are simply representations of possible structures that can be filled in by empirical interpretation.[15]

However, the fact of alternative geometries is irrelevant to the present case. After all, prior to any geometrical systematization, a person has acquired, through everyday experience, the concept 'cube'. And the question concerns the content of this concept, not the content of some related concept incorporated within a geometry created by someone else. It may turn out that empirical science at some future time will utilize a geometry that has no place for the concept 'cube' that we are now in possession of through everyday experience. It may be that all the things we thought were cubes or approximate cubes are really nothing of the kind. Perhaps we will discover empirically that there are no cubes in the actual world. In that case, we would interpret "A cube has 12 edges" nonexistentially as not applying to any actual item. It would be equivalent to "If anything is a cube, it has 12 edges." Nevertheless, it would still be a necessary truth. So the claim that the analytic propositions exhaust the necessary truths is not plausible.

4. Logic and Analyticity

Kant noticed that the logical principle of contradiction plays a special role in ascertaining analytic truths.

> That a body is extended is a proposition that holds *a priori* and is not empirical. For, before appealing to experience, I have already in the concept of body all the conditions required for my judgment. I have only to extract from it, in accordance with the principle of contradiction, the required predicate, and in so doing can at the same time become

conscious of the necessity of the judgment – and that is what experience could never have taught me.[16]

If being extended is contained in the concept 'body', then to claim that a body is *not* extended is self-contradictory. So one test for conceptual containment is this: deny that the predicate belongs to the subject, and see if you get a contradiction; if you do, the proposition is analytic.

Later philosophers have used this criterion not merely as a test for conceptual containment, but as the basis for an extended notion of analyticity. A proposition is analytic if and only if its negation is a logical contradiction or, equivalently, if the proposition is entailed by the laws of logic. For example, if by 'body' we mean an extended thing, then "All bodies are extended" is equivalent to "All extended things are extended," which is a case of the logical principle "Anything that is both A and B is A." Equivalently, its negation is a case of "Something that is both A and B is not A," an example of a self-contradictory logical structure.

In his influential *Foundations of Arithmetic*, Frege made use of this criterion to determine the status of mathematical propositions. To determine whether or not a mathematical proposition is analytic,

> The problem becomes, in fact, that of finding the proof of the proposition, and of following it up right back to the primitive truths. If, in carrying out this process, we come only on general logical laws and on definitions, then the truth is an analytic one . . . If, however, it is impossible to give the proof without making use of truths which are not of a general logical nature, but belong to the sphere of some special science, then the proposition is a synthetic one.[17]

What, then, is a law of logic? What is the criterion for distinguishing a logical law from other laws? Presumably a law of logic is a general truth whose negation entails a logical contradiction. But how are we to distinguish a logical contradiction from a necessary falsehood? According to Frege, logic is not a "special science." Its task is that "of discovering the laws of truth."[18] But these characterizations simply raise new questions, none of which possesses a clear answer.

Under the influence of the work of Frege and later of Russell and Whitehead on the foundations of mathematics, the logical positivists claimed that arithmetic and number theory generally consist of analytic propositions, because the propositions of arithmetic are deducible from the laws of logic, together with definitions of the meanings of terms. This is sometimes called the 'logistic thesis', or 'logicism' for short.[19] It is now generally conceded that efforts to work out the logistic thesis have uncovered a number of intractable difficulties. One of them is founded upon Gödel's incompleteness proof, according to which there are true propositions of arithmetic that are not provable. A second stems from Russell's discovery that Frege's system implies a contradiction; none of the methods used to avoid the contradiction – such as the theory of types or dropping the law of excluded middle – have the intuitive obviousness of the uncontroversial cases of logical laws.

Another difficulty, and the one that is most important for our purposes, is that in order to deduce arithmetic from logic, it is necessary to use not only the principles of first-order logic, but also the principles of identity theory and of the theory of sets. Are these principles laws of logic? If logic is not just another special science, then its principles must be topic-neutral, applicable to any subject matter whatever. That is why first-order logic is, uncontroversially, logic: it presents us with patterns of valid reasoning applicable to reasoning on any topic. Is set theory topic-neutral? After all, its use commits us to the existence of some specific subject matter – namely, sets – and thus it can be classified as a special science. Moreover, its principles are controversial and involve ontological claims that are quite unintuitive.[20]

In recent years, there has been a proliferation of systems that have been classified as logics: modal logic, deontic logic, doxastic logic, intuitionist logic, free logic, many-valued logic, higher-order logic, and so on. These logics are extensions of, or alternatives to, standard first-order logic. As a result, the very notion of logic has been blurred. Earlier, I said that first-order logic is uncontroversial; that claim needs to be qualified, because it too has been subject to deep philosophical criticism from various points of view.

Perhaps what we should conclude from all this is that logic has no essence that enables us to distinguish it sharply from other sciences. Logic is concerned with the principles of valid reasoning. This is a characterization that almost everyone would agree to; but it is vague, and fails to provide objective answers to many questions, such as: Is set theory a branch of logic? Thus, there is an element of sheer decision involved in asserting that this or that system belongs to logic. Moreover, there are many views regarding the nature of the principles of valid reasoning, which have produced alternatives to the standard logic.

The notion of an analytic proposition is clear and well defined if we restrict it to Kant's account in terms of conceptual containment. But if we extend it according to the logical criterion, the distinction between the analytic and the synthetic becomes blurred; it is as vague as the notion of logic itself.

However, none of these worries about the analytic–synthetic distinction casts doubt upon Kant's distinction between necessary and contingent truths. Even if arithmetic fails to be analytic according to either criterion, it seems, intuitively, to consist of propositions that are necessarily true. In what possible world could "$7 + 5 = 12$" turn out to be false? If such propositions are necessary, then, according to Kant, our mode of access to them is a priori. However, there is a line of thought that has been pursued with great tenacity in recent philosophy, according to which the very category of necessary truth is suspect. Let us see what lies behind this skepticism.

5. Ontology and the A Priori

Intuitive knowledge is a type of knowledge that we arrive at by reflecting upon the content of our concepts and coming to realize that a certain proposition must be true just in virtue of its content. Demonstrative knowledge consists in constructing a proof of a proposition whose ultimate premises are known intuitively and whose validity is ascertained by the intuitive knowledge of the truth-preserving character of its steps. If there is a priori knowledge, this is the form it takes. On this score, both Descartes and Locke were correct. There is plenty of room to argue about how extensive the a priori is. Descartes thought that there was an a priori argument for God's existence. Kant thought that the principle of universal causality – that every event has a cause – is a priori. But however we decide these cases, the minimum claim of traditional rationalism, that some of our nontrifling beliefs are a priori, seems to be true. This also tends to support the foundationalist position on the structure of our systems of belief: some of our beliefs are basic – namely, those that constitute intuitive knowledge.

Locke thought that there was no ontological bite in this viewpoint. He was a nominalist: there are no objectively existing universal entities, as Plato thought. "All Things, that exist, [are] particulars."[21] It was his empiricist theory of the origin of ideas that bolstered his nominalist prejudice. The material universe consists of particulars; our sensory input – ideas of sensation – consists of particulars; general ideas are formed by abstraction, which consists in modifying the representative function of ideas of particulars by subtracting individuating features from them:

> *Ideas* become general, by separating from them the circumstances of Time, and Place, and any other *Ideas*, that may determine them to this or that particular Existence. By this way of abstraction they are made capable of representing more Individuals than one; each of which, having in it a conformity to that abstract *Idea*, is (as we call it) of that sort.[22]

For example, by leaving out of his ideas of particular people what is peculiar to each and retaining only "what is common to them all,"[23] a person is able to construct the general idea of a human being.

On the basis of this account of the origin of general ideas, Locke thought he could demonstrate the irrelevance of *conceptual realism*, which claims that there are real, nonparticular universals in the realm of being:

> *General and Universal*, belong not to the real existence of Things; but *are the Inventions and Creatures of the Understanding*, made by it for its own use, *and concern only Signs*, whether Words, or *Ideas*. . . . *Ideas* are general, when they are set up, as the Representatives of many particular Things: but

universality belongs not to things themselves, which are all of them particular in their Existence, even those Words, and *Ideas*, which in their signification, are general. When therefore we quit Particulars, the Generals that rest, are only Creatures of our own making, their general Nature being nothing but the Capacity they are put into by the Understanding, of signifying or representing many particulars.[24]

There is a problem here that Locke is only dimly aware of. According to his view, my idea or concept 'human being' is a particular mental entity whose generality consists in its function in my thinking process of representing particular human beings. However, when I employ this concept, as when I think, for example, that Socrates is human, I do not have all humans in mind; in fact, the only human I have in mind when I think this is Socrates. My thought that Socrates is human characterizes Socrates in a specific way: namely, as being human. Since what I think is, in this case, true, we can ask how it is that my characterization of Socrates succeeds in being true of him. How is it that my concept 'human' is able to latch onto Socrates?

Locke's answer is that Socrates, the real individual person I am representing to myself by means of my idea of Socrates, has "a conformity to that abstract *Idea*." But what does that mean? Socrates conforms to or exemplifies or participates in the concept 'human'. What sort of relation is that? An obvious answer is that my concept 'human' applies to Socrates and to any other human being I happen to think about because it has as its content a certain complex property, the property of being human, and Socrates exemplifies this property. Thus my concept 'human' latches onto Socrates because he exemplifies its content.

The content of a general idea, then, consists of a certain property that anything correctly represented by that idea exemplifies. We are now in a position to realize that there is a certain ambiguity in the notion of a concept or idea. When we speak of an idea as being in someone's possession, we are referring to a mental entity, something in his brain/mind system that has a representative function analogous to the representative function of words. But there are also the properties that form the contents of general concepts, and these properties are not themselves mental entities.

The property 'human' does not characterize my idea when I think that Socrates is human; it characterizes Socrates. So a concept or idea has both a subjective and an objective aspect; it includes a mental vehicle for a certain content, and it includes the content itself. The content is not itself a mental entity; it is needed to explain how the concept manages to latch onto the particulars that exemplify it. A general idea, then, has a twofold representative function: in order to represent particulars, it must represent certain properties; these latter constitute the content of the idea.

But properties, being objective features of things that exist independently of the mind, are not creatures of the understanding. And since they are exemplifiable by numerous particulars, they are not themselves particulars; so it seems as if, contrary to Locke's thought, general and universal do belong to the real existence of things.

Locke dimly perceives this problem, and tries to resolve it in a manner consistent with nominalism.

> Nature in the Production of Things, makes several of them alike . . . But . . . the *sorting* of them under Names, *is the Workmanship of the Understanding, taking occasion from the similitude* it observes amongst them, to make abstract general *Ideas*, and set them up in the mind, with Names annexed to them, as Patterns, or Forms . . . to which, as particular Things existing are found to agree, so they come to be of that Species.[25]

The objective basis for the formation of general ideas consists not in real universals, but in resemblances, or similitudes, among particulars. I observe, for example, a variety of different people; I form the concept 'human' by subtracting their points of difference and retaining only the points in which they resemble one another.

The great stumbling block for the resemblance theory of concept formation is the very notion of a point of resemblance. Does not this entail the very universals that the nominalist intends to exclude? Can we understand the notion of resemblance without introducing the one over the many?[26] Locke frequently speaks as if the qualities and properties of things are as real as the things that exemplify them. Perhaps he thinks of qualities as being themselves particular. The snub-nosedness of Socrates was a property of him as much as the snub-nosedness of Susan Hayward was a property of her; but they are not identical: qualities are particulars which are capable of resembling one another. But the introduction of abstract particulars simply reproduces the problem of understanding resemblance at another level; it delays, but does not prevent, the introduction of real universals.

The disagreement between Locke's nominalism and conceptual realism is not about the existence of concepts or ideas – they are both versions of conceptualism – but about the ontological analysis of generality. In this century, the manner of thinking typified by Locke's "way of ideas" has come under attack from a variety of philosophical quarters. The turn towards language has encouraged the notion that thinking is just a form of talking and that we should stop concerning ourselves with concepts and instead concern ourselves with the meanings of words and other units of discourse. We should worry not about the concept 'human', but about the meaning of the word 'human'. The linguistic turn has replaced talk of mental entities by talk of linguistic entities.

However, there is little gain in this change as far as the question of the a priori is concerned. There are two reasons for this. First, issues about meaning reproduce the same ontological questions that concepts raise. Is the meaning of the word 'human' a universal? How does it manage to represent and apply to many different particulars? The vehicle of representation has changed, but the nature of representation remains a puzzle.

Second, the basic assumption underlying the linguistic turn is problematic. It assumes that we can intelligibly understand the nature of meaning without reference to mental entities such as ideas and concepts. Yet a word token, of its nature, is just a physical particular. It has meaning as a result of its being a token of a type used by human beings speaking a language. And humans choose the words they use to express the thoughts they have; the meanings of words are determined by the concepts available to the speech community. Teaching someone the meaning of a word presupposes their possession of the concept whose content is that meaning. Learning a word's meaning involves associating the word with a meaning, and both must be available if the association is to take place. A computer may be able to send messages to its user; but in the human case the messages sent are expressions of thoughts.

We may wonder about the very possibility of conceptual representation. What is the mechanism by which human beings acquire and store and have access to and make use of concepts? What is the inner nature of the mental entity which represents a content? And what is the nature of representation itself? These are excellent questions about which there is much speculation and little certainty. However, ignorance of the explanation of a phenomenon need not lead to skepticism about the phenomenon itself. Yet the question of the nature of meaning has produced a denial of the very existence of a priori knowledge and necessary truth. Let us turn now to this skepticism about meaning.

6. Skepticism about Meaning

If nominalism is rejected in favor of conceptual realism, then the epistemological claim that there is a priori knowledge, whether of trifling or instructive propositions, acquires a significant ontological weight. Russell brought this out clearly in his bold formulation: *"All a priori knowledge deals exclusively with the relations of universals."*[27] The analysis of what it is we know when we know something a priori brings with it an ontological commitment to "the real existence" of universals.

The nominalist prejudice is a product not exactly of empiricism, but rather of an assumed corollary of an empiricist epistemology: namely, that sensory input acquaints us with particulars alone, and further processing of the sensory input by the mind/brain system cannot produce entities of a new ontological type. Russell rejects this corollary as much as he rejects – in *The Problems of Philosophy*, at least – the underlying empiricism. "We are acquainted with such universals as white, red, black, sweet, sour, loud, hard, etc., i.e. with qualities which are exemplified in sense-data."[28]

For Russell, general words mean or denote universals. This *semantic realism* about words is bolstered by a *conceptual realism* about ideas. Since every sentence includes at least one general word, it follows that "no sentence can be made up without at least one word which denotes a universal. . . . Thus all truths involve universals, and all knowledge of truths involves acquaintance with universals."[29] Both semantic and conceptual realism can be defended as part of the explanation of how it is possible for a speaker of a language to apply the general terms in his language to new cases. The explanation is that the speaker knows the meaning of the term – that is, he possesses the appropriate concept – and this knowledge consists in his knowing which properties fix the term's reference or determine its extension. The semantic rules for the application of a general term are formulated in terms of the property or conjunction of properties or disjunction of properties that tell us the type of object to which the term applies. Speakers do not apply words to objects blindly, but in the light of the information about word meanings in their possession. And in the case of general terms, this information takes the form of reference to universals.

In a series of papers, W. V. Quine has challenged both conceptual and semantic realism. He denies, first of all, that general terms denote universals or, for that matter, properties or qualities.

> One may admit that there are red houses, roses, and sunsets, but deny, except as a popular and misleading manner of speaking, that they have anything in common. The words 'houses', 'roses', and 'sunsets' are true of sundry individual entities which are houses and roses and sunsets, and the word 'red' or 'red object' is true of each of sundry individual entities which are red houses, red roses, red sunsets; but there is not, in addition, any entity whatever, individual or otherwise, which is named by the word 'redness', nor, for that matter, by the word 'househood', 'rosehood', 'sunsethood'. That the houses and roses and sunsets are all of them red may be taken as ultimate and irreducible.[30]

Quine's objection to semantic realism is that the universals that the realist posits as the *denotata*, or meanings, of general terms are "occult entities."[31] For the realist, meanings are intermediaries between a word and the items it is true of, and their role as intermediaries is to explain how it is that the word can be true of just those items. For Quine, however, "meanings themselves, as obscure intermediary entities, may well be abandoned."[32]

But why are meanings as understood by the realist occult and obscure? For Quine, our ontological commitments are logical consequences of the conceptual scheme we adopt to understand the world as we know it through experience.

> We adopt, at least insofar as we are reasonable, the simplest conceptual scheme into which the disordered fragments of raw experience can be fitted and arranged. Our ontology is determined once we have fixed upon the over-all conceptual scheme which is to accommodate science in the broadest sense.[33]

Quine mentions the physicalist conceptual scheme (as contrasted to the phenomenalist one), which contains an ontological commitment to external physical objects. "Physical objects are postulated entities which round out and simplify our account of the flux of experience."[34]

According to Quine, from the standpoint of physicalism, a Platonistic ontology (that is, the ontology of universals and other abstract objects implied by semantic and conceptual realism) is just a myth. He does not think that a myth is necessarily to be rejected if it is better at simplifying our account of the flux of experience than alternative myths. What he seems to be saying is that if we start out as physicalists, then the burden of proof lies on the realist to establish his case. But why should the realist accept this burden? After all, as Russell pointed out, universals and abstract objects are presented in our immediate sense experience, so the portion of our conceptual scheme which analyzes the nature of experience implies an ontological commitment to the very universals that later assume the function of meanings, once linguistic behavior comes to be explained. Thus the commitment to universals is epistemically prior to the postulation of physical objects; universals are no more occult and obscure than are physical objects.

Moreover, an assumption subscribed to by most nominalists is that particularity is more intelligible than universality. But there is no reason why the realist should agree with this. If universals are among the items we are acquainted with, and if we have intuitive knowledge of relations among them, they are as intelligible as anything else in our conceptual scheme. In addition, there are deep, intractable problems in making sense of the very idea of a particular, or individual, thing. In its classical Aristotelian formulation, an individual thing, such as Socrates or a spherical globe, is an ultimate subject of predicates. It is something that exemplifies properties and stands in relation to other things but is not itself a property or relation that is capable of being exemplified. There is a dilemma that the friends of particulars must face. Either the particular consists of nothing but the sum of the properties that it is said to exemplify, or it consists of an item over and above the properties. In the former case, a particular is just a bunch of universals, and particularity turns out to be a special case of universality. In the latter case, a particular turns out to be an entity distinct from the properties that exemplify it. But such a "bare" particular is something unintelligible: we are acquainted with it only through its properties; at best, it is an item that is postulated for explanatory purposes – but what does it explain? So the friends of universals conclude that particulars are either just bunches of universals or obscure and occult entities with no rationale or explanatory role.

A behaviorist view of language learning lies behind Quine's rejection of conceptual realism. "I think that the behaviorists are right in holding that talk of ideas is bad business even for psychology."[35] The explanation of the ways in which words latch onto objects must be in terms of conditioning and response. "Words mean only as their use in sentences is conditioned to sensory stimuli, verbal and otherwise."[36] A person's current language consists of "his current dispositions to respond verbally to current stimulation."[37]

The problem with a behaviorist approach to language, and with behaviorism generally, is that behavioral dispositions are not ultimate explanatory points of reference. We can see this clearly in the physical sciences. If, for example, a certain metal possesses the behavioral disposition to melt at a certain temperature, we seek an explanation of that fact in terms of its atomic structure and what happens to it when heat is applied to it. We do not say, "It just melts at that temperature and that's that." Dispositions are just the sort of things that need explanation.

Moreover, explanations of dispositions to verbal behavior are ready at hand in the light of information available to the speaker. I know what I mean when I use the word 'bachelor'. I mean "unmarried man," and that makes "Bachelors are unmarried" expressive of an analytic proposition, something whose truth I know a priori in virtue of my knowledge of what I mean. Of course, in order to make use of that information, it is necessary to have recourse to the subjective point of view, to what the speaker knows about himself. What the subjective point of view contains is not reducible to what is available objectively. For example, correlations between words and the objects they are true of does not determine meaning, since different properties may yield the same extension. The only way to determine which property belongs to the meaning is to infer the content of the speaker's concept or, if the speaker is oneself, to remind oneself of what one already knows.

What makes someone a behaviorist is skepticism concerning the possibility of knowing the contents of the human mind, especially when that requires gaining access to the subjectivity of another person. Let us turn to that issue.

7. Other Minds

Conceptual realism is plausible only if we are in a position to identify the concepts that others possess. For example, when I classify the proposition that someone expresses in using the sentence "Bachelors are unmarried" as analytic, I claim to know that the concept he expresses by 'bachelors' contains the concept he expresses by 'unmarried'. The interpretation of the speech of others, the understanding of what others express in their speech acts, depends, according to the conceptual realist, upon the existence of a human ability to apprehend the thoughts of others as well as one's own thoughts. Clearly, one is not directly acquainted with the thoughts of others. When someone speaks to me, I am acquainted with certain sounds, which I interpret as instances of certain sentences in a language; then, in the light of my own knowledge of the language, I interpret the sentences as speech acts of a certain type – for example, assertions or questions – and as expressing a certain content – for example, propositions – that the speaker meant or intended. A series of interpretations is necessary in order to reach the speaker's intended meaning.

My beliefs about what others mean, then, depends upon a sequence of interpretations, at the end of which I apprehend the contents of their speech acts, which are composed of the contents of the concepts in their possession. Of course, I am not usually aware of making such interpretations, or even of paying attention to the sounds that others produce. I appear to grasp the meaning of another directly and effortlessly. But in reconstructing the process, we can see that my grasp depends upon utilizing my knowledge of the language in order to identify words and sentences in the sounds I hear and to identify concepts and meanings expressed in them. My knowledge that Smith's utterance of "Bachelors are unmarried" expresses an analytic proposition depends on my identifying which of the several concepts we express by 'bachelor' in the English language was the one meant by Smith. To do that, I need to know the various meanings of 'bachelor' in the language, together with the particular content meant by Smith at the time of utterance.

Is the inference to the contents of the minds of others justifiable? On the face of it, there seems to be no particular difficulty here, once we have accepted the making of transcendent inferences generally. My beliefs about the minds of others are conclusions of transcendent inferences which can be made explicit and which, it would seem, are no more and no less problematic than the variety of such inferences we make in daily life and in science and in other human activities.

Philosophers have frequently argued, however, that there is some special problem here that distinguishes our beliefs about other minds from our accepting the unobservables of physics. In order to form such beliefs, I must already have available the concepts in which they are formulated. I must know, for example, what it is for another to have a concept or idea if I am to infer his meanings. Or, if what I believe is that he has certain pains or emotions, I must already have attained knowledge of what a pain is or what an emotion is. But if the only data pertaining to others available to me is their bodily behavior, including the sounds they produce that I classify as speech, then the original source of these concepts is my own individual mental life. I know what a pain is because I have felt pain myself; I know what it is to feel anger because I have felt angry myself; I know what it is to mean something because I have meant something. So the conceptual repertoire that I use to learn about other minds is gained through my knowledge of my own mind.

The picture is this, then. Each person knows about their own mind directly; they have also acquired a general knowledge of the connection between the contents of their mind and their public actions whereby they express and communicate this content. When another person acts in a certain way, they infer that something is going on in that individual's mind similar to what goes on in their own mind when they act in that way. I conclude, for example, that another person has a pain in their knee when they hold their knee, utter certain sounds, and behave in a certain way, because I know that when I do such things, I usually have a pain in my knee. Because each of us starts from our own case, it is necessary to learn the meanings of our mentalistic vocabulary from our personal experience. I learn, for example, what "pain" means on the basis of my own pains; that is the only basis available to me.

A central feature of "my own case" is that it is marked by a certain privacy. I have access to my own pains, for example, directly, whereas others gain knowledge of them only through transcendent inferences based on their perceptions of my behavior. Even if another knew everything there was to know about my body and my nervous system, they would still have to infer that I have a pain in my knee, relying, this time, on their own case.

One problem that has been alleged to be inherent in this picture is that no one can acquire the required conceptual abilities just from his own case. Thus Wittgenstein writes:

> When one says "He gave a name to his sensation" one forgets that a great deal of stage-setting in the language is presupposed if the mere act of naming is to make sense. And when we speak of someone's having given a name to pain, what is presupposed is the existence of the grammar of the word "pain"; it shews the post where the new word is stationed.[38]

The argument seems to be that in order to identify items in one's own mind as the referents of certain words in the language, the language itself is presupposed, together with its grammatical and semantic categories. But language is a social phenomenon; one learns it through interaction with others. One's knowledge of one's own case emerges gradually in combination with one's knowledge of the minds of others as one acquires knowledge of the language through social interaction.

Wittgenstein offers the following interpretation of the "my own case" picture of language learning (which he ascribes to St Augustine):

> Augustine describes the learning of human language as if the child came into a strange country and did not understand the language of the country; that is, as if it already had a language, only not this one. Or again: as if the child could already *think*, only not yet speak. And "think" would here mean something like "talk to itself".[39]

So the criticism is that the picture presupposes that the child already has the very conceptual abilities that need to be accounted for. One cannot explain how one acquires the ability to think about the minds of others on the basis of one's own case, because one would already have to know how to think about one's own mind, and one could not do that until one had the rudiments of language – that is, until one had already engaged the minds of others.

The conclusion that Wittgenstein seems to want to draw is that the picture must be rejected; in particular, the idea that our knowledge of the minds of others is knowledge of something marked by privacy must be rejected. It is not clear what alternative picture, if any, he wants us to adopt. Since Wittgenstein tends to want to reject all pictures and models put forward in the philosophical tradition, perhaps what he is aiming at is that we simply stop asking the questions which generate the "my own case" picture. This is unsatisfactory, however, because the question of the origin of our abilities to apply mentalistic concepts to ourselves and others is certainly a legitimate topic of psychological and philosophical inquiry, so if one picture has insurmountable difficulties, one should not discourage efforts to formulate a better picture.

Further, Wittgenstein's criticism of St Augustine's view confuses two different questions. One question is the origin of the conceptual abilities presupposed in the "my own case" picture. This question is connected to a host of other questions concerning how language is learned, what a language is, whether or not language is a social phenomenon, and so forth. These are very interesting questions, but they are not obviously pertinent to the epistemological issue.

The epistemological question begins with the fact that each of us has a system of beliefs that includes beliefs about the minds of others. So it already supposes that we have acquired by some means or other the whole conceptual repertoire embedded in our belief system. The question, then, is whether those beliefs about the minds of others can be justified. How the conceptual repertoire was acquired in the first place is not really pertinent. Even if the acquisition of it already depends upon our being in possession of beliefs about other minds, it does not follow that these beliefs are justified. So the epistemological question remains.

Wittgenstein does make a point that is pertinent, though. "If I say of myself that it is only from my own case that I know what the word 'pain' means – must I not say the same of other people too? And how can I generalize the *one* case so irresponsibly?"[40] The point is that the transcendent inference from one's own case to the minds of others is based upon a sample with only one member, and that sample is too small to justify our beliefs about the minds of many others. For example, if I believe generally that human beings have minds, that they have thoughts, feelings, emotions, and sensations of the sort I have, then I am claiming that all creatures who look and behave in ways similar to me have a private world similar to mine. So I take myself as the sole basis for a generalization to billions of others. Wittgenstein evaluates such a generalization as "irresponsible."

He continues with his famous beetle in the box example:

Now someone tells me that *he* knows what pain is only from his own case! – Suppose everyone had a box with something in it: we call it a "beetle". No one can look into anyone else's box, and everyone says he knows what a beetle is only by looking at *his* beetle. – Here it would be quite possible for everyone to have something quite different in his box.[41]

I must admit that it would be *possible* for everyone to have something quite different in his box. But the question is whether or not it is *probable*.

The criticism that one is limited to a sample too small to justify inferences to other minds rests upon a superficial account of the nature of the data. After all, I am not restricted to a single occurrence of a feeling a thought or an emotion; I have my whole mental history to rely upon. Moreover, I have evidence in my own case that the connections between my mental life and my outward behavior are not sheer accidents, but illustrate causal connections. That a certain blow to my knee accompanies this pain is based upon a series of causal connections between outer events and events in my body. Moreover, my inferences to other minds tend to be confirmed over time. In addition, I can confirm directly the inferences that others draw about me. In this way, I gradually form a system of generalizations – a theory, if you like – concerning the connections between mind and body which continues to be sustained by subsequent experience and forms the basis for numerous successful predictions about the actions and minds of others. Although it is *possible* that those to whom I ascribe minds are actually robots, this is not very likely, given the mass of data that confirm how similar those others are to me.

Therefore, the question about our knowledge of other minds does not push us in the direction of a behaviorist conception of mind that undermines the argument for the reality of a priori knowledge.

Further Readings

René Descartes, *Rules for the Direction of the Mind.*

H. P. Grice and P. F. Strawson, "In Defense of a Dogma," *Philosophical Review*, 65 (1965), repr. in Paul Grice, *Studies in the Way of Words* (Cambridge, Mass.: Harvard University Press, 1989), pp. 196–212.

Immanuel Kant, "Introduction" to *Critique of Pure Reason.*

John Locke, *An Essay Concerning Human Understanding*, Bk IV, chs i, vi–viii.

Paul Moser (ed.), *A Priori Knowledge* (Oxford: Oxford University Press, 1987).

Arthur Pap, *Semantics and Necessary Truth* (New Haven: Yale University Press, 1958).

W. V. Quine, "On What There Is" and "Two Dogmas of Empiricism," in *From a Logical Point of View* (Cambridge, Mass.: Harvard University Press, 1980), pp. 1–19, 20–46.

Ludwig Wittgenstein, *Wittgenstein's Lectures on the Foundations of Mathematics, Cambridge, 1939*, ed. Cora Diamond (Ithaca, NY: Cornell University Press, 1976).

7

Epistemology

1. Epistemology

The discussions in the previous sections of this book fall under the general heading of epistemology, or the theory of knowledge, a philosophical endeavor that began with Plato's *Theaetetus*, if not earlier. Descartes's *Meditations* formulated the problems which subsequent epistemologists have taken seriously, and philosophers such as Locke, Berkeley, Hume, and Kant have worked the agenda that Descartes instigated. The main question has been: What are the foundations of human knowledge? A great deal of the energy behind traditional epistemological inquiries was generated by the thought that perhaps human knowledge has no foundation. Lacking a foundation, we are reduced, so it was believed to skepticism, or, even worse, solipsism.

Descartes sought certainty, as did many of his successors. The basic propositions that were to constitute the ultimate foundation of knowledge were thought to be arrived at by processes deemed infallible or immune from error. Dewey provided a rhetorically resounding label for the Cartesian position in the title of his book *The Quest for Certainty*. Dewey's verdict was negative, as was the verdict of dominant trends of philosophy in the twentieth century. With a few exceptions, the contents of our belief systems lack the absolute certainty that Descartes thought they required if knowledge were to be possible. Peirce's term 'fallibilism' is now thought to be a more accurate characterization of the human condition as far as belief is concerned.

However, the repudiation of the quest for certainty does not necessarily undermine the quest for the foundations of knowledge. Even if there are no, or only very few, absolutely secure basic propositions, it is not necessary for a proposition to be basic that it be secure. Instead of supposing that basic propositions are certain and that they lend their certainty to those derived from them, we can suppose instead that they possess a degree of credibility and that they transmit to derived propositions whatever degree of credibility they possess. We can search for the foundations in good conscience, while dropping the quest for certainty.

However, another aim of the Cartesian project has also been questioned in recent philosophy. Traditional epistemology was thought to have the function of providing criteria for demarcating justified from unjustified belief, and the search for foundations was thought to be aimed at revealing such criteria. Once armed with criteria, philosophers would then be in a position to play the role of umpire with respect to our beliefs, proclaiming some of them "safe" and others "out." Take something controversial, such as the question of the existence of God. Does God exist? Well, first apply your criteria to determine the set of basic propositions; then see whether "God exists" is among them; if it isn't, see if it is among the derived propositions. If it is, then belief in God is justified; if it isn't, it isn't justified.

Many of our beliefs are controversial. Since our social and political lives depend upon our actions and since our actions are motivated by what we believe, epistemology was thought to have an indispensable cultural role in the fixation of belief. To the extent to which we are rational, we seek to believe only what we have an epistemic right to believe. And to determine that, we need epistemology.

However, epistemology has turned out to be somewhat of a disappointment. First of all, epistemologists disagree with one another about the nature of the criteria. There are empiricists who want us to rely upon sense awareness alone. There are rationalists who favor clear and distinct ideas. And there are numerous disagreements within these camps as to the nature of the deliverances of sense awareness and intellectual intuition. Thus no single story has emerged in the epistemological marketplace. Each epistemologist has done the best he could, but no class of favored umpires has emerged. Within our democratic culture, we are unable to identify a body of wise men, or Platonic rulers, who are able to distinguish truth from falsehood by the use of a set of criteria to which all rational persons would be willing to give their assent.

In the second place, the Cartesian foundational project was itself thrown into doubt.[1] Dewey pointed out that the biological purpose of thinking is to solve problems that human and other animals are confronted with because of changes in their circumstances; what is wanted is a successful resolution of our problems, in order that we may cope better with our difficulties and satisfy our desires. It is the criterion of success in action that fixes our beliefs and separates the sheep from the goats, not the appeal to ultimate foundations. The doubts that occur with regard to our beliefs are not the pretended doubts of Descartes's first *Meditation*, but real doubts arising from a problematic situation. The resolution of these doubts does not depend upon epistemology, upon some set of criteria imposed from without by wise men engaged in philosophical reflection, but upon actual thinking relevant to the context in which the problem arose. In this regard, recall Peirce's recommendation: "Let us not pretend to doubt in philosophy what we do not doubt in our hearts."[2]

A further difficulty with the foundational project appeared as a result of Hume's discussion of induction. A belief is epistemically warranted if it is produced by a method or procedure that produces truth more often than not – that is, by a procedure that is reliable. But, as Hume showed, there is no guarantee that inductive procedures are reliable. There is no guarantee that the methods of science in general are productive of truth. We think they are. And we are convinced by the technological and predictive successes of some of the sciences that they are reliable. But if we simply stick with what is successful and stop worrying about what is epistemically reliable, we would be no worse off than we are now.

In other words, the project of tracing our beliefs to their origin in sense impressions or intellectual intuitions has no point with regard to the fixation of belief.

As though an explanation as it were hung in the air unless supported by another one. Whereas an explanation may indeed rest on another one that has been given, but none stands in need of another – unless *we* require it to prevent a misunderstanding. One might say: an explanation serves to remove or to avert a misunderstanding – one, that is, that would occur but for the explanation; not every one that I can imagine. . . . The sign-post is in order – if, under normal circumstances, it fulfils its purpose.[3]

Wittgenstein here joins hands with Peirce in rejecting Descartes's paper doubt.

What, then, becomes of epistemology? Wittgenstein provides us with a clue. "If I have exhausted the justifications I have reached bedrock, and my spade is turned. Then I am inclined to say: 'This is simply what I do.'"[4] So perhaps there is room for an enterprise that investigates "what I do." Epistemology then becomes the study of human cognitive practices. The ways in which people actually fix their beliefs is a topic as amenable to scientific study and investigation as any other. Epistemology becomes transformed into a branch of cognitive psychology. Since fixation of belief is to a great extent a social process, the psychology will be social as well as individual. Just as natural philosophy merged into physics and metaphysics merged into science in general, so epistemology, liberated from the Cartesian program, disappears as an autonomous philosophical inquiry, only to reappear within psychology with a new agenda.

Quine has provided a sharp formulation of this new "naturalized" epistemology.

Epistemology, or something like it, simply falls into place as a chapter of psychology and hence of natural science. It studies a natural phenomenon, viz., a physical human subject. This human subject is accorded a certain experimentally controlled input – certain patterns of irradiation in assorted frequencies, for instance – and in the fullness of time the subject delivers as output a description of the three–dimensional external world and its history. The relation between the meager input and the torrential output is a relation that we are prompted to study for somewhat the same reasons that always prompted epistemology; namely, in order to see how evidence relates to theory, and in what ways one's theory of nature transcends any available evidence.[5]

Since one of the great aims of traditional epistemology, starting with Descartes, was to validate the scientific enterprise, to show that science is productive of knowledge, it is unclear how epistemology could reappear as a science when the very validity of science is in question. Quine urges us not to worry over an incipient circularity. For, by reminding ourselves that "the Humean predicament is the human predicament,"[6] we realize that there is no external philosophical standpoint from which science as such and as a whole can be validated. Giving up the Cartesian project means giving up the attempt to provide a wholesale validation of science. There is no circularity in using the science of psychology to understand the production of human knowledge. "If we are out simply to understand the link between observation and science, we are well advised to use any available information, including that provided by the very science whose link with observation we are seeking to understand."[7]

"Why not settle for psychology?," Quine asks.[8] But there *is* a reason why we cannot simply merge epistemology with psychology. It is that the categories of epistemological evaluation are not reducible to the categories of psychological description and explanation. We can see this in one of Quine's own formulations. He describes the input into the human subject as "certain patterns of irradiation in assorted frequencies," the study of which is supposed to illuminate "how evidence relates to theory." But the category of evidence is not the same as the category of sensory input, even if one agrees with Quine that "whatever evidence there is for science is sensory evidence."[9] When we characterize something as evidence, we are saying that it provides a reason for thinking that a proposition is true, whereas no such implication is contained in characterizing something merely as sensory input. To describe something as evidence is to evaluate it epistemically; to call it sensory input implies no such evaluation. In psychology, we study sensory input as one of the factors that *cause* us to acquire and modify our beliefs. In epistemology, we study sensory input to assess its role in *justifying* our beliefs and in providing us with an epistemic right to believe.

Understanding the relation between the meager input and the torrential output in causal terms leaves us somewhat in the dark as to how much of the output is justified and how much of the input succeeds in justifying anything. Take color skepticism as an example. The input consists of color sensations, the output of beliefs about the colors of objects. I have argued that this output is entirely mistaken; so none of the input has any evidential status, all things considered, even though we think it does. Evolution is capable of creating a cognitive apparatus that causes certain animals to form a variety of beliefs that are useful, though false. Of course, the argument for color skepticism made use of certain premises drawn from the sciences. So I must agree with Quine that we cannot exclude scientific information from epistemology. But certain normative epistemological principles that are not simply descriptive of our psychology were also involved. When we have finished explaining and arguing for the epistemological principles that we think are essential for the quest after truth, perhaps Wittgenstein is correct in saying that the last thing there is to be said is "This is simply what I do." But between saying this and doing cognitive psychology, there stands the inquiry into the meaning and import of our epistemological categories and norms. We may find that the notions of basic and derived belief have some legitimate role to play in understanding how some of the torrential output can be valid.

Moreover, I think that classical epistemology was not simply the game of a few philosophers pretending to be wise men, but a historically significant enterprise which contributed to the formation of our present-day scientific culture. Locke's *Essay Concerning Human Understanding*, to take just one example, was not an isolated work of detached philosophizing, but had enormous reverberations throughout European intellectual life in the eighteenth century. It influenced the formation of liberal views in religion and ethics; it provided a rationale for the scientific enterprise well before science-based technology came to have much effect on the lives of ordinary individuals. Today we look back on Locke's *Essay* and on other epistemological works as ancient history, forgetting their impact on all aspects of the culture. Nowadays, we tend to think of philosophy as one subject among others, somewhat insulated from the intellectual life of the culture; we forget that philosophy was once of interest to the educated classes generally, not just to professors of philosophy. Perhaps the current isolation of rigorous philosophy from the rest of the culture, together with recent skepticism about epistemological inquiries, is itself just a temporary trend that will be reversed by new ideas that we are at present in no position to anticipate.

2. The Ethics of Belief

The heading of this section is taken from the title of an essay by W. K. Clifford in which he argued that "it is wrong always, everywhere, and for anyone, to believe anything upon insufficient evidence."[10] He supports his claim by considering the case of a shipowner who fails to investigate whether his ship is seaworthy; it sinks, and everyone on board drowns. In Clifford's story, the shipowner's error consists in his not paying sufficient attention to evidence showing that his ship was not seaworthy. The point is that neglect of evidence can have terrible consequences. Clifford applies his rule to all cases of belief, not just to those in which a false belief really matters. His reason is that:

> No real belief, however trifling and fragmentary it may seem, is ever truly insignificant; it prepares us to receive more of its like, confirms those which resembled it before, and weakens others; and so gradually it lays a stealthy train in our inmost thoughts, which may some day explode into overt action, and leave its stamp upon our character forever.[11]

Every violation of the rule weakens our loyalty to it and makes it more likely that terrible consequences will ensue.

In his discussion of the relation between faith and reason, Locke adopted a similar view: his rule consists of "the not entertaining any Proposition with greater assurance than the Proofs it is built upon will warrant."[12] If you do not adopt this rule, then you do not love truth for truth's sake, thinks Locke. It is important for religious reasons to love truth for its own sake; otherwise rational religion will be replaced by "the ungrounded Fancies of a Man's own Brain." He calls this state of mind "enthusiasm," which arises "from the Conceits of a warmed or over-weening Brain."[13]

Locke's formulation includes an idea that is absent in Clifford's. We hold our beliefs with various degrees of assurance or conviction. Locke claims that the strength of our convictions should match the strength of the evidence. We can combine both formulations in this principle of *evidentialism*: A person is entitled to believe that a proposition P is true (a) only if the evidence that is available to him at the time supports its truth and (b) only to the degree that the evidence supports its truth.

There is an ambiguity in this rule, because there are at least two ways of interpreting the term 'entitled'. On the one hand, it may refer just to what one is epistemically entitled to believe; on the other hand, it may represent an ethical or moral entitlement.

The ultimate basis of epistemic entitlement is truth. After all, what we aim at in belief is truth. The relation between belief and truth is internal: whenever we believe something, we believe that it is *true*. That X believes P entails that X believes that P is true. There is no conceptual distance between belief and truth. Thus, what makes a person epistemically entitled to a belief is that the basis of the belief, whatever it is, is a good reason for thinking that it is true. I shall interpret the term 'evidence' in the formulation of the rule to refer to whatever it is that amounts to a good reason that a person has or could give for thinking that one of their beliefs is true.

On these interpretations, the evidentialist principle says that a person is epistemically entitled to believe that P is true (a) only if the reason they have for believing it is a good reason for thinking that it is true and (b) only to the degree that the reason supports its truth. Someone who accepts this rule would then be willing to examine their beliefs, the strength of their convictions, and the reasons they have for them to determine whether the reasons support them to the degree that they are convinced of them.

Suppose upon examination a person finds that a certain belief P is not supported by the reasons they have for it and that another belief Q is believed with greater conviction than the evidence warrants. Does this mean that they should cease believing in P and reduce the strength of their conviction about Q? Locke thinks they should, because for him the love of truth is an unconditional *moral* requirement. Thus the principle of evidentialism is not merely an epistemic norm; it is also, for Locke, an absolute ethical norm:

Light, true Light in the Mind is, or can be nothing else but the Evidence of the Truth of any Proposition; and if it be not a self-evident Proposition, all the Light it has, or can have, is from the clearness and validity of those Proofs, upon which it is received. To talk of any other light in the Understanding is to put our selves in the dark, or in the power of the Prince of Darkness, and by our own consent, to give ourselves up to Delusion to believe a Lie.[14]

It is clear that for Clifford as well, evidentialism is not just an epistemic principle, but an ethical one. Consider the tone of his argument: "we ought not to do evil that good may come."[15] Aiming at the truth via evidence is an unconditional moral requirement for him as well as for Locke.

Suppose the evidence supports P no more and no less than it supports its negation, not-P. According to evidentialism, we should believe neither, but should suspend our judgment until new evidence tilts us in one direction or another. William James argued against Clifford that in certain cases we should allow our desires and emotions to fix belief: "*Our passional nature not only lawfully may, but must, decide an option between propositions, whenever it is a genuine option that cannot by its nature by decided on intellectual grounds.*"[16] In this formulation James restricted the loosening of the rule to cases of propositions whose truth cannot, because of their very nature, be determined by evidence. Among the beliefs he had in mind are those of religion; even though we can neither prove God's existence nor disprove it, we need not remain agnostics. If religious belief provides us with important goods, if it satisfies our emotions, if it better represents the way we hope and want the world to be, then, for James, no moral wrong is done by having faith in God.

One difficulty with James's view is his claim that there are some questions that, in the nature of the case, cannot be decided on intellectual grounds. After all, plenty of people think that there are good reasons for believing in God, and many think that there are good reasons for rejecting religious belief. The argument continues; there is no end to giving reasons for and against. No criterion for determining whether a proposition is permanently inaccessible to rational considerations has ever been substantiated.

Perhaps James would be willing to weaken his exception to allow belief in cases where the evidence has not yet settled the issue and where the goods forfeited by disbelief are very great.

A different approach is to reject the claim that truth is an unconditional good. There are other values besides truth, and in some situations they may have greater urgency. So it may be morally acceptable in those situations to fix one's belief by reference to goods other than truth.[17]

There is something strange about this whole debate. After all, if truth is internally related to belief, then one's reasons for one's beliefs are reasons for thinking they are true. Thus to adopt a policy of appealing to reasons that have nothing to do with the determination of truth is incoherent. In fact, it is just plain wrong to say that a certain reason is a good reason for believing that something is true even though that reason does not support its truth; for in that case it just isn't a good reason for believing it to be *true*.

I think what happens is something like this. A person may have a motive for believing that something is true that, unlike a good reason, does not pertain to the determination of truth. For example, a person who finds comfort and consolation in religious belief has a motive to believe, even though these goods have no bearing on the question of its truth. Such a person may then have a motive for not paying much attention to the evidence, particularly if the evidence would tend to show that their belief is false. They may ignore it, or put it out of their mind, or assign a low priority to examining it, or deceive themselves about its strength. In such a case, they may end up believing things they are not epistemically entitled to believe. They do this not because they adopt an epistemic principle other than evidentialism (for that is incoherent), but because they have strong motives to ignore epistemic considerations entirely.

Let us say that a person who thus ignores epistemic considerations in the fixation of a belief is *dogmatic* with respect to that belief. I think that everyone is dogmatic about some beliefs. Dogmatism cannot be justified epistemically, because it consists in putting epistemic considerations aside. So the only question left is whether it can ever be justified morally or prudentially.

One reason why we are all dogmatists to some extent is that

there is not enough time to examine with care the grounds for all our beliefs. We have other things to do, other goods to seek. So sometimes we ignore our epistemic responsibilities because other matters are more urgent. Not all of us have the leisure or the ability of Descartes to meditate on the overall cogency of our systems of belief. For that reason, a certain degree of relaxation about the satisfaction of our epistemic duties is morally justified. We do not have a moral obligation to be epistemic Puritans. In this respect, William James's "Will to Believe" points in the right direction.

However, rejection of moral Puritanism does not justify epistemic anarchy.[18] It is not true that anything goes in matters of belief. It is frequently quite important that our beliefs be true, and our welfare and the welfare of others may depend upon it. In such cases, we have a moral, not merely an epistemic, obligation to follow the evidentialist principle. Clifford's negligent shipowner is an example of someone justifiably subject to moral condemnation.

It goes without saying that in those activities whose primary aim is to discover the truth, such as scientific and philosophical inquiry, we have no option but to be evidentialists if we wish to be members of the community of inquirers in good standing.

Further Readings

W. K. Clifford, "The Ethics of Belief," in *The Theory of Knowledge*, ed. Louis Pojman (Belmont, Calif.: Wadsworth, 1993), pp. 502–5.

Alvin Goldman, *Epistemology and Cognition* (Cambridge, Mass.: Harvard University Press, 1986).

William James, *Pragmatism: A New Name for Some Old Ways of Thinking* (New York: Longmans, Green, 1907).

William James, "The Will to Believe" and "The Sentiment of Rationality," in *The Will to Believe and Other Essays in Popular Philosophy* (New York: Longmans, Green, and Co., 1919), pp. 1–31, 63–110.

W. V. Quine, "Epistemology Naturalized," in *Ontological Relativity and Other Essays* (New York: Columbia University Press, 1969), pp. 69–90.

Notes

Chapter 1 Sense Awareness
1 Berkeley, *Three Dialogues between Hylas and Philonous*, in *Philosophical Works*, p. 172.
2 Ibid.
3 Berkeley, *Philosophical Works*, p. 144.

Chapter 2 Appearance and Reality
1 Locke, *Essay Concerning Human Understanding*, pp. 9–10: "The Epistle to the Reader."
2 Ibid., II. viii. 9.
3 Ibid., II. viii. 10.
4 Ibid., II. viii. 15.
5 Ibid., II. viii. 16.
6 Ibid.
7 The classical formulation of this objection to efforts to subjectivize the objects of awareness is contained in Moore, "The Refutation of Idealism."
8 Planck, "The Unity of the Physical World Picture," p. 5.
9 The question of the objective status of color is discussed at greater length in the chapter entitled "Color Objectively Considered" in my book *The Eye and the Mind*. The criticism of the scientific definition of color follows Berkeley's discussion in the first of his *Three Dialogues between Hylas and Philonous*.
10 Locke argued against Descartes that extension is not sufficient to characterize something as a body, because extension can also belong to empty space devoid of matter. For Locke, a body is an extended thing that is solid or that fills space: "By this *Idea* of Solidity, is the Extension of Body distinguished from the Extension of Space" (Locke, *Essay*, II. iv. 5).

11 One of the papers responsible for the revival of materialism in recent years is Smart's "Sensations and Brain Processes."
12 See Hume, *Treatise of Human Nature*, I. iv. 2, 6, and James, "Does Consciousness Exist?"
13 I have defended color skepticism at length in *Color and Consciousness* and "Why Nothing Has Color."
14 Price, *Perception*, p. 3.
15 Ibid.
16 Ryle, *Concept of Mind*, pp. 150–2.
17 Locke, *Essay*, IV. ii. 14.
18 Kant, *Critique of Pure Reason*, A51.
19 Strawson, *Individuals*, p. 10.
20 Sellars, *Science, Perception and Reality*, p. 27.

Chapter 3   Skepticism
1 Hume, *Treatise of Human Nature*, p. 187.
2 Ibid., p. 188.
3 Descartes, *Philosophical Writings*, ii. 12.
4 Ibid.
5 Ibid., p. 9.
6 Ibid., p. 12.
7 Ibid., p. 13.
8 Ibid.
9 Ibid.
10 Ibid., p. 12.
11 Ibid., p. 16.
12 Ibid., p. 17.
13 Hume, *Enquiry Concerning Human Understanding*, pp. 102–3.
14 Ibid., p. 105.
15 Ibid.
16 Hume, *Treatise*, p. 269.
17 Kant, *Critique of Pure Reason*, p. 34n.
18 Boswell, *Life of Samuel Johnson*, p. 285.
19 Hume, *Treatise*, pp. 208–9.
20 Ibid., p. 209.
21 von Glasersfeld, "An Introduction to Radical Constructivism," p. 30.
22 Hume, *Treatise*, p. 247.
23 Ibid.
24 Moore, *Philosophical Papers*, p. 144.
25 Ibid.
26 Ibid., p. 145.
27 Ibid., p. 147.

28 Ibid.
29 Ibid., pp. 147–8.
30 Ibid. p. 148.
31 Sellars, *Science, Perception and Reality*, p. 27.
32 Ibid.
33 Ibid., p. 28.
34 Russell, *Problems of Philosophy*, pp. 131–2.
35 The most widely discussed criticism of the true justified belief defi-
    nition of knowledge is by Edmund Gettier, in "Is True Justified
    Belief Knowledge?" In my *The Eye and the Mind*, pp. 133–4, I have
    argued that the examples Gettier presents are not genuine counter
    examples to the definition.
36 I had accepted a weakened conception of justification in *The Eye and
    the Mind*, p. 137.
37 Peirce, *Collected Papers*, v. para. 384.
38 Nozick, *Philosophical Explanations*, p. 178.
39 On this point see Wittgenstein, *On Certainty*, para. 13.
40 Peirce, *Collected Papers*, v. para. 265.
41 Descartes, *Philosophical Writings*, ii. 12.
42 Peirce, *Collected Papers*, v. paras. 370–3.
43 Ibid., i. para. 152.
44 This is an enduring theme of pragmatism. See, e.g., Dewey's *The
    Quest for Certainty*.
45 Peirce, *Collected Papers*, v. para. 265.
46 Aristotle, *Metaphysics*, 982b12.

Chapter 4 Self-Knowledge

1 Freud provides an example of this projection in primitive man's
   personification of objects in his environment. See Freud, *The Future
   of an Illusion*, p. 22.
2 Descartes would claim that the *cogito* is an exception: we can't be
   mistaken about that. In the next section, I shall examine certain
   criticisms of the *cogito*.
3 Descartes, *Philosophical Writings*, iii. 55.
4 The White Knight in Lewis Carroll's *Through the Looking Glass*
   appears to be a substance dualist. "How can you go on talking so
   quietly head downwards?" asked Alice, as she dragged him out by
   the feet and laid him in a heap on the bank. The Knight looked
   surprised at the question. "What does it matter where my body
   happens to be?" he said. "My mind goes on working all the same.
   In fact the more headdownwards I am, the more I keep inventing
   new things."

5 Blanshard, *The Nature of Thought*, i. 336–7.

6 *Basic Writings of Nietzsche*, p. 214.

7 Ibid., p. 213.

8 Ibid.

9 Ibid.

10 Hume's criticisms of the substantial self were anticipated 2,000 years earlier in the Buddhist no-soul theory. Even in modern Western philosophy, Locke's notion of self-identity departed significantly from Cartesian conceptions. See Locke's discussion of personal identity in his *Essay Concerning Human Understanding*, II. xxvii.

11 Hume, *Treatise of Human Nature*, p. 16.

12 Ibid., p. 251.

13 Ibid., p. 252.

14 Ibid., pp. 252–3.

15 Russell, *Problems of Philosophy*, p. 51.

16 Chisholm, "On the Observability of the Self," pp. 97–8.

17 Some years ago, the *New Yorker* printed a cartoon showing a computer saying "Cogito, ergo sum."

18 Locke, *Essay*, II. i. 2.

19 Ibid., II. i. 4.

20 Ibid.

21 John Searle uses the term 'derived intentionality' and contrasts it with 'intrinsic intentionality'. See Searle, *Intentionality*, introduction and ch. 1.

22 'Illocutionary force' is a term used by J. L. Austin to indicate the speech-act potential of a sentence. Thus, "The cat is on the mat" can be used to make a definite statement, whereas "Is the cat on the mat?" asks a question. These sentences possess different forces, even though their contents are similar. See Austin, *How to Do Things with Words*.

23 Locke, *Essay*, III. ii.

24 Searle, *Intentionality*, p. vii.

25 For a defense of this view, see Fodor, *The Language of Thought*.

26 Freud, *Autobiographical Study*, p. 53.

27 Ibid.

28 An interesting discussion of this issue is contained in Fodor, "Methodological Solipsism Considered as a Research Strategy in Cognitive Psychology," repr. in his *Representations*.

29 An interesting discussion along these lines is Nagel, "What is it Like to be a Bat?," in his *Mortal Questions*.

30 Frege's paper "The Thought" is a brilliant investigation of the nature of propositions. It is included in his *Collected Papers on Mathematics, Logic, and Philosophy*.

31 Russell, *Problems of Philosophy*, p. 124.
32 Ibid., pp. 126–7.
33 See, e.g., Wittgenstein, *Philosophical Investigations*, Part I, paras. 109–11.
34 Locke, *Essay*, II. xxiii. 2.
35 For a recent discussion of this issue focusing on the question of language acquisition, see Chomsky, *Rules and Representations*.

Chapter 5   Beyond Basic Belief
 1 Peirce, *Collected Papers*, v. para. 365.
 2 Ibid., para. 367.
 3 Ibid., para. 369.
 4 See W. V. Quine, "On What There Is," in *From a Logical Point of View*, pp. 1–19, for the view that reference involves ontological commitment to the existence of the object referred to.
 5 For a discussion of this point, as well as a criticism of Quine's point of view, see my "Remarks on Reference and Action."
 6 Horwich, *Truth*, p. 24.
 7 Ibid., p. 36.
 8 Ibid., p. 110.
 9 Ibid., p. 115.
10 For this emotive theory of ethical language, see Ayer, *Language, Truth and Logic*, ch. 6.
11 Hume, *Enquiry Concerning Human Understanding*, p. 21.
12 Ibid., p. 22.
13 Ibid., p. 23.
14 Ibid., p. 27.
15 Ibid., p. 29.
16 For a recent defense of pragmatism in these terms, see Rorty, *Philosophy and the Mirror of Nature*.
17 Quine, *From a Logical Point of View*, pp. 44–5.
18 Freud, *Introductory Lectures on Psychoanalysis*, pp. 562–3.
19 Grünbaum, *Foundations of Psychoanalysis*, ch. 2.

Chapter 6   A Priori Knowledge
 1 Locke, *Essay Concerning Human Understanding*, IV. viii. 4.
 2 Ibid., IV. viii. 1.
 3 Kant, *Critique of Pure Reason*, A6.
 4 Locke, *Essay*, IV. viii. 5.
 5 Ibid., IV. viii. 6.
 6 Ibid., III. ii. 1.
 7 Ayer, *Language, Truth and Logic*, pp. 78, 79, 80.
 8 Lewis, *Analysis of Knowledge and Valuation*, pp. 150–1.

9 Locke, *Essay*, IV. viii. 8.
10 Kant, *Critique of Pure Reason*, A9.
11 Locke, *Essay*, IV. ii. 1.
12 Ibid., IV. i. 2.
13 Kant, *Critique of Pure Reason*, B15.
14 Ayer, *Language, Truth and Logic*, p. 78.
15 For a clear presentation of this view, see Hempel, "Geometry and Empirical Science."
16 Kant, *Critique of Pure Reason*, B11–12.
17 Frege, *Foundations of Arithmetic*, p. 4.
18 Frege, "The Thought," in *Collected Papers*, p. 508.
19 For a clear formulation and discussion of logicism, see Hempel, "On the Nature of Mathematical Truth." A more extended, but equally readable, account is Russell, *Introduction to Mathematical Philosophy*.
20 For a critique of set theory on ontological grounds, see Goodman, "A World of Individuals," in *Problems and Projects*, pp. 155–72.
21 Locke, *Essay*, III. iii. 1.
22 Ibid., III. iii. 6.
23 Ibid., III. iii. 7.
24 Ibid., III. iii. 11.
25 Ibid., III. iii. 13.
26 See Russell, *Problems of Philosophy*, pp. 95–6, for an elaboration of this criticism of the resemblance theory.
27 Ibid., p. 103.
28 Ibid., p. 101
29 Ibid., p. 93.
30 Quine, *From a Logical Point of View*, p. 10.
31 Ibid.
32 Ibid., p. 22.
33 Ibid., pp. 16–17.
34 Ibid., p. 18.
35 Ibid., p. 48.
36 Quine, *Word and Object*, p. 17.
37 Ibid., p. 28.
38 Wittgenstein, *Philosophical Investigations*, Part I, para. 257.
39 Ibid., para. 32.
40 Ibid., para. 293.
41 Ibid.; emphasis original.

Chapter 7 Epistemology
1 For an influential version of the story that alleges the demise of the Cartesian project, see Rorty, *Philosophy and the Mirror of Nature*.

2   Peirce, *Collected Papers*, v. para. 265.
3   Wittgenstein, *Philosophical Investigations*, Part I, para. 87.
4   Ibid., para. 217.
5   Quine, *Ontological Relativity*, pp. 82–3.
6   Ibid., p. 72.
7   Ibid., p. 76.
8   Ibid., p. 75.
9   Ibid.
10 Clifford, "Ethics of Belief," p. 505.
11 Ibid., pp. 503–4.
12 Locke, *Essay Concerning Human Understanding*, IV. xix. 1.
13 Ibid., IV. xix. 3, 7.
14 Ibid., IV. xix. 13.
15 Clifford, "Ethics of Belief," p. 505.
16 James, "Will to Believe," p. 11.
17 For this view, see Meiland, "What Ought We to Believe?"
18 For an interesting defense of epistemic anarchism, see Feyerabend, *Against Method*.

Bibliography

The bibliography includes only those items mentioned or quoted in the text.

Aristotle, *Metaphysics*, trans. W. D. Ross (Oxford: Clarendon Press, 1954).

Austin, J. L., *How to Do Things with Words* (Cambridge, Mass.: Harvard University Press, 1975).

Ayer, A. J., *Language, Truth and Logic* (New York: Dover, 1952).

Berkeley, George, *Philosophical Works*, ed. Michael R. Ayers (London: J. M. Dent, 1993).

Berkeley, George, *Three Dialogues between Hylas and Philonous*, in *Philosophical Works*, pp. 155–252.

Berkeley, George, *A Treatise Concerning the Principles of Human Knowledge*, in *Philosophical Works*, pp. 71–153.

Blanshard, Brand, *The Nature of Thought* (London: George Allen and Unwin, 1948).

Boswell, James, *The Life of Samuel Johnson* (New York: Modern Library, n.d.).

Chisholm, Roderick, M., "On the Observability of the Self," in *Self-Knowledge*, ed. Quassim Cassam (Oxford: Oxford University Press, 1994), pp. 94–108.

Chomsky, Noam, *Rules and Representations* (New York: Columbia University Press, 1994).

Clifford, W. K., "The Ethics of Belief," in *The Theory of Knowledge*, ed. Louis Pojman (Belmont, Calif.: Wadsworth, 1993), pp. 502–5.

Descartes, René, *The Philosophical Writings of Descartes*, trans. John Cottingham, Robert Stoothoff, and Dugald Murdoch (Cambridge: Cambridge University Press, 1984).

Dewey, John, *The Quest for Certainty* (New York: Minton, Balch, and Co., 1929).

Feigl, Herbert, and Sellars, Wilfrid (eds), *Readings in Philosophical Analysis* (New York: Appleton-Century-Crofts, 1949).

Feyerabend, Paul, *Against Method* (London: Verso, 1978).

Fodor, Jerry, *The Language of Thought* (New York: Thomas Y. Crowell, 1975).

Fodor, Jerry, *Representations* (Cambridge, Mass.: MIT Press, 1986).

Frege, Gottlob, *Collected Papers on Mathematics, Logic, and Philosophy*, ed. Brian McGuinness (New York: Blackwell, 1984).

Frege, Gottlob, *The Foundations of Arithmetic*, trans. J. L. Austin (Oxford: Blackwell, 1953).

Freud, Sigmund, *An Autobiographical Study*, trans. James Strachey (New York: W. W. Norton, 1963).

Freud, Sigmund, *The Future of an Illusion*, trans. James Strachey (New York: W. W. Norton, 1961).

Freud, Sigmund, *Introductory Lectures on Psychoanalysis*, trans. James Strachey (New York: W. W. Norton, 1989).

Gettier, Edmund, "Is True Justified Belief Knowledge?," *Analysis*, 23 (1963), pp. 121–3.

Glasersfeld, Ernst von, "An Introduction to Radical Constructivism," in *The Invented Reality*, ed. Paul Watzlowick (New York: W. W. Norton, 1984), pp. 17–40.

Goodman, Nelson, *Problems and Projects* (Indianapolis: Bobbs-Merrill, 1972).

Grünbaum, Adolf, *The Foundations of Psychoanalysis* (Berkeley: University of California Press, 1984).

Hempel, Carl, "Geometry and Empirical Science," in *Readings in Philosophical Analysis*, ed. Herbert Feigl and Wilfrid Sellars (New York: Appleton-Century-Crofts, 1949), pp. 238–49.

Hempel, Carl, "On the Nature of Mathematical Truth," in *Readings in Philosophical Analysis*, ed. Herbert Feigl and Wilfrid Sellars, pp. 222–37.

Horwich, Paul, *Truth* (Oxford: Blackwell, 1990).

Hume, David, *Dialogues Concerning Natural Religion*, ed. Norman Kemp Smith (Indianapolis: Bobbs-Merrill, n.d.).

Hume, David, *An Enquiry Concerning Human Understanding*, ed. Eric Steinberg (Indianapolis: Hackett Publishing Co., 1983).

Hume, David, *A Treatise of Human Nature*, ed. L. A. Selby-Bigge, 2nd edn rev. P. H. Nidditch (Oxford: Clarendon Press, 1985).

James, William, "Does Consciousness Exist," in *Essays in Radical Empiricism* (New York: E. P. Dutton, 1971), pp. 3–22.

James, William, "The Will to Believe," in *The Will to Believe and Other Essays in Popular Philosophy* (New York: Longmans, Green, and Co., 1919), pp. 1–31.

Kant, Immanuel, *Critique of Pure Reason*, trans. Norman Kemp Smith (New York: St Martin's Press, 1965).

Landesman, Charles, *Color and Consciousness: An Essay in Metaphysics* (Philadelphia: Temple University Press, 1989).

Landesman, Charles, *The Eye and the Mind* (Dordrecht: Kluwer Academic Publishers, 1993).

Landesman, Charles, "Remarks on Reference and Action," in *Issues in the Philosophy of Language*, ed. Alfred F. MacKay and Daniel D. Merrill (New Haven: Yale University Press, 1976), pp. 105–18.

Landesman, Charles, "Why Nothing Has Color: Color Skepticism," in *The Theory of Knowledge*, ed. Louis Pojman (Belmont, Calif.: Wadsworth, 1993), pp. 121–6.

Lewis, C. I., *An Analysis of Knowledge and Valuation* (La Salle, Ill.: Open Court, 1946).

Locke, John, *An Essay Concerning Human Understanding*, ed. Peter Nidditch (Oxford: Clarendon Press, 1988).

Meiland, Jack, "What Ought We to Believe?," in *The Theory of Knowledge*, ed. Louis Pojman (Belmont, Calif.: Wadsworth, 1993), pp. 514–25.

Moore, G. E., *Philosophical Papers* (New York: Collier Books, 1962).

Moore, G. E., "The Refutation of Idealism," in *Philosophical Studies* (London: Routledge and Kegan Paul, 1922), pp. 1–30.

Nagel, Thomas, *Mortal Questions* (Cambridge: Cambridge University Press, 1979).

Nietzsche, Friedrich, *Basic Writings of Nietzsche*, trans. Walter Kaufmann (New York: Random House, 1968).

Nozick, Robert, *Philosophical Explanations* (Cambridge, Mass.: Harvard University Press, 1981).

Peirce, Charles Sanders, *Collected Papers*, ed. Charles Hartshorne and Paul Weiss (Cambridge, Mass.: Harvard University Press, 1934, 1935).

Planck, Max, "The Unity of the Physical World Picture," in *Physical Reality*, ed. Stephen Toulmin (New York: Harper and Row, 1970), pp. 1–27.

Pojman, Louis (ed.), *The Theory of Knowledge* (Belmont, Calif.: Wadsworth, 1993).

Price, H. H., *Perception* (London: Methuen, 1954).

Quine, W. V., *From a Logical Point of View* (Cambridge, Mass.: Harvard University Press, 1980).

Quine, W. V., *Ontological Relativity and Other Essays* (New York: Columbia University Press, 1969).

Quine, W. V., *Word and Object* (Cambridge, Mass.: MIT Press, 1960.)

Rorty, Richard, *Philosophy and the Mirror of Nature* (Princeton, NJ: Princeton University Press, 1979).

Russell, Bertrand, *Introduction to Mathematical Philosophy* (London: George Allen and Unwin, 1953).

Russell, Bertrand, *The Problems of Philosophy* (London: Oxford University Press, 1959).

Ryle, Gilbert, *The Concept of Mind* (London: Hutchinson's University Library, 1952).

Searle, John, *Intentionality* (Cambridge: Cambridge University Press, 1983).

Sellars, Wilfrid, *Science, Perception and Reality* (London: Routledge and Kegan Paul, 1963).

Smart, J. J. C., "Sensations and Brain Processes," *Philosophical Review*, 68 (1959), 141–56.

Strawson, P. F., *Individuals: An Essay in Descriptive Metaphysics* (London: Methuen, 1959).

Watzlowick, Paul (ed.), *The Invented Reality* (New York: W. W. Norton, 1984).

Wittgenstein, Ludwig, *On Certainty* (New York: J. and J. Harper Editions, 1962).

Wittgenstein, Ludwig, *Philosophical Investigations* (Oxford: Blackwell, 1953).

Index